ROUTLEDGE LIBRARY EDITIONS: THE OIL INDUSTRY

Volume 3

THE COMMUNITY OF OIL EXPORTING COUNTRIES

THE COMMUNITY OF OIL EXPORTING COUNTRIES

A Study in Governmental Co-operation

ZUHAYR MIKDASHI

LONDON AND NEW YORK

First published in 1972 by George Allen & Unwin Ltd

This edition first published in 2024
by Routledge
4 Park Square, Milton Park, Abingdon, Oxon OX14 4RN

and by Routledge
605 Third Avenue, New York, NY 10158

Routledge is an imprint of the Taylor & Francis Group, an informa business

British Library Cataloguing in Publication Data
A catalogue record for this book is available from the British Library

ISBN: 978-1-032-55944-5 (Set)
ISBN: 978-1-032-57580-3 (Volume 3) (hbk)
ISBN: 978-1-032-57581-0 (Volume 3) (pbk)
ISBN: 978-1-003-43998-1 (Volume 3) (ebk)

DOI: 10.4324/9781003439981

Publisher's Note
The publisher has gone to great lengths to ensure the quality of this reprint but
points out that some imperfections in the original copies may be apparent.

Disclaimer
The publisher has made every effort to trace copyright holders and would
welcome correspondence from those they have been unable to trace.

THE COMMUNITY OF OIL EXPORTING COUNTRIES

A Study in Governmental Co-operation

Zuhayr Mikdashi
D.Phil. (Oxon.)

London George Allen & Unwin Ltd
Ruskin House   Museum Street

First published in 1972

ISBN 0 04 350035 8

Printed in Great Britain
in 10 point Times Roman
by Alden & Mowbray Ltd
Oxford

Preface

This book is prompted solely by the author's personal academic interest, and does not purport to defend views held by any party or group. The author has benefited greatly from guest speakers, colleagues, participants and students in his seminars on the economics of the world oil industry held at the Kuwait Institute for Economic and Social Planning in the Middle East and at the American University of Beirut with the assistance of several colleagues, notably Dr George W. Stocking, Professor Emeritus of Vanderbilt University; Dr A. J. Meyer, Associate Director of Harvard University Center for Middle Eastern Studies, and Dr Thomas R. Stauffer, Research Associate at the Center; and Professor Sherill Cleland of Kalamazoo College; and more recently in 1970–71 at Indiana University's Graduate School of Business, where he had a fine group of M.B.A. and doctoral students in his course, and stimulating discussions with several colleagues.

To carry out this research, the author has had the opportunity of visiting major oil exporting and oil importing countries, as well as several other mineral exporting or importing countries where international organizations or mineral companies have their head-quarters – in both the Eastern and the Western hemispheres. He has been privileged in his access to published and unpublished documentation, and has discussed the subject with a large number of highly placed government and industry policy- and decision-makers. His consulting assignments to the United Nations Secretariat, to OPEC, and to individual governments have been of great value to this study.

For scrutinizing and helpful comments on preliminary drafts of this study, a special debt of gratitude is due Professor M. A. Adelman of the Massachusetts Institute of Technology; Professor Edith Penrose of London University; Messrs U. W. Kitzinger, L. E. Baragwanath and Wilfred Knapp of Oxford University; Mr J. E. Hartshorn, author and petroleum consultant.

Several others spared their valuable time to comment on various aspects of the work, notably Professor Cleland, Professor Wayne Leeman of the University of Missouri, Professor William Snavely of the University of Connecticut, Professor Ingo Walter of New York University, Professor Abbas Alnasrawi of the University of Vermont, Mr F. R. Parra, ex-Secretary General of OPEC, Mr J. A. Van den Heuvel, former head of the OECD Energy Division, Mr I. N. H. Seymour of the *Middle East Economic Survey*, and Mr. J. Masseron of the French Petroleum Institute. A large number of government and company officials interviewed by the author have requested anonymity, due to the delicate nature of the issues discussed.

The research was started at the American University of Beirut with the support of a grant there. Additional valuable support has come from the Ford Foundation which is sponsoring the author's study of several minerals. The work was completed at Indiana University's Graduate School of Business, in the congenial atmosphere of the International Business Department, where, thanks to Professor Richard N. Farmer, the author received all the assistance needed to prepare the final draft for publication.

The author is naturally alone responsible for all the information and conclusions of this study.

14 May 1971
ZUHAYR MIKDASHI
Visiting Professor at
Graduate School of Business
Indiana University

Contents

Preface   *page* 8
Abbreviations   15

1 THE PROBLEM AND ITS SETTING
  A. Purpose and Approach   17
  B. The Genesis of OPEC: Early Attempts at Co-operation   22
    I. *Early Venezuelan Contacts*   22
    II. *The Iraqi–Saudi Agreement of 1953*   24
    III. *The Arab League and the Origins of Oil Co-operation* 27
    IV. *Price Cuts and the Establishment of OPEC*   29

2 THE PROTAGONISTS, AND THE OLIGOPOLY MODEL
  A. Control by the Few of Supplies and Markets   35
  B. Vertical Integration and Posted Prices   40
  C. The Concession System and Governmental Control   42
  D. The Undermining of the Oil Oligopoly and Vertical
    Integration   45
  E. The Dilemma of OPEC   50
    I. *Oil Suppliers: the OPEC Objectives*   50
    II. *Consumer Markets*   53
  F. OPEC and its Environment   62

3 CO-OPERATION AMONG OIL EXPORTING COUNTRIES
  A. Measuring Compatibility   70
  B. The OPEC Group   78
    I. *The Conception of OAPEC*   83
    II. *The 'Revolutionary' Countermoves*   87
    III. *Evaluation of Sectoral Integration in Oil* 91

4 INSTITUTIONAL ASPECTS OF OPEC AND OAPEC
   A. OPEC and its Secretariat   96
   B. OAPEC's Organizational Structure   103
   C. OAPEC and the European Communities   107

5 THE JOINT REGULATION OF PRODUCTION
   A. Aims of Production Programming   111
   B. Production Programming and Market Realities   114
   C. Industry's Co-operation   123
   D. Disparities Among OPEC Countries: a 'Rational' Versus a
      'Workable' Formula   127
   E. A Historical Precedent   134

6 BARGAINING FOR ECONOMIC BENEFITS: GOVERNMENT
   REVENUES
   A. Company Profitability   137
   B. Payment of Royalty   142
   C. Raising Posted Prices and Tax Rates   145

7 BARGAINING FOR ECONOMIC BENEFITS: TERMS OF
   TRADE
   A. The Significance of Terms of Trade   157
   B. OPEC and Industry Measures of Terms of Trade   165
   C. The Concepts and the Tools   176
   D. Statistical Limitations and Measurement   183
   E. Inferences   191

8 THE FUTURE OF CO-OPERATIVE EFFORT
   A. The Achievements   196
   B. The Opportunities   207
   C. Expected Structural Changes   214

      Appendix

1 BIOGRAPHICAL NOTES ON OPEC'S SECRETARIES-
   GENERAL

2 SELECTED BIBLIOGRAPHY
   A. Published Official   225
   B. Published Private   228
   C. Selected Trade Journals and Periodicals   231
   D. Unpublished   232

      Index   234

Tables

1.1 Inter-Area Total Oil Movements, 1970 *page* 19

1.2 Oil Production and Proved Reserves in Selected Areas and Years 20

1.3 Value of Six Most Important Commodities Exported by Less Developed Countries, 1950–68 22

2.1 Leading Joint Ventures in the OPEC Arabian–Persian Gulf Countries 38

2.2 Approximate Shares of the Eight Majors in Oil Operations Outside U.S. and Communist Areas 49

2.3 OPEC Policies and External Critical Variables, 1971 63

4.1 Selected Data on OPEC's Secretaries-General 99

5.1 Comparison Between Actual Production Increment and Planned Programme Increment, OPEC Area, July 1956-June 1966 115

5.2 Per Capita GNP and Energy, by Region, 1960–66 120

5.3 Selected Information on OPEC Member Countries, 1969 132

6.1 Production, Earnings and Government Payments of Seven International Oil Companies, Eastern Hemisphere, 1957–70 139

6.2 Summary of Royalty Expensing: Phase-Out of Percentage and Gravity Allowances, 1964–75 144

7.1 Value of Petroleum as a Percentage of Exports for Selected Countries, 1961–70 158

7.2 OPEC (Middle East) Terms of Trade 166

7.3 Selected Price Data with Reference to Kuwait Crude Oil 1951–71 169

7.4 Indices of Unit Values of Imports for Selected OPEC Countries and Years 185

7.5 Indices of Government Take per Unit of Export for Selected OPEC Countries Under the Profit Sharing Agreements, 1952–69   187

7.6 Quantum Indices of Oil Exports for Selected OPEC Countries, 1952–69   188

7.7 Indices of Mid-Year Population for Selected OPEC Countries, 1952–69   189

7.8 Indices of Gain from Oil for Selected OPEC Countries, 1962–69   192

7.9 OPEC Countries' Population (mid-1964 and mid-1969), GNP Per Capita (1968) and Average Annual Growth Rates (1961–68)   195

Charts

3.1 Partial Profiles of Iran and Kuwait with Respect to Co-operation in the OPEC Production Programme of 1966–67 *page* 73

5.1 U.K. Wholesale Price and Wage Indices 118

5.2 Per Capita GNP and Energy, by Region, 1960–66 121

Abbreviations

AIOC	Anglo-Iranian Oil Co.
API	American Petroleum Institute oil gravity measure
Aramco	Arabian American Oil Co.
ARPEL	Association for Reciprocal Assistance by the State-owned Petroleum Companies of Latin America
bbl.	barrel(s)
BP	British Petroleum Co. Ltd
CFP	Compagnie Française des Pétroles
CIPEC	Conseil Intergouvernemental des Pays Exportateurs de Cuivre (Intergovernmental Council of Copper Exporting Countries)
ECSC	European Coal and Steel Community
EEC	European Economic Community
ENI	Ente Nazionale Idrocarburi
ERAP	Entreprise de Recherches et Activités Pétrolières
Gulf	Gulf Oil Corporation
INOC	Iraq National Oil Co.
IPC	Iraq Petroleum Co. Ltd
Jersey	Standard Oil Co. (New Jersey)
KOC	Kuwait Oil Co. Ltd
MEES	Middle East Economic Survey
Mobil	Mobil Oil Corporation
NIOC	National Iranian Oil Co.
OAPEC	Organization of Arab Petroleum Exporting Countries
OECD	Organization for Economic Co-operation and Development
OPEC	Organization of Petroleum Exporting Countries
PIF	Petroleum Information Foundation

PIW	Petroleum Intelligence Weekly
PPS	Petroleum Press Service
RCD	Regional Co-operation for Development
Shell	Royal Dutch/Shell Group
Socal	Standard Oil Co. of California
SONATRACH	Société Nationale pour la Recherche, la Production, le Transport, la Transformation, et la Commercialisation des Hydrocarbures

Chapter 1
THE PROBLEM AND ITS SETTING

Oil is of major economic and strategic importance in the world. It is both the most important source of energy and the largest internationally traded commodity. For several less-developed countries, it has a special significance; it is, by far, their principal foreign exchange earner. Naturally, such countries are unwilling to leave their economic fate to the vagaries of competition; they tend to support arrangements that will protect them from fluctuations in, or deterioration of, their trade receipts. Accordingly, since shortly after World War II they have sought to adopt co-operative schemes. After a number of attempts to overcome political and economic differences, their efforts culminated in 1960 in the creation of a permanent Organization of the Petroleum Exporting Countries (OPEC), the subject of this study.

A. *Purpose and Approach*

A distinguished economist has written that 'the world oil problem is political before it is economic.'[1] The purpose of this study is to examine the political and economic conditions which have affected co-operation among a group of developing countries concerned with promoting their interests in the export of a single commodity, petroleum. Any such analysis raises a number of questions. How was OPEC created, what influence did the international oil industry have on its creation, and what are its objectives? What has been the role of the OPEC Secretariat, and what has been its relation to member governments? Has OPEC influenced the industry's structure? Has OPEC been able to go beyond the few immediate interests common to its members at the time of its establishment and develop new common

[1] M. A. Adelman, 'Efficiency of Resource Use in Crude Petroleum', *The Southern Economic Journal* (October 1964), p. 114.

B   17

interests? To what extent can major factors which shaped it in the past also shape it in the future, and what others will become relevant? OPEC is evaluated in this work with respect to how well it has fulfilled the member's collective and individual objectives; the members' success in manipulating controllable variables to their advantage; its capacity to respond quickly to demands and stresses; and its growth in influence or functions.

This study suggests that OPEC is an original type of international organization; an effort is made to demonstrate that any unique features OPEC may have it owes largely to the special characteristics of the international oil industry (notably concentration, vertical integration, and concession systems), and to its administrative set-up and methods of operation.

This study attempts to prove that OPEC, like a cartel, has endeavoured to control production and prices. The successful enforcement of unanimous collective policies and decisions in this field would necessitate, among other things, delegation of authority and responsibility to a central agency such as the OPEC Secretariat. OPEC member countries have not, however, been willing to grant the Secretariat any supranational role. Moreover, as a result of the economic and non-economic pressures at work in each member country, of the characteristics of the international energy market, and also of the policies of oil importing countries, the OPEC institution has encountered serious problems in formulating and administering production and price controls. This failure is not due to negligence but to some basic difficulties which this study will define and analyse. The fact that OPEC has been generally loosely knit, as far as collective and central decision-making power is concerned, has helped it to accommodate newcomer oil exporting countries and to avoid losing members, thus enabling it to survive as a policy co-ordinating agency.

Furthermore, this study shows that OPEC's scope has remained narrowly confined to its original objectives. The nature of its members' individual needs and requirements has precluded widening its functions. Prospects, however, are probably brighter for regional or subregional groupings composed of fewer and more compatible countries. Nevertheless, OPEC has set an example for groupings among other developing countries, such as the Intergovernmental Council of Copper Exporting Countries (CIPEC) and the Organization of Arab Petroleum Exporting Countries (OAPEC).

OPEC as of 1971 has ten members: seven Arab countries (Abu Dhabi, Algeria, Iraq, Kuwait, Libya, Qatar, and Saudi Arabia)

18

Table 1.1

INTER-AREA TOTAL OIL MOVEMENTS, 1970

(Millions of Tons)

From / *To*	*U.S.A.*	*Canada*	*Other Western Hemisphere*	*Western Europe*	*Africa*	*South-East Asia*	*Japan*	*Australia*	*Other Eastern Hemisphere*	*Destination Not Known*	*Total Exports*
U.S.A.	—	1¼	1¼	3¼	—	3½	3½	—	¼	—	13
Canada	34¼	—	—	—	—	—	—	—	—	1¼	35½
Caribbean	106	25¼	11¼	26½	1	1	1¼	—	—	—	172¼
Other Western Hemisphere	¼	—	1¾	—	—	—	—	—	—	—	2
Western Europe	10½	¼	1½	—	4	—	¼	—	¼	14¼	31
Middle East	8¾	7½	12	309	20¾	39¾	173	17¼	21¼	22¼	631½
North Africa	3¾	—	2¾	220½	¼	—	2	¼	2¼	—	231¾
West Africa	2½	1¾	7¾	44¼	—	—	½	—	—	—	56¾
South-East Asia	3½	—	½	½	—	—	30	4¾	¼	—	39½
U.S.S.R., Eastern Europe	¼	—	4¾	39½	1½	—	¾	—	½	—	47¼
Other Eastern Hemisphere	¼	—	—	—	¼	2	—	—	—	—	2½
Total Imports	170	36	43½	643½	27¾	46¼	211¼	22¼	24¾	37¾	1,263

* Includes changes in stock and increased quantities in transit, transit losses, minor movements not otherwise shown, military use, etc.

Source: BP, *Statistical Review of the World Oil Industry, 1970*, p. 10.

and three non-Arab countries (Indonesia, Iran, and Venezuela).[1] Since 1960, OPEC countries have accounted for the bulk of world oil trade (about 85 per cent), which moves largely to the developed

Table 1.2

OIL PRODUCTION AND PROVED RESERVES IN SELECTED
AREAS AND YEARS

(Millions of Tons)

	1938	*1951*	*1960*	*1970*
U.S.A.				
Production	162	298	342	478
Reserves at end of year	2,300	3,645	4,190	6,100
Production as % of reserves	7·04	8·17	8·16	7·84
Caribbean				
Production	33	97	163	212
Reserves at end of year	430	1,510	2,780	2,300
Production as % of reserves	7·67	6·42	5·86	9·22
Middle East				
Production	15	94	257	689
Reserves at end of year	670	6,875	24,475	47,000
Production as % of reserves	2·23	1·36	1·05	1·47
U.S.S.R., Eastern Europe, China				
Production	35	47	166	390
Reserves at end of year	770	1,070	4,535	13,700
Production as % of reserves	4·54	4·39	3·66	2·84
Africa				
Production	—	—	—	300
Reserves at end of year	—	—	—	9,800
Production as % of reserves	—	—	—	3·06
World				
Production	268	580	1,041	2,353
Reserves at end of year	4,585	13,935	39,960	84,100
Production as % of reserves	5·84	4·16	2·60	2·80

Source: B P, *Statistical Reviews of the World Oil Industry.*

industrial world (Table 1·1). Their share in world production and reserves for 1970 was over 50 per cent and 70 per cent, respectively.

Other large oil exporting countries in 1971 were the Soviet Union, Nigeria, Muscat and Oman, and U.A.R. (Egypt). Most have objectives somewhat similar to those of OPEC members, but have followed paths dictated by their own particular circumstances. The

[1] Nigeria joined as the eleventh member in July 1971.

United States, although the largest oil producer in the world (about 20 per cent of world production in 1970), is a net oil importer – the second largest after Japan (see Tables 1.1 and 1.2). In 1970, the United States imported about 23 per cent of its oil supply, close to 15 per cent of world oil trade; whereas Western Europe and Japan imported 95 per cent of their oil requirements, over two-thirds of world oil trade.

A common feature of major oil exporting countries is their dependence – in varying degrees – on oil as a foreign exchange earner and as a major element in state receipts (see Tables 5.3 and 7.1). The desert countries – for example, Kuwait, Qatar, and Abu Dhabi – depend almost completely on oil for their livelihood and prosperity, in contrast to countries with more diversified economies, such as Indonesia. The majority of the oil exporting countries also belong to the group defined broadly as developing countries, whose prosperity is generally affected by the export conditions of one or two commodities.

The study spans the whole post-World War II period. Important developments occurred in the Middle East during that period: several of the countries in the area attained independence, and the Middle East and North Africa emerged as the major oil producing and exporting area of the world after the discovery of vast and low-cost reserves.

The significance of a study of the community of oil exporting countries relates to the fact that the majority of these countries are situated in a crucial area of the world – the Middle East – and to the fact that oil is a commodity of major international importance, supplying in 1970 about three-fourths of world energy needs. UN statistics indicate that petroleum alone constituted over 9 per cent of world exports by value in 1960–70. For the less-developed countries, it represents by far the most important commodity exported; its value amounts to over five times that of copper, the next most important commodity. Moreover, petroleum exports from these countries have risen dramatically since World War II, about 9 per cent per annum (Table 1.3). Furthermore, oil has weighed importantly in political and military decisions.

The study relies almost exclusively on primary sources for information concerning the areas dealt with, obtained by the author from various parties. These include OPEC and its member countries, other oil exporting countries, various international or regional agencies, various agencies of major oil importing countries, and the oil companies. The author has also had access to responsible officials, and unpublished information. He has, however, taken care

21

whenever possible to quote only evidence or information available to the public.

Table 1.3

VALUE OF SIX MOST IMPORTANT COMMODITIES EXPORTED BY
LESS DEVELOPED COUNTRIES, 1950–68*

(Billions of U.S. Dollars)

Year	Petroleum	Copper	Coffee	Sugar	Cotton	Rubber†
1950	2·50	0·39	1·69	0·90	1·20	1·54
1951	3·06	0·52	2·06	1·04	1·44	2·67
1952	3·40	0·67	2·15	1·00	1·33	1·40
1953	3·34	0·70	2·38	1·03	1·30	0·94
1954	4·00	0·66	2·48	0·92	1·33	0·94
1955	4·45	0·92	2·21	1·01	1·36	1·57
1956	4·75	1·12	2·44	1·04	1·26	1·39
1957	5·21	0·80	2·27	1·35	1·04	1·34
1958	5·67	0·61	2·02	1·19	1·04	1·19
1959	6·05	0·88	1·89	1·07	1·07	1·68
1960	6·32	1·04	1·85	1·22	1·09	1·71
1961	6·66	0·99	1·79	1·34	1·10	1·52
1962	7·54	1·05	1·82	1·19	1·14	1·45
1963	8·34	1·03	1·95	1·69	1·30	1·35
1964	8·94	1·10	2·29	1·74	1·24	1·21
1965	9·51	1·34	2·14	1·44	1·33	1·24
1966	10·37	2·11	2·29	1·38	1·32	1·25
1967	11·64	2·21	2·15	1·50	1·18	1·09
1968	13·14	2·36	2·30	1·46	1·30	1·13

* The commodities mentioned were the most important in the years 1960–68.
† Including gums.

Source: International Bank for Reconstruction and Development, *Trends in Developing Countries*, Washington, D.C., June 1970, Table 4.7.

B. *The Genesis of OPEC: Early Attempts at Co-operation*

Attempts at formal and effective economic co-operation among oil exporting countries can be traced back to the late 1940s and early 1950s. Co-operation occurred in both bilateral and multilateral forms.

I. *Early Venezuelan Contacts*
In 1947, diplomatic contacts were made in Washington between the

22

Venezuelan and Iranian diplomatic missions, at the time of the start of Iran's eventful negotiations with its concessionaire the Anglo-Iranian Oil Co. (AIOC). In 1949, an official Venezuelan delegation paid a series of visits, for the first time, to Middle East oil producing governments. Arab and Iranian official oil delegations were invited to visit Venezuela in the summer of 1951.[1] These contacts were prompted by Venezuela's apprehension over the rapid growth of sales of and competition from Middle East oil extracted at tax-paid costs much lower than Venezuela's. The Venezuelan government hoped at that time to induce Middle East governments to raise fiscal charges on concessionary companies.

In fact, the information the Venezuelan delegation gave in 1947–50 on their own income tax arrangements to the Iranian, Saudi, and other governments in the Middle East was partly responsible for changing the method and for raising the level of payments of oil companies to host governments in the Middle East. The system then current called for a fixed royalty per unit of production or export, generally 4 shillings gold per ton (about 22 cents a barrel). It was first replaced in Saudi Arabia in December 1950 in order to raise government receipts to 50 per cent of imputed notional income on oil exports. Expatriate companies, particularly U.S. companies, have not suffered from that arrangement to the extent they are eligible for tax credit in their countries of origin on tax payments made overseas.[2]

Nevertheless, the pattern of terms which emerged in the Middle East was different from that in Venezuela in two major respects: first, Middle East governments did not receive separate royalty payments over and above income tax payments (as was the practice in Venezuela); and second, even more significant, Middle East governments could not legislate unilateral changes in concession terms, in particular, fiscal terms. Thus under the Middle East 50–50 arrangements, the 50 per cent rate of income tax was limited to a maximum, whatever later tax changes. In Venezuela, as in most developed countries of Northern America and Western Europe, concession agreements do not fix the income tax; the government is entitled to change this like any other tax. Although companies have complained

[1] See OPEC, *Background Information* (Geneva, 1964), p. 11; also, Abdallah Tariki, 'The Organization of Petroleum Exporting Countries – Why it was established and what objectives it has fulfilled since its establishment', *The Arab Oil and Gas Journal* (Arabic), Beirut (November 1965), pp. 13–17.

[2] See a detailed analysis of this subject in Zuhayr Mikdashi, *A Financial Analysis of Middle Eastern Oil Concessions: 1901–65* (New York: Praeger, 1966), pp. 135–45.

23

on economic grounds when the Venezuelan government has increased its tax take, they have not been able to complain that such
action is in breach of the agreements.

II. *The Iraqi-Saudi Agreement of 1953*

The first formal agreement of co-operation concluded between oil
exporting countries was signed on 29 June 1953 between Iraq and
Saudi Arabia. It prescribed the exchange of oil information and the
holding of periodical consultations about petroleum policies.

It is revealing that the Iraqi–Saudi agreement was signed in the
aftermath of the abortive nationalization of the Iranian oil industry
on 1 May 1951. Iranian oil exports were almost brought to a stand-
still from May 1951 to October 1954, as a result of a successful
collective boycott instituted by international oil companies in
support of the nationalized Anglo-Iranian Oil Co. (renamed British
Petroleum Co. Ltd (BP) in 1954). Private companies with sufficient
market outlets to handle a substantial volume of Middle East oil
were, as a matter of principle, against buying nationalized Iranian
oil, they were aware that the ownership of this production was in
dispute and that they ran the risk of legal action outside Iran if it
were exported. Bearing in mind the gravity of the deadlock between
Iran and the international oil companies, Iraqi and Saudi officials
sought co-operation with a view to improving their bargaining
position *vis-à-vis* the companies.

Among the varied and complex reasons that sparked the Iranian
nationalization movement was the dissatisfaction of the Iranian
government with British hegemony in oil matters. Moreover,
financial terms won after protracted negotiations with the Anglo-
Iranian Oil Company, the British concessionaire, appeared to
Iranian politicians far less attractive than terms already obtained by
neighbouring Saudi Arabia from its respective concessionaires.[1]

Host governments have always tried to obtain terms in line with
the best available in the region, or even internationally. The Iraqi–
Saudi agreement of 1953 was intended to be a first step in assisting
host governments to win the so-called best-terms clauses from their
concessionaires. These clauses first found their way into the Middle
East oil agreements in the 1950s. A feature common to these clauses
is that host governments can call on their concessionaires to discuss
possible revisions of agreements if neighbouring countries obtain
better terms.

Thus, the Iraqi government in 1956, learning of an improvement in

[1] *Ibid.*, pp. 153–60.

the Saudi government's financial terms with Aramco, sought and obtained an improvement in its own terms. It obtained a reduction from 2 to 1 per cent in the so-called selling expense allowable to the concessionaire off the relevant price used for Iraq income tax purposes on oil exports. That expense was supposed to represent a commutation of actual costs incurred by the parent companies of the producing companies while arranging for the marketing of oil exports. But since most Middle East oil moved in integrated channels or on long-term contracts, little or no out-of-pocket costs were incurred by the producing companies in selling their oil to affiliates of their parent companies. The 1 per cent reduction in selling expense led in 1956 and in 1957 to an increase in the Iraqi government revenues, averaging about £1,000,000 annually.[1]

Beginning in 1958, the Iraqi government – again in line with a precedent set by Saudi Arabia in 1955 – refused to allow volume discounts on prices to concessionaire companies for income tax purposes. These discounts represented reductions in tax liabilities and were originally intended as an incentive to increase exports. Volume discounts in Saudi Arabia prior to 1955 averaged 18·5 per cent of posted prices;[2] they amounted in Iraq in 1956–57 to 5 per cent of prices for the first 8 million tons exported beyond the agreed minimum of 30 million tons, a 7·5 per cent discount for the next 8 million tons, and a 10 per cent discount for all additional exports.[3] The elimination of these discounts for income tax purposes increased the Iraqi government's revenues per unit of exports in 1958 by about 7 per cent. The Saudi Director-General in 1960 (in 1961 the Minister of Petroleum and Mineral Resources) commented on these discounts as follows:

In the past the oil companies did not give us the peace of mind to take all what they said to be in our best interest, and I am going just to give you one example. When we made the 50–50 agreement [in 1950], after a year or so we discovered that Aramco was putting $1.42 in their books [for Saudi income tax purposes].

[1] Nadim al-Pachachi, *Iraqi Oil Policy. August, 1954–December, 1957* (Official Documents), The Research and Translation Office (Beirut, June 1958), pp. 13–18.

[2] The first to start posting prices in the Middle East for sales to third parties was Mobil which announced on 1 November 1950 for Saudi Arabian crude (36–36·9° API) a price of $1.75/bbl. f.o.b. Ras Tanura, and for Qatar crude (37–37·9° API) a price of $1.77/bbl. f.o.b. Umm Said. *Platt's Oil Price Handbook for 1950* (Cleveland, Ohio; 1951), p. 307.

[3] Memorandum of Agreement between the government of Iraq and the Iraq Petroleum Company Ltd. (IPC) and its Associated Companies (24 March 1955).

25

When we asked, they said this was a [18·5 per cent] discount for the parent companies to build marketing facilities. . . . We didn't sign that agreement, in effect, the 50–50 was only 32–68.[1]

The Director-General's statement should be carefully scrutinized in the light of pricing practices then current in the international oil industry. In fact, the 18·5 per cent discount yields a price of $1·42 per barrel, which is roughly equivalent to the weighted average of realized prices obtained by a major seller of crude (see author's primary price data in Table 7.3 on Gulf Oil Corporation sales of Kuwait oil to non-affiliates) after due allowance for the differential in quality (mostly that of a 3 degree API gravity) and freight in favour of Saudi oil. Needless to say, Aramco's parents were then resorting to some price differentiation among buyers with a view to maximizing their sales revenues and reducing their tax burden.[2]

The attempts of host governments to make profitable use of the best-terms clauses were, more often than not, met with staunch resistance from the oil companies. These clauses are artfully worded by concessionaires to spare themselves commitment to accept changes in their fiscal obligations *vis-à-vis* host governments; understandably, they wish to protect their profits. The concessionaires' only commitment is willingness to review and discuss the possibility of raising their payments to host governments in the light of changes taking place in certain specified countries and/or concessions.

Attempts by oil exporting countries to improve the fiscal terms of their concessions by bilateral negotiations with companies were, on several occasions, successful, although the parties concerned (whether companies or governments) often managed to delay negotiations, to waver about acceding to each other's demands for more favourable arrangements or to water down these demands. Further, to promote their interests, oil exporting countries have sought collective multilateral action; their increasing sense of political independence *vis-à-vis* Western nations has undoubtedly encouraged them to do so.

[1] Abdallah Tariki, 'Minutes of the 4th Meeting', *Second Arab Oil Congress* (Beirut, 21 October 1960).

See also for evidence on these discounts: George W. Ray, Jr., General Counsel, *Arbitration between the Government of Saudi Arabia and Arabian American Oil Company – Memorial of Arabian American Oil Co. 1955*, Vol. IV, pp. 2282–98. (Not published).

[2] See Mikdashi, *op. cit.*, pp. 185–7.

III. *The Arab League and the Origins of Oil Co-operation*

Formal multilateral multipurpose co-operation in modern times among Middle East countries began with the signing on 7 October 1944 of the Alexandria Protocol calling for the establishment of the League of Arab States. The league's pact was signed on 22 March 1945 by the heads of states of the then independent Arab countries: Egypt, Iraq, Lebanon, Saudi Arabia, Syria, Trans-Jordan, and Yemen. A Palestinian delegation participated with an observer-status, since Palestine was then a British mandate.

The objectives of the league are primarily 'defensive' (Article 2):

> The League has as its purpose the strengthening of the relations between the member states; the co-ordination of their policies in order to achieve co-operation between them and to safeguard their independence and sovereignty; and a general concern with the affairs and interests of the Arab countries.

The league 'has also as its purpose the close co-operation of the member states' in economic and financial affairs, communications, nationality affairs, social affairs, and health affairs.

The league in no way limits members' sovereignty. Its governing body is a council assisted by specialized committees. All member states are represented on the council with one vote each. Resolutions are binding only on those states which accept them.

The defensive or common threat factor which prompted Arab statesmen to launch the Arab League in 1945 became more compelling after 1948 when the highly dynamic and resourceful state of Israel came into being in a hitherto predominantly Arab Palestine.[1] The presence of an expansive state in their midst was, and has remained, a matter of grave concern to Palestinians and other Arabs, and has markedly influenced the area's economic and political life. Following that momentous event, five members of the Arab League (Egypt, Lebanon, Saudi Arabia, Syria, and Yemen) signed a collective security pact known as the Joint Defence and Economic Co-operation Treaty on 17 June 1950; they were joined in 1952 by Iraq and Jordan, in 1961 by Morocco and Kuwait, and in 1964 by Algeria, Tunisia, Libya, and Sudan.[2]

[1] To a historian of modern times, 'the core of the Pact lay in the anxieties of the Arab states over the Jewish question'. Wilfred Knapp, *A History of War and Peace, 1939–1965* (Oxford: Oxford University Press, 1967), p. 163.

In 1948, 'the creation of the Jewish state of Israel had destroyed the Arab state of Palestine', p. 176.

[2] The treaty provided for the establishment – under the supervision of the Arab League Council – of two councils: a Joint Defence Council consisting of

The 1950 treaty was obviously intended to meet external threats, and economic co-operation among member states was sought originally as a by-product of joint defence. Thus the Permanent Military Commission, besides its military functions, is required to 'submit proposals for the exploitation of natural, agricultural, industrial, and other resources of all Contracting States in favour of the inter-Arab military effort and joint defence'.

That provision was to prove of some significance to oil, the most important natural resource in the Arab world, as subsequent events have shown. It has often been argued that it is only in self-defence that many functional organizations get started at all. Certainly, the league's and the treaty's economic activities are by-products of defence requirements, and are reminiscent of European functionalism since World War II. Mandatory membership in the treaty for those members wishing to join the league's Economic Council was removed in 1960.

The Political Committee of the Arab League pioneered co-operation in oil affairs by sponsoring a Committee of Oil Experts, which first convened on 14 June 1952. The reason behind the establishment of the committee was primarily political, namely the national security of Arab countries. This meant the protection of the political independence and the territorial integrity of Arab states. It was hoped it would be achieved at that time by instituting a general economic boycott, including a boycott of oil supplies to Israel with a view to cutting the latter's military capacity for expansion into neighbouring Arab countries.[1] The Committee of Oil Experts was also concerned with co-ordination of Arab states' oil policies, and with studying oil projects which would result in common benefits for the Arab world.

In order to assist the committee, the league's council decided on 20 January 1954 to establish a permanent Petroleum Bureau (renamed Department of Oil Affairs in 1959) under the supervision of the league's Political Committee. Some ten years elapsed before Oil Affairs was shifted from the League's Political Committee to its Economic Committee on 23 March 1964. The shift represents a change of outlook in the league's oil policy. In the first two decades of its existence, the league considered oil essentially a strategic in-

Foreign Ministers and Defence Ministers, and an Economic Council consisting of Ministers in charge of economic affairs. The latter can enlist the services of the Economic and Financial Affairs Committee of the Arab League.

[1] Arab League – Oil Affairs Department, *The Efforts of the League of Arab States in Oil Affairs* (Cairo, 16 April 1959), p. 9.

strument of defence; more recently it has increasingly emphasized oil's role as an instrument of socio-economic development in Arab countries.

One of the major activities of the League's Department of Oil Affairs has been the sponsoring of Arab oil congresses. The general purpose of these congresses, as originally set, was educational – to 'spread petroleum knowledge among Arab populations, in order to induce the responsible quarters to create a generation of young people trained in oil affairs, and to acquaint individuals in these populations with the importance of oil as a principal source of national income'[1].

Besides the preparation of oil congresses, the Oil Affairs Department has, since 1957, produced a number of 'paper' agreements and projects: the Agreement on the Co-ordination of Oil Policies; a draft Treaty on an Arab Petroleum Organization; a project for an Arab Oil Pipelines Company; a project for an Arab Oil Tankers Company; a project for an Arab Oil Producing Company; and a draft agreement on an Arab Petroleum Research Institute. These agreements and projects have never been ratified or implemented, and the parties concerned have shown little willingness to co-operate effectively in the oil sector. The decision to co-operate is in essence a political one, and bickering among Arab governments has occasionally ended up in fratricidal bloodshed.

Given its proven inadequacy as a framework for oil policy formulation and execution, the league has in recent years been relegated by major Arab oil exporting countries to a secondary economic role. More specifically, a number of Arab countries have attempted to achieve closer co-operation and co-ordination of oil policy through separate organizations, such as the Organization of Arab Petroleum Exporting Countries (OAPEC) established in 1968.

IV. *Price Cuts and the Establishment of OPEC*
Reductions in posted prices of oil exports are of grave concern to host countries, since the latter's income tax receipts are based on these prices. Moreover, uneven reductions of posted prices may favour the oil exports of one country or area at the expense of others. Thus the Venezuelan government protested to the British ambassador in February 1959 against the excessive reductions in Middle East posted prices (about 8 per cent and averaging 18 cents a barrel) initiated by BP, since the British government was then a majority

[1] *The Efforts of the League of Arab States in Oil Affairs* (Cairo: Arab League – Oil Affairs Department, 16 April 1959), p. 33 (author's translation).

shareholder (51 per cent) in that comapny. It is doubtful, however, whether the British government had any direct say in deciding on these price changes. The Venezuelan government argued that BP (which does not operate in Venezuela) was undermining the international price structure with a view to invading the traditional markets of Venezuela with Middle East crude. The government's protest said:

On February 6 [1959], the Shell Oil Company of Venezuela announced a price reduction ranging from 5 to 15 cents per barrel according to the type of oil. . . . *The price reduction adopted by Venezuela was kept within the limits dictated by the United States market situation.*

But the reductions announced by the British Petroleum Company on February 12, for their Kuwait, Iran and Qatar production, went much further than those put into effect in Venezuela and the United States. . . .

. . . It has been said that the British Petroleum Company took advantage of the readjustment which followed the Suez crisis [1956] and now of the economic recession in the American Continent in order to break the logical tie between the international petroleum price structure and prices in the United States, which is not only the largest producer but also the most important consumer in the world.[1]

One month later, crude oil price postings in Venezuela had to be reduced further to match the higher reductions already in effect in the Middle East.[2] This change upset the Venezuelan government, which realized the degree of interdependence and competition between Venezuela and Middle East oil sources in major markets. Accordingly the Venezuelan government strove to join Middle East governments in their endeavour to protect prices and per-barrel oil revenues from declining further.

To claim that there is or has been a so-called single logical tie between prices in the U.S. market and prices outside it does not stand the test of market realities. But prior to World War II, Texas was the world's largest oil exporting area; this fact made the Gulf of

---

[1] Memorandum from the Ministry of Mines and Hydrocarbons to the British Ambassador in Caracas relative to the British Petroleum Company and the reduction in the price of petroleum, March 1959, in: Republic of Venezuela, *Venezuela and OPEC*, Imprenta Nacional, Caracas, 1961, pp. 99–100 (their italics).

[2] Ref. *Platt's Oil Price Handbook 1959*, pp. 227–9.

Mexico the basing point for most oil prices in international trade. By 1943, the Arabian–Persian Gulf started to become a major exporting area, and consequently developed into another basing point, thus leading to the formation of a dual-basing point system in world oil trade.[1]

Shortly after the above-mentioned reductions in posted prices, the First Arab Oil Congress, to which Iran and Venezuela were invited as observers, met in April 1959 in Cairo. Its significance – for oil exporting countries, oil importing countries, and international companies – went far beyond mere education. The Oil Congress offered a handy forum for expressing oil exporting countries' dissatisfaction and apprehension over these reductions although, by the terms of their agreements, concessionaires had no obligation to consult Middle East governments on changes in posted prices.

The fact that Arab oil exports have never exceeded 30 per cent of world oil demand may have led Arab policy-makers of oil exporting countries to look for effective international co-operation beyond the frame of the Arab League, to non-Arab oil exporting countries. The first such attempt at multinational co-operation came on the heels of the First Arab Oil Congress; it took the form of an Oil Consultation Commission, a forerunner of the Organization of the Petroleum Exporting Countries (OPEC). According to Abdallah Tariki, Saudi Arabia's Minister of Petroleum and Mineral Resources in 1961, the OPEC idea owes its existence to the First Arab Oil Congress.[2]

Venezuela played an active role in starting multinational co-operation in oil affairs. Early in 1959, the Venezuelan Minister of Mines and Hydrocarbons, Pérez Alfonzo, proposed the establishment of an international agreement 'in order to avoid the continued waste of a basic energy source such as oil with its detrimental effects to producers and consumers.[3] In April 1959, on the occasion of the First Arab Petroleum Congress, he sponsored the idea of constituting an Oil Consultation Commission to 'permit the discussion of common problems so as to arrive at coincident conclusions'. This commission was to include Iran and Venezuela, besides the Arab oil exporting countries and the Arab League Organization.[4] It is interesting to note that the U.A.R. (Egypt) – though not at that time a net oil exporting country – was among its founding members. The

[1] See Mikdashi, *op. cit.*, pp. 95–7 and 169–73.
[2] Proceedings of Group I at the Third Arab Petroleum Congress (Alexandria, 19 October 1961), p. 6.
[3] *Venezuela and OPEC, op. cit.*, p. 135.
[4] *Ibid.*, pp. 103–4.

fact that it was the host country to the League of Arab States and to the First Arab Petroleum Congress, that it owned promising oil areas, and that it operated the Suez Canal – then a vital artery for oil traffic – had much to do with its participation. Venezuela's politicians believed also that to achieve their country's objective of co-operating with Arab oil countries, they must operate through Cairo which loomed large in Arab politics.

The Oil Consultation Commission advocated the stabilization of posted or tax reference prices on crude oil exports. Further, it wanted companies contemplating changes in these prices first to seek approval by the host countries concerned. Moreover, it advised host governments in the Middle East to raise their tax-take on oil exports. This last recommendation was prompted by Venezuela's wish to see its Middle East competitors producing lower cost crudes raise their levies on oil exports. They would thereby narrow the differential between Venezuelan and Middle East tax-paid costs for similar crudes sold in major importing centres. The short-run impact of the recommended policy would be to reduce the economic advantage of Middle East crudes available to producing companies. The long-run impact would be to reduce these companies' incentive to explore for new deposits in the Middle East; this impact would not worry unduly those host governments which have vast proved oil reserves.

But the Oil Consultation Commission was short-lived. According to Venezuelans, its demise was attributable to 'the opposition of interested parties'[1] – presumably the opposition of Iran and certain Arab leaders (notably General Kassem of Iraq) to the U.A.R.[2]

On 13 May 1960 Venezuela's Minister of Mines and Hydrocarbons, still Pérez Alfonzo, and Saudi Arabia's Director-General of Petroleum Affairs, Abdallah Tariki, once again sought concerted action. They called for the formulation and execution of a common petroleum policy to safeguard the legitimate interests of the oil exporting countries.

In August 1960, the international oil companies further reduced posted prices by about 8 to 10 cents a barrel (approximately 6 per cent). A top executive of the world's largest oil company admitted the responsibility of the majors. He acknowledged that cuts in Middle East posted prices were made because of 'competitive offers and sales made at sizable discounts below posted prices by major

[1] *Ibid.*, p. 140.
[2] See David Hirst, *Oil and Public Opinion in the Middle East* (Faber & Faber; London, 1966), p. 110.

32

suppliers'[1]. The August 1960 posted price cut implied an imputed 'loss of tax proceeds' to Middle East host governments of 4 cents a barrel assuming an inelastic demand; this 'loss' was imputed at some $300 million for exports over the period of August 1960 to the end of 1963.[2] Following this price reduction, representatives from the governments of Iran, Iraq, Kuwait, Saudi Arabia and Venezuela conferred in an atmosphere of crisis in Baghdad[3] from 10 to 14 September 1960. They agreed – a decision later to prove momentous – to create a permanent Organization of the Petroleum Exporting Countries (OPEC) 'with a view to coordinating and unifying the policies of the Members' (Res. I.2).

Besides Alfonzo and Tariki, credit for OPEC's creation should go to Shah Mohammad Riza Pahlavi of Iran and the former ruler of Iraq, General Abdul-Karim Kassem. The Shah was offended at the way in which the companies had reduced posted prices in August 1960. He said that 'even if the action was basically sound it could not be acceptable to us as long as it was taken without our consent'[4]. His indignation caused him to overcome his suspicion of collaborating with Arab regimes, and particularly with the revolutionary anti-monarchical regime of General Kassem in neighbouring Iraq. Furthermore, the presence of Venezuela allayed his fears, and provided him with the hedge that Iran would not be the only non-Arab country in such a group.

Kassem acted as host to OPEC's first conference partly to enhance his personal prestige, and partly to obtain support from participating countries to strengthen his hand in his negotiations with the concessionaire (The Iraq Petroleum Co. Ltd) with whom he was then in acute conflict. The ruling family of Kuwait (the al-Sabbah) also sought active participation in OPEC with a view to gaining economic as well as political advantage. Politically, the al-Sabbah family hoped to gain international recognition for their sheikhdom, then still under British political tutelage in foreign affairs, defence matters, and legal jurisdiction over foreigners.[5]

[1] *Oil and Gas Journal*, 15 August 1960, p. 15.

[2] *Background Information, op. cit.*, p. 5.

[3] Tariki claimed that he suggested (then as Saudi Arabia's top oil official) holding such a conference in Baghdad, *Arab Oil and Gas Journal*, November 1965, *op. cit.*, p. 15.

[4] *Press Conferences of His Imperial Majesty Mohammad Reza Shah Pahlavi of Iran, 1960–1961*, Office of Information (Tehran, 1961), p. 36.

[5] Before independence on 19 June 1961, the U.K. had an exclusive treaty with the Ruler of Kuwait in which he does *inter-alia* 'pledge and bind himself, his heirs and successors not to receive the Agent or Representative of any Power or

C

OPEC's creation was generally well-received in all member countries; it is difficult, however, to detail the various shades of opinion regarding its creation and its growth. Most of these countries, although with diverse political systems and experiences, have predominantly monolithic states, and lack the freedom of expression allowed various interest groups in pluralist societies. Nevertheless, one can detect, as shown later, that support for OPEC has not been uniform in all members at all times. Domestic and international pressures of an economic and non-economic nature faced by each member government have, in fact, affected the solidarity of member countries.

Government at Kuwait, or at any other place within the limits of his territory, without the previous sanction of the British Government; and he further binds himself, his heirs and successors not to cede, sell, lease, mortgage, or give for occupation or for any other purpose any portion of his territory to the Government or subjects of any other Power without the previous consent of Her Majesty's Government for these purposes'.

See document entitled 'Agreement between Great Britain and Kuwait providing for non-Cession of Territory within the Sheikhdom – 23rd January 1899' in *British and Foreign State Papers, 1961–62*, vol. 166, Her Majesty's Stationery Office, London, 1968, p. 112; also in J. C. Hurewitz, *Diplomacy in the Near and Middle East, A Documentary Record: 1535–1914*, Vol. I, Van Nostrand, New York, 1956, pp. 218–19.

Other territories in Eastern Arabia (Bahrain, Qatar, Abu Dhabi, Dubai, Sharjah, Ajman, Umm al-Qaiwain, Ras al-Khaima, Fujairah, and Muscat and Oman) have had until 1971 broadly similar 'special treaty relationships'. See: J. B. Kelly, *Britain and the Persian Gulf, 1795–1880*, Oxford University Press, Oxford, 1968, pp. 834–6.

Chapter 2
THE PROTAGONISTS, AND THE OLIGOPOLY MODEL

OPEC's creation and development have been influenced by three major characteristics of the international oil industry: the highly concentrated structure, vertical integration of oil companies operating on an international basis, and certain features of the traditional oil concession system. An analysis of these characteristics will contribute to a better understanding of the relationships between oil companies and OPEC countries.

The OPEC idea embodies the belief that the economic benefits of member countries are, in the long run, likely to be greater if they stick together. Concessionaire companies and their parent countries see OPEC as a threat, and consumer countries generally are concerned about the political and economic implications of OPEC's actions. The relationships among the protagonists in the world oil industry can be summarily described with a matrix model. The model should be useful for identifying major collective OPEC policies and key external variables of various groups which constrain or favour OPEC's goal of benefits optimization.

A. *Control by the Few of Supplies and Markets*

The international oil industry, outside the United States and the Communist bloc, has had a highly concentrated structure (see Table 2·2); it is oligopolistic in the sale market for crude and products, and oligopsonistic in the purchase market for oil production or oil supply rights. Eight large companies have dominated, controlling close to 80 per cent of world crude oil trade in 1970. Of these companies five are American: Standard Oil Company of New Jersey (Jersey), Texaco, Gulf Oil Corporation (Gulf), Standard Oil Company of California (Socal), Mobil Oil Corporation (Mobil); one is Anglo-Dutch: Royal-Dutch Shell (Shell); one is British: British

Petroleum Company Ltd. (BP); and one is French: Compagnie Française des Pétroles (CFP).

Even in the United States, petroleum refining and distribution has a relatively high concentration ratio. In petrol sales, eight companies have raised their total share of the U.S. market from 60 per cent in 1960 to over 80 per cent in 1968.[1]

No single measure commands general acceptance for ranking oil companies by size, and each measure produces a different result. For instance, the list based on volume of crude oil production differs from that based on product sales. Other dimensions of size are oil reserves, equity capital, earnings, assets, and employees.[2] In product sales for 1970, Jersey ranked first with 5,684 thousand barrels per day, followed by Shell with 5,246, Texaco with 2,917, Mobil with 2,145, BP with 2,118, Socal with 1,919, Gulf with 1,545, and CFP with close to 1,000. Figures for 1970 show that Jersey and Texaco are reasonably well 'balanced' in their integrated operations; their crude oil supplies approximately match their refinery facilities and their sales of products. By comparison, BP, Gulf, and to a lesser extent CFP and Socal are 'long' on crude, whereas Shell and Mobil are relatively 'short'.

Under conditions of so-called rational economic behaviour, it is generally acknowledged and reasonably well-proved that an oligopolistic industrial structure tends to develop awareness of interdependency. The few firms involved lean toward a 'don't-rock-the-boat' policy with respect to business policies or practices which can be readily matched by competitors, primarily the pricing of standardized or homogeneous products and to some extent the financial terms of oil contracts with host governments. This behaviour can be attributed to the fact that every move of a rival is noticed and its impact soon felt by the other firms; fear of retaliation and chain reaction leading eventually to price wars (or spiralling costs in the case of oil contracts) may well induce an oligopolist to refrain from starting open competition. Such understanding among the oligopolistic firms (whether they are buyers or sellers) can, generally, only be tacit; explicit, formal or even informal arrangements are subject to legal prosecution in several countries under antitrust legislation.

Avoiding the dangers of price wars calls for a level of 'maturity' among individual firms, an awareness of interdependence, and

---

[1] *Fortune*, Chicago, June 1969, p. 108; see also L. W. Weiss, *Case Studies in American Industry*, John Wiley, New York, 1967, pp. 7 and 237–48.

[2] See, for example, M. A. Adelman, 'The Measurement of Industrial Concentration', *The Review of Economics and Statistics*, XXXIII (1951), pp. 269–96.

knowledge of what retaliation to expect from rivals. The harmony reached within a mature industry does not necessarily mean the absence of competition. Competition among firms is then likely to be mostly non-price and non-financial competition, as the industry may have a cluster of prices or financial terms that are tolerable to all from the point of view of profits.

Regarding the significance of the low number of international oil companies, Adelman surmises that 'had there been a large group – say of the order of twenty or more – prices would have started to fold earlier [than 1958], and then the [host] governments would have intervened earlier. But a small interrelated group [of eight] was able, without any consultation, to stand fast, try to gain business by all possible non-price methods, and leave the price alone . . .'[1]

An understanding among businesses – supported by barriers to entry of new operators – is likely to lead to less competition among the interested parties; more stable but higher prices to consumers, if the latter happen to be many and non-organized; and probably higher company profits, as compared with the situation in an openly competitive industry.[2] Attractively higher company profits cannot be maintained for long since they will invite entry and competition, as well as governmental action in the form of antitrust action and increased taxation. As far as oil exporting countries are concerned, business concentration and *entente* among major companies in their bids for oil rights is likely to yield host governments less attractive financial terms – other things being equal – than would be the case if these same companies were competing.

The concentrated structure of the international oil industry has been supported by joint ventures and interlocking directorates[3] among major oil companies in one or more of the integrated stages of the industry; interlocking directorates exist when an individual serves on the boards of directors of two or more companies. Joint ventures are most common at the exploration and production stage (see Table 2.1), and less so at the refining or marketing stages. Co-operation among oil companies at the production level does not necessarily lead to co-operation at the marketing end; partners in a

---

[1] M. A. Adelman, 'The World Oil Outlook', *Natural Resources and International Development*, ed. Marion Clawson, Resources for the Future (Baltimore: The Johns Hopkins Press, 1964), p. 86.

[2] Higher company profits may also be due to efficiency, innovation or economic rent. See, for example, J. S. Bain, *Industrial Organization* (New York: Wiley, 1959), pp. 411–16; and Weiss, *Case Studies in American Industry*, pp. 317–28.

[3] See also Peter C. Dooley, 'The Inter-locking Directorate', *The American Economic Review* (June 1969), pp. 314–23.

37

joint producing venture are likely, however, to exercise some restraint and not resort to cut-throat competition in marketing their products.

Joint control of oil operations has been encouraged by a number of factors. In addition to averting severe competition, it has allowed companies short of crude to buy their way into already proven large oil reserves, and has allowed companies long on crude the advantage of obtaining ready access to certain markets. In addition, joint

Table 2.1

LEADING JOINT VENTURES IN THE OPEC ARABIAN–PERSIAN GULF COUNTRIES

Country	Operating Company	Parent Companies	
Iran	The Consortium	BP	40%
		Shell	14%
		Jersey, Texaco, Gulf, Stancal, Mobil	7% each
		CFP	6%
		U.S. independents	5%
Iraq Abu Dhabi Qatar	The Iraq Petroleum Co. Ltd & Associated Companies	Shell, BP, and CFP	23·75% each
		Jersey and Mobil	11·875% each
		One independent	5%
Kuwait	Kuwait Oil Co. Ltd	BP and Gulf	50% each
Saudi Arabia	Aramco	Jersey, Texaco, and Socal	30% each
		Mobil	10%

control has allowed heavy investments – as well as geologic risk and business uncertainty – to be distributed over a number of ventures. Major oil companies became international in character prompted by profits. They sought geographical diversification to take advantage of favourable economic and political conditions, and to hedge against adverse contingencies in any one single area. Their world-wide activities enabled them to gain in leverage *vis-à-vis* individual host governments, and to improve their control over oil supplies or markets in relation to rivals.

International oil companies have not always behaved closely in accordance with the oligopolistic model which provides for concerted action. In fact, they do not form a homogeneous group. Too many differences stand in the way – differences in resources, degree of integration, geographical spread, costs, interest, background, managerial philosophy and methods of operation, nature and scope of functions, and nationality of their major share-holding groups. Some are fully integrated, others concentrate on one or two functions of the oil trade. Some are strong in their home markets, others strong in international markets. Some are privately owned, others state-owned or controlled, and so on. All these differences have contributed to competition.

Nevertheless, oil companies' joint operations in several host countries, and their common stands on several occasions have fomented reactions leading eventually to the creation of the OPEC front, and the development of further links among individual oil exporting countries with a view to improving their bargaining position.[1] A spokesman of OPEC commented as follows:

> Through OPEC, the exporting countries could, for the first time, face the international major oil companies as a team. Previously, only the major companies were in a position, through joint ownership of concessionaire companies in the Middle East, to practice collective bargaining in their dealings with the exporting countries.[2]

With the creation of OPEC, a bilateral oligopoly, though broad and loose, has evolved in the market for oil rights. On the demand side are the international companies, and on the supply side are the oil exporting countries. In the dynamic conditions of the energy market, the degree of understanding within each group varies, and entries or exits take place as competing sources of energy supplies grow or decline in attractiveness and importance. Chapter 6 describes two situations in which the organization and the industry came close to becoming a bilateral oligopoly, with full co-operation among members of each group. In the first, OPEC countries agreed in 1964 and 1968 with major oil companies on royalty expensing without prior consultation with the smaller independent companies or with the countries outside the OPEC area. In the second, OPEC countries and the international companies (both majors and in-

[1] See Z. Mikdashi, 'An Introduction to Middle Eastern Oil Relations Prior to 1960', in *Continuity and Change in the World Oil Industry*, eds. Z. Mikdashi, S. Cleland, and I. Seymour (Beirut: The Middle East Research and Publishing Center, 1970), pp. 85–101.

[2] *OPEC and the Principle of Negotiation*, Vth Arab Petroleum Congress (Cairo, 16–23 March 1965), pp. 7–8.

dependents) negotiated in 1971 changes in posted prices and tax rates.

B. *Vertical Integration and Posted Prices*

In addition to the oligopolistic structure and behaviour of the international oil industry, OPEC's creation has been influenced by the growing dissatisfaction of host countries with the 50–50 profit-sharing system as originally formulated in the Middle East in the early 1950s. The system's keystone is the posted price concept, and posted prices are the basis for imputing concessionaires' taxable income.

Prices posted by concessionary companies were supposed in the early 1950s to reflect open market prices. To illustrate, a hypothetical oil company sells a substantial portion of its crude oil production in the open competitive market (say 80 per cent), and the balance (20 per cent) to its affiliates. Under conditions of a buyers' market with widespread price discounting, that company can actually increase net profits after taxes by reducing its posted prices, as shown below, assuming there would be no further change in market prices if posted prices were reduced:[1]

	Cents per Barrel	
	(A)	(B)
If the posted price is . . . . . ·	200	180
If operating costs are	20	20
Then for host government tax purposes, profits are	180	160
And host government tax at 50 per cent is . .	90	80

	Cents per Barrel
If, when the posted price was 200 ¢/bbl., 20% of actual sales were made at the full posted price of	200
and 80 per cent at a discount of 20¢/bbl. . .	180
the over-all weighted average price becomes .	184
then a reduction in the posted price to . . .	180
would involve the company in a reduction of sales proceeds by only	4
compared with their income tax-savings of .	10
or a net increase in company profits of . .	6

[1] See also *MEES Supplement*, 'Crude Oil Prices – A Link with the Price of Manufactures', 22 March 1963.

40

The findings of the example can be summarized by comparing the company take and the government take under the three relevant market conditions: prior to discounting, after discounting but prior to reducing posted prices, and after reducing posted prices:

Market Position	Company Take (cents)	Government Take (cents)
(1) Posting 200¢/bbl., 100% sold at posting	90	90
(2) Posting 200¢/bbl., 20% sold at posting 80% sold at 180¢/bbl.	74	90
(3) Posting reduced to 180¢/bbl., 100% sold to new posting	80	80

In this illustration, the oil company bears in position (2) the total loss resulting from a decline in market price until the posting is changed in position (3), when the loss is shared equally between government and company. Therefore, the largely non-integrated crude oil producer selling to third parties in the open market has a financial incentive to decrease posted prices when discounts are widespread.[1] If most crude sales in the open market are made at a given posted price, then a reduction in the posted price would reduce company income by more than the saving in taxes.

It is well established that the greater part of the international oil trade is (and has been) carried out by international companies with largely vertically integrated operations.[2] It is unrealistic, therefore, to calculate international oil companies' profits on the basis of posted prices of crude oil; their profits depend primarily on product prices.

A vertically integrated oil company carries operations from exploration and production via transport and refining to distribution and marketing. Incentives for vertical integration are several. First, oil companies with distribution networks want assured and regular crude oil supplies to refine and market; similarly, companies owning crude oil producing facilities want certain outlets for their production, and seek their own refining and distribution network. Second, oil companies generally find it commercially attractive to carry out all the functions of oil trade rather than depend on facilities belonging to outside firms. These firms may 'foreclose' competion in oil sources or outlets in order to exploit their economic advantage

[1] For an analysis of price elasticity of demand, see Chapter Five, section B.
[2] First National City Bank, *Premium on Raw Material*, Energy Memo, Vol. VII, No. 1, New York, January 1971, pp. 2–3.

and charge excessive prices. No such foreclosure is possible in an 'atomistic' industry with numerous operators.

Third, management can achieve a higher degree of administrative efficiency and a better control of costs by avoiding duplication of facilities and by smoothing operations from production to marketing. Management can thereby enjoy greater flexibility in meeting fluctuations in demand and other market requirements. Fourth, management of a vertically integrated company can reduce its over-all tax burden by setting transfer prices and notional profits for the movement of crude and products in interaffiliate transactions. One executive candidly admits that managed book-keeping prices and allocation of profits among various segments of the integrated operations of an international oil company are arbitrary:

> Any attempt to allocate profit as between phases of the integrated operation is bound to involve some purely arbitrary decisions which may differ as between companies. For example, some companies treat marine transportation as purely a service function, allocating no profit element to it, while others follow a contrary policy.[1]

With the growth of independents and increase in arms'-length sales, the flexibility of international companies in pricing their goods within the integrated system has become restricted; most governments of oil consuming countries currently require vertically integrated international companies to base their transfer prices on open market prices.[2]

C. *The Concession System and Governmental Control*

The international oil industry has numerous varieties of owner-producer relationships controlled in various degrees by governments. In fact, the development of oil resources may take many forms: private ownership, government ownership, service-contract arrangements, lease arrangements, joint ventures, or concessions.[3] Until today, concessions have been most common in the Middle East.

In a Middle East concession agreement of the conventional type,

[1] Elston R. Law, Middle East Co-ordinator, Gulf Oil Corporation, *Financing of Integrated International Oil Companies*, paper delivered at the Kuwait Institute for Economic and Social Planning in the Middle East, 22 November 1967, p. 4.

[2] Geoffrey Chandler, Trade Relations Co-ordinator, Shell International Petroleum Co., 'The Myth of Oil Power – International Groups and National Sovereignty', in *International Affairs*, London, October, 1970, Vol. 46, No. 4, p. 717.

[3] See OPEC, *From Concessions to Contracts*, March 1965.

the state – as owner of the nation's natural resources – entrusts a company (usually a foreign one) with the right to search for, develop, and export freely certain natural resources (here hydrocarbons) from large areas over a long period of time (several decades) in return for certain financial payments and others benefits. Changes in the concession terms are to be made by mutual agreement. A top oil policy-maker in Indonesia once equated concession with 'transfer of sovereignty'. He also claimed that 'the foreign oil companies understood that the concession system allowed them extraordinary freedom to build up and develop their giant companies internationally ... They [also] could topple a government or set up another one'.[1]

The power of concessionaires to change governments in mineral exporting countries is becoming a thing of the past.[2] Moreover, any international agreement – be it of a concession type or otherwise – 'abrogates sovereignty to a degree'.[3] This is true in any business or a non-business partnership where a measure of freedom has to be sacrificed.

Concession agreements offer a large measure of freedom to expatriate companies and require prior company approval for a change in concession terms. Individual host governments in the Middle East originally abrogated, for relatively long periods of time, their right to decide unilaterally on some fiscal matters and to legislate in other matters covered by the concession agreements. In addition, concessionaires have insisted on company prerogatives to set posted prices,[4] budget for investments, and determine the volume of oil production in excess of certain minima stipulated in the agreements; disputes with their host governments were to be arbitrated in international tribunals. That provision may have been necessary in some of the host countries, for example in sheikhdoms with only rudimentary judicial systems; it has, however, proved

---

[1] Ibnu Sutowo, *The Role of Oil in the National Life* (Djakarta: Hong Boon Printing Company), p. 21.

[2] See Chandler Morse', 'Potentials and Hazards of Direct International Investment in Raw Materials', in *Natural Resources and International Development*, ed. Marion Clawson, Resources for the Future, Inc. (Baltimore: The Johns Hopkins Press, 1965), pp. 367–414.

[3] C. P. Kindleberger, *American Business Abroad* (New Haven: Yale University Press, 1969), p. 203.

[4] In the United States, the 'Renegotiation Act of 1951' empowers the government to demand the renegotiation of financial terms of contracts entered into between a government agency and private companies should the latter be deriving 'excessive' profits from prices charged to a government agency. But companies are well aware of the act's provisions before they enter into contracts with the U.S. government.

undesirable, from a nationalist point of view, for countries which have developed court systems judged adequate by their own standards. Expatriate companies, however, fear even the remote possibility that legal proceedings in host countries could be tainted by prejudice arising from the nationality of the judges, public opinion pressures in the area, and other considerations or events in the immediate vicinity of the litigation.

Furthermore, individual oil exporting countries have attempted on several occasions to assert their sovereign right unilaterally to change terms of concession agreements made several years ago, when their governments were generally unsophisticated, weak, or subordinate to Western powers.[1] Viewed within a historical perspective, these agreements played an essential role in attracting venture capital into the developing countries, and were instrumental in the process of oil discovery and development. The oil exporting countries' attempts to force the rate of change were not always successful. One telling example was the Iranian nationalization crisis of 1951–54. Later, through OPEC, oil exporting countries became able for the first time to exercise a measure of collective bargaining with oil companies with a view to changing, to their advantage, certain terms of their concession agreements, long before the expiry dates.

OPEC's creation in 1960 coincided with the Middle East countries' progress in political sophistication and confidence. These countries refused to tolerate any further unilateral action to change posted prices (the basis of their fiscal receipts) by concessionaire companies. Moreover, the oil exporting countries were not, at that time, solely concerned with the strictly economic impact of reductions in posted prices; they were, and still are, deeply concerned with the political significance of the international oil companies' actions. They consider company decisions on posted prices made in a unilateral manner and without prior consent to be an encroachment on their sovereign rights, and tantamount to initiating a reduction in the companies' fiscal charges. Furthermore, oil in OPEC countries is the major source of income; therefore, these countries consider the oil industry as 'having the character of a public utility' on which their development programmes heavily depend (Res. IV.32).

The Shah of Iran expressed this point of view in August 1960, on the eve of OPEC's creation, emphasizing the permanent sovereignty of the state over its natural resources and the Iranian government's desire to share with companies in vital decisions such as the alteration

[1] See Mikdashi, 'An Introduction to Middle Eastern Oil Relations Prior to 1960', *op. cit.*, pp. 85–101.

44

of posted prices:

> The question facing us was whether the oil companies could take such a unilaterial action, even if justified, without consulting the real owners of the oil. The logical and right way would have been for the companies to discuss their problems with us, the owners of the oil. If their claim was justified we could certainly have been convinced. Otherwise, we would have convinced them. Our objection is directed against this kind of unilateral action.[1]

OPEC's creation coincided with a sensitive period of the Cold War between East and West. Soviet influence, furthermore, was making successful inroads into developing countries. It is possible that, in these circumstances, the parent countries of major oil companies (principally the United States and the United Kingdom) did not then want to alienate oil exporting governments. The Western governments may have feared that certain Middle East oil exporting countries and other mineral exporting countries from the developing world would succumb to Soviet propaganda. Moreover, the United States and the United Kingdom are partners with Iran in the CENTO alliance, and are on friendly terms with several other OPEC countries, notably Venezuela, Saudi Arabia and Kuwait; also at the time of OPEC's establishment, Kuwait's foreign relations were the responsibility of the U.K. government.

D. *The Undermining of the Oil Oligopoly and Vertical Integration*

Structural and behavioural changes in the international oil industry have had a remarkable impact on government–company relationships, and on the achievement of OPEC objectives. Certain of these changes were favourable to host countries, notably intercompany competition over oil rights and the accompanying spread of information through the bidding process, thereby precluding the 'exploitation of knowledge' by any single company.[2] In addition, the improved bargaining position of OPEC countries, acting individually or collectively, has won for them larger shares of company earnings, notwithstanding the deterioration of market prices within the industry.

Other changes – for example, increased competition in the international market and host countries' policies concerning ex-

[1] Conference of 27 August 1960, in *Press Conferences of His Imperial Majesty Mohammad Reza Shah Pahlavi of Iran, 1960–1961*, pp. 25–6.
[2] Chandler, 'The Myth of Oil Power,' *op. cit.*, p. 716.

tensive sales of oil rights to newcomers – have helped undermine the oligopolistic concentration of the international oil industry and its vertical integration, thereby adding to the difficulties encountered by OPEC in regulating production and controlling market prices.

Enticed by profits and undeterred by heavy capital requirements overseas, several so-called newcomer independent companies (outside the group of eight majors) acquired oil rights shortly after World War II by offering what then appeared to be attractive terms to host governments. By the middle 1960s, these companies had discovered and developed substantial oil reserves world-wide.

Newcomer companies – private or state-owned – have ventured, initially at least, into one segment of the oil industry's operations. Their entry has caused larger volumes of oil to move outside integrated channels. But as these companies settle into the market, they often find it more profitable to integrate downstream from production to marketing, or upstream from marketing to production.[1]

Restrictions on oil imports into the United States effective since 1957 frustrated the expectations of several companies that had invested heavily overseas in the hope of selling to the U.S. market.[2] These companies have consequently been forced to sell outside the United States the bulk of the oil produced from discoveries made in the 1950s and 1960s in Venezuela, North Africa, and the Middle East. To edge into the international market, newcomers have resorted to price competition.

Other causes of price competition in an industry where prices have significantly exceeded long-run supply costs include the successful attempts of the U.S.S.R. to force its way into markets outside the Soviet bloc and the impact of oil consuming countries' policies aimed at reducing the cost of oil imports.[3] Nevertheless, the major oil companies first resorted to price competition, beginning in the early 1950s and long before the advent of Russian and newcomer oil,

[1] See John G. McLean, President, Continental Oil Company, 'The Importance of the Newcomers in the International Oil Business', paper presented at the American University of Beirut, 8 April 1968, reproduced in *MEES Supplement*, 12 April 1968. Several newcomer companies joined the majors in the OPEC negotiations of 1971 (see their listing in Chapter Six, Section C).

[2] U.S. oil import restrictions started 'voluntarily' on 29 July 1957, and have become mandatory since March 1959, in accordance with Presidential Proclamation 3279 of 10 March 1959.

[3] Indian official sources claimed that Russian competition was instrumental in making majors offer price discounts on their oil exports to India. See Government of India, Ministry of Steel, Mines and Fuel, *Report of the Oil Price Inquiry Committee*, July 1961, p. 22; see also National Petroleum Council, *Impact of Oil Exports From the Soviet Bloc*, 2 vols., Washington, 1961; and *Supplement*, 1964.

by offering general discounts off posted prices. These discounts rose over the years and reached close to 20 per cent on increasing volumes of oil sold[1] (see also Table 7·3).

OPEC countries have, through policy and action, been largely responsible for disturbing the concentration of the international oil oligopoly, thereby leading to further price weakness. This development is due primarily to policies of reclaiming acreage from established concessionaires, of selling oil rights to newcomer independents, and of exhorting all operators to increase exports. Most countries have been motivated in their deals with independents by their wish to increase their economic choices among oil companies and gain economic and non-economic leverage, take advantage of better financial terms offered by some independents in comparison with majors, and use these terms to seek more favourable conditions from established companies. The impact of non-economic factors must be borne in mind, principally the politically motivated desire of some host countries to 'break the yoke' of the so-called 'oil cartel' composed of 'imperialist' major companies.[2]

OPEC's dilemma is that individual host governments are not generally mindful of the global impact of independents. It appears advantageous to a single host government to grant oil rights to a few independents offering larger shares of profits, but the cumulative impact of rival independents on the international petroleum market is bound to lead to lower prices and lower company profit margins. The ultimate effect is lower tax take per unit of oil exports for all host governments, assuming demand for petroleum to be relatively price inelastic. The major beneficiaries would be the industrially developed countries (mostly the OECD), which import the bulk of world oil trade (over 80 per cent).

Another factor undermining oligopoly and vertical integration in the international oil industry is the role of the host government-owned companies. The impact of these companies on international

[1] See, for example, M. Suzuki, *Competition and Monopoly in the World Oil Markets – A Review in the Light of Price Analysis of Imported Crude Oils in Japan*, The Institute of Energy Economics, Supplement to *Energy in Japan No. 4* (Tokyo, February 1968), pp. 5, 8, 9, 10, 12 and 13; and U.S. Senate, *Governmental Intervention in the Market Mechanism, The Petroleum Industry, Part 1*, 'Statement by Walter L. Newton' in Hearings before the Subcommittee on Antitrust and Monopoly of the Committee on the Judiciary, Washington, March–April 1969, pp. 41–76.

[2] See, for an example, Adib al Jader, then Chairman of INOC, 'Address Upon the Signature of the ERAP Deal', in Arabic, *Arab Oil and Gas Journal* (January 1968), pp. 20–1.

47

markets will be increasingly felt; they possess large amounts of crude oil and will possess even more in the not-so-distant future. That oil, in contrast to major companies' oil, does not flow as yet in integrated channels. It has to be sold by the national companies to other companies which have downstream operations, that is, transport, refining, distribution, and marketing facilities. Also, a number of consuming countries are promoting their own national companies in order to buy or produce oil independently from the traditional international companies.

It is not unusual or unlikely that national companies, seeking a foothold in international markets, are willing to offer potential buyers attractive terms, mostly in the form of price discounts. As early as 1964, the National Iranian Oil Co. (NIOC) took the lead in offering significant price discounts on crude oil produced jointly with an independent oil company (Pan American Oil Co., an affiliate of Standard Oil Co. of Indiana). NIOC went to the extent of offering crude oil to an Indian refinery at prices that undercut all the major oil companies. The latter, already in unending dispute with India over their import transfer prices on other large oil supplies, were of course further inhibited in resorting to price competition. As *The Economist* commented: 'In this price-cutting the international oil majors, mindful of repercussions in other markets, were left far behind, even though they added frill upon frill to their bids on the processing.'[1]

The price-weakening impact of national oil companies with no marketing outlets in consuming countries is of great concern to OPEC officials, with respect to both crude and products. A weakening of market prices of petroleum is bound in the long run to adversely affect 'posted prices', which are the basis of host countries' tax calculations; reduce the value of host countries' uncommitted acreage; and harm the earning prospects of all companies, including national companies.[2] OPEC's apprehension was clearly stated in 1968 by Ashraf Lutfi, one of its Secretary-Generals:

> They are entering a buyers' market where crude supplies are abundant and promise to remain so for some years to come; where for one reason or another, the local independent refiner is already committed to certain suppliers for his crude oil requirements. . . .

[1] *The Economist* (London, 15 November 1964), pp. 741–2; the statement, according to a well-informed contributor to that journal, is exaggerated in using the words 'left far behind'.

[2] See F. R. Parra, 'OPEC and the Stabilization of Petroleum Prices', *OPEC Bulletin* (December 1968), p. 2.

For the export of refined products to a certain destination our national oil company will not only have to compete with the refinery on the spot but also with the surplus distress products offered in that same area by other refineries next door. . . .

It is here in the final analysis that one finds a real conflict of interests: OPEC's desire for equitable (higher) *prices* and the eagerness of its national oil companies for profits whatever the price.[1]

The OPEC Co-ordination Committee for national oil companies, with the support of the Secretariat, is endeavouring to reach a 'gentlemen's agreement' that will dissuade national companies from

Table 2.2

APPROXIMATE SHARES OF THE EIGHT MAJORS IN OIL OPERATIONS OUTSIDE U.S. AND COMMUNIST AREAS

(Figures in Percentage of Total)

Year	Production	Refining	Product Sales
1955	92	81	n.a.
1960	84	74	70
1965	76	58	66

Source: Data supplied through OPEC Secretariat.

resorting to severe price competion in international markets. Whether national companies will exercise the necessary restraint remains to be seen.

Selected figures for 1955, 1960, and 1965 (see Table 2.2) show a decline in the shares of majors outside the U.S. and Communist areas. The majors' 1960–65 share of world oil production fell from 84 to 76 per cent, of refining from 74 to 58 per cent, and of product sales from 70 to 66 per cent.

Using other bases for computations, Penrose shows that in the 1950–66 period the seven major companies' share (excluding CFP) in world production and refining (outside Northern America and Communist countries) fell from 85 to 76 per cent and from 72 to 61 per cent, respectively.[2] Shell estimated that the seven majors accounted in 1952 for more than 90 per cent of the non-Communist world

[1] Ashraf T. Lutfi, *OPEC Oil*, Middle East Research and Publishing Centre (Beirut, 1966), p. 35; his *italics* and brackets.

[2] Edith Penrose, *The Large International Firm in Developing Countries: The International Petroleum Industry* (London: Allen & Unwin, 1968), p. 78.

production outside North America, 72 per cent of refining, and more than 75 per cent of product sales. In 1968, Shell calculated that these companies' share of production had fallen to under 80 per cent, of refining to just over 60 per cent, and of product sales to about 60 per cent. The projected figures for 1971 are 77, 56, and 56 respectively. The companies to suffer most, according to Shell, are the three largest; Jersey, Shell, and BP.[1]

E. *The Dilemma of OPEC*

That producers' and consumers' objectives and interests are in conflict is axiomatic. This section reviews the objectives and policies of the protagonists.

I. *Oil Suppliers: the OPEC Objectives*

As is apparent from the Conference's resolutions and the Secretariat studies, OPEC considers certain objectives to represent common interests among its members. It has attempted to use them to promote collective action in the face of forces tending to split members, whether these forces originate from within or outside the group.

The members' common objectives as seen by the organization can be broadly divided into two groups; those which depend largely on members' common action and those dependent on action or consent by others (mainly importing countries). In the first group of objectives the most important is the stabilization of petroleum prices (in real terms) and, more generally, larger economic benefits from oil exports in terms of balance of payments and gross national product. Other objectives of growing importance are diversification of economic activities through oil-based or oil-sponsored industrialization, and direct and active participation of national agencies in the ownership and management of various stages of the domestic and international oil industry.

The second group of objectives is concerned mainly with the elimination, reduction, or at least the preclusion of further increases in trade restrictions and barriers (for example, quotas, tariffs, and foreign exchange licences) and in fiscal discrimination (mostly through heavy excise duties) against the import and consumption of

---

[1] See Geoffrey Chandler, 'The Function of the Major Integrated Oil Companies', *International Oil and Energy Policies of the Producing and Consuming Countries* (hereafter *International Oil*), a collection of papers presented at OPEC's Seminar held in Vienna in July 1969, pp. 25–32; and 'The Myth of Oil Power', *op. cit.*, p. 712.

OPEC area oil and derived products, as compared with other sources of energy including domestic sources. OPEC also seeks to ensure continued and regular reliance on OPEC area oil and the discouragement of high cost exploration outside the area.[1]

The OPEC Conference and the Secretariat have not come out with a priority listing of common objectives nor endeavoured to ensure their consistency. A number of the Conference's resolutions have been expedients chosen to meet the wish of one or more member countries, and incompatible goals sometimes result. For example, the objective of oil price stabilization is at variance with the aim of maximizing host countries' oil income per unit of exports, as some individual member countries have been striving to do.

That OPEC's policies may contain conflicts is not unique. The same problems occur elsewhere in the fields of energy or other commodities. National or intergovernmental policies are bound to reflect competing or even incompatible interests and goals if economic exigencies are to blend with sociopolitical necessities. A search for an expedient accommodation among conflicting interests was considered desirable by a one-time policy-maker in the U.S. oil industry who stated:

> Much has been said about the inherent conflicts in energy policy – the incompatibility of the goals of security, diversity of supply, low cost, fiscal solvency, and pollution abatement. In view of these conflicts, one of my colleagues once observed that energy policy is necessarily a compromise, and that a good test of its wisdom be that it satisfy no one. In my experience in administering the oil imports program, I found this test most comforting on many occasions.[2]

One should remark, however, that U.S. oil imports programmes do satisfy domestic oil producers; this in fact means that governmental policy can very well tilt to the side of one interest group.

Putting aside the consistency test we find that OPEC's policy objectives are founded on generalizations which lack adequate supporting empirical evidence. For example, one objective advocates a reduction in the heavy indirect taxes on petroleum products (notably on petrol) in major consuming countries to reduce the price to consumers. This implies that the consumption of products is price

---

[1] For a listing of objectives, see *OPEC Bulletin*, No. 6, 16 November 1970.
[2] U.S. Department of the Interior, Assistant Secretary J. Cordell Moore, *Observations and Remarks on United States Energy Policy*, presented to OECD's Energy Committee, January 1967.

elastic. But OPEC went so far as to admit that 'all the evidence points towards the demand for refined products as a whole being relatively price inelastic.'[1] What it needs is a realistic analysis of the elasticity of each product in major consuming areas under various market conditions, and an assessment of repercussions of price changes in different ranges on the demand for crude and products.

In the context of price policy, OPEC statements have often used the elusive concept of 'equitable', which has been explained differently. Secretary-General Ashraf Lutfi took it to mean higher prices,[2] whereas Secretary-General Francisco Parra thought it meant prices 'at levels which will result in a more adequate sharing as between consumer and producer of the rent accruing to petroleum from the difference between its cost and the cost of the principal alternative sources of energy. . . .'[3]

In seeking the highest possible prices they can get, OPEC members do not differentiate between sales made to the developed industrial countries and the less-developed countries. Indeed, the visit of an official Uruguayan delegation to OPEC's headquarters in Vienna on 23 March 1971 to solicit a preferential price treatment for developing nations has proved of little immediate avail.[4] The Shah of Iran believes that joint oil ventures between OPEC countries and developing oil importing countries is the key solution to establishing reasonable terms:

Question: Any increase in prices of course is bound to hit particularly hard the developing countries . . . who have to import oil and who need oil to develop their industries. Now is there anything that can be done to ease the burden on them?

Answer: Well, that is a very good question. Which are these developing countries which really have either huge populations or will need oil in very great quantities? But I take India, which has about 550 million people. India's oil consumption is 13 million tons, about the same that we consume here in this country, and to make a striking difference I will tell you that Holland is consuming 30 million tons against 13. But even now with India we have some special agreements. We are participating for instance in the Madras refinery. We are selling oil to that country, with, I

[1] See OPEC, *Elasticity of Demand for Crude Oil; Its Implications for Exporting Countries,* by Isam K. Kabbani, 1966, p. 21.
[2] Ashraf T. Lutfi, *OPEC Oil,* Middle East Research and Publishing Centre (Beirut, 1966), p. 35.
[3] See *OPEC Bulletin,* April 1968, p. 7.
[4] *Le Monde,* Paris, 25 March 1971, p. 40.

think very, very reasonable prices. The day that this country will become a developed country like yours, I promise you that I will help the not-yet-developed countries of the world at least as much as you developed countries. This I can promise you.[1]

The Secretary-General of OPEC, Nadim Pachachi, went farther and said that OPEC would readily support developing countries in their attempts to obtain better prices for their primary products from the industrialized countries:

Question: Some press commentators have made much of the possible adverse repercussions of the [1971] Tehran settlement on the underdeveloped oil consuming countries with acute foreign exchange problems. What do the OPEC countries feel about this?

Answer: Yes, we do realize that the developing countries, as well as the industrialized nations, will have to pay more for their oil imports. We, as developing countries ourselves, sympathize with them. We, like them, are raw material producers trying to get an equitable price for the primary product on which our economies depend. They too should follow our example in getting the industrialized countries to pay a better price for raw materials and primary commodities in general. And we in OPEC are always ready to co-operate with other developing countries and/or commodity price stabilization organizations and to put our experience at their disposal.[2]

II. *Consumer Markets*

Concessionaire companies and their parent countries consider OPEC a threat to their prosperity. Indeed, prior to the opening of financial negotiations in 1963 between the oil companies and the organization's Secretary-General (then Fuad Rouhani of Iran), the major oil companies (all of them represented in the Iran Consortium) informed the press that their representatives would be negotiating with a representative of the Iranian government, and not with a representative of the OPEC countries. They argued that their contracts were with individual governments, and it was with these governments that the companies wanted to deal. The trade press associated with the oil industry originally offered hostile comments; as Francisco Parra, at the time head of OPEC's Economics Department pertinently remarked:

[1] Interview the Shah granted to the British Broadcasting Corporation on 17 February 1971, reproduced in OPEC *Weekly Bulletin*, 19 February 1971, p. 28, and *Iran Oil Journal*, February 1971, p. 13.

[2] *MEES*, 19 February 1971, p. 6.

... Some industry sectors and some sectors in the consuming countries ... wish that OPEC would pack its things and go home. These people see in OPEC a threat to their security and they think they would prefer things as they were before, with Member Countries weak and divided.[1]

Toward the end of 1964, the trade press acknowledged that 'it is now abundantly clear that OPEC is a force to be reckoned with by oil companies in all their negotiations with producing countries'.[2]

Though they have acquiesced, in some cases, in the maintenance of, or increase in, host government takes per unit of oil exports, oil importing countries are nevertheless opposed to an OPEC cartel. The major importing countries have favoured competition among the oil exporters, since competition is claimed to exist among oil importing countries – as the French Secretary-General of energy put it.[3]

The objectives of the major oil importing countries are chiefly to import oil at the lowest long-run price[4] and minimize outlays in foreign currencies; to protect domestic energy producers – especially with reference to earnings, employment, and market opportunities (such protection has been achieved through government expenditures on research, subsidies of capital and operating costs of domestic

[1] OPEC, *OPEC and the Oil Industry in the Middle East*, by F. R. Parra, October 1962, p. 10.

[2] *Petroleum Press Service* (PPS), London, September 1964, p. 324.

[3] 'Il est inévitable et sain qu'entre les pays producteurs s'établisse une certaine concurrence, de même qu'elle existe entre les pays acheteurs.' Jean Couture, 'L'Energie en France', *Bulletin de l'Industrie Petrolière* (*BIP*) No. 840, 22 May 1967, p. 11.

At the First United Nations Conference on Trade and Development (UNCTAD) held in Geneva in the summer of 1964, the United States led industrial countries in refusing recognition and encouragement to international organizations set up by the principal exporters of non-renewable natural resources, including fuels (Annexes A.II.9 and A.VI.2.) They probably anticipated and apprehended cartellization by groupings of countries exporting primary products, in whose decisions and plans they would be excluded.

See OECD, *Energy Policy, Problems and Objectives*, Paris, July 1966; also Japan, Advisory Committee for Energy, *Report on Energy Policy*, 20 February 1967, p. 36; U.K. Ministry of Power, *Fuel Policy*, October 1965 and November 1967 in Cmds 2798 and 3438 respectively; Cordell Moore, *op. cit.*, and M. A. Adelman, 'Security of Eastern Fuel Supply', 6 December 1967, condensed in *PPS*, January 1968, pp. 2–4.

[4] For example, Japan (the world largest oil importing country in 1970) aimed in 1965 at a price reduction for imported crude oil of at least 15 cents a barrel by 1970 below the average price in the latter half of 1965. See Japan, *Report on Energy Policy*, p. 19. Japan's target was realized: *Japan Petroleum News*, Tokyo, 15 April 1970.

energy producers, and trade and fiscal barriers on oil imports); and to safeguard the regularity and continuity of oil flows, the adequacy of stocks, the diversity of sources, and the competitiveness of overseas suppliers. In addition, the countries seek to reserve an important portion of the domestic petroleum industry for national agencies (private or state-owned), and to help these agencies in overseas oil exploration and development. Leading state-owned or supported agencies are ENI of Italy, ERAP of France, Hispanoil of Spain, Deminex of West Germany. Last, the countries seek to protect the physical environment.

Understandably, these objectives vary in emphasis or in method of implementation from one country to another. Concern for balance-of-payments effects of oil imports is not uniform. In some countries, governments protect domestic energy industries. In others, they influence or manipulate the amounts and pattern of energy imports to take advantage of foreign exchange savings and to improve the export prospects of certain industries dependent on cheap energy.[1] This balance-of-payments policy requires more petroleum imports at lower prices with the same import bill of foreign exchange.[2] At lower prices, the consumption of petroleum can be expected to increase, especially by those industries in which energy is a significant element of cost, and which have scope to substitute among different sources of energy. But an oil importing country can also have balance-of-payments benefits from higher prices of petroleum to the extent that its oil companies derive larger earnings from international operations, and these earnings are repatriated home. Other contributions to the parent country's foreign exchange receipts arise from company and oil exporting countries' disbursements for equipment, materials, personnel, or investments in the country concerned. This has been the case with the United States, the United Kingdom, France and the Netherlands.

A recent statement by the British Petroleum Co. (BP) regarding its sizable contribution to the U.K. balance of payments in 1970 is

[1] See European Economic Community, *L'influence économique du prix de l'énergie*, Brussels, 1966.
[2] See Bulletin de la Communauté Européenne du Charbon et de l'Acier, *Nouvelles réflexions sur les perspectives énergétiques à long terme de la Communauté européenne*, Brussels, April 1966; and Communauté Européenne, Service d'Information, *L'Europe et l'Energie*, Luxembourg, 1967.
See also M. A. Adelman, 'Oil Prices in the Long Run (1963–75)', *The Journal of Business* of the University of Chicago, April 1964, pp. 143–61; and M. A. Adelman, 'The Future of World Oil', Parts I and II, *The Transportation Center* at Northwestern University, 27 and 28 March 1966, edited transcript.

most revealing:

> The group's U.K. exports consisted of approximately 10 million tons of oil products, the value of which, given to comply with the requirements of the Companies Act 1967, was £93·9 million. The value of chemical exports was £17·4 million.
>
> Over 90 per cent of the group's trade of 189·7 million tons was carried on overseas and the majority of the crude oil and products was neither imported into nor exported from the U.K. The oil export figure given above is therefore not indicative of the group's contribution from oil activities to the U.K. balance of payments which for 1970 is estimated at £145 million.
>
> £75 million of this contribution arises from overseas trade (including sales of quantities exported from the U.K.) less capital investment abroad, to which is added £40 million representing the estimated saving to the country by reason of the group importing oil to the U.K. for consumption as compared with the foreign exchange cost of buying the same quantity from a foreign based oil company. There is also a further £30 million representing the approximate saving of overseas expenditure by reason of carrying the oil in British flag tankers and the value of British materials exported for our account by contractors.[1]

Major oil importing countries which have had until recently independent energy policies are currently making serious attempts – not without some difficulty – at closer co-ordination (including the sharing and rationing of oil supplies in times of emergencies). Such attempts are made through the consultative Oil Committee of the Organization for Economic Co-operation and Development (OECD), through the European Economic Community (EEC),[2] or through the nationally owned oil companies of some of these countries. The co-operation of major oil importing countries has increased in response to their common concern for assured imports.

Spokesmen of certain oil exporting countries (for example, Venezuelan, Saudi and Kuwaiti ministers) have welcomed the formation of a counterpart organization for the petroleum importing countries, probably similar to OPEC.[3] Furthermore, Venezuela's

[1] BP, Annual Report and Accounts for 1970, as reproduced in *The Economist*, 10 April 1971, p. 13.

[2] See *PPS*, December 1969, p. 462; and *ibid.*, 'Consumers' Community', March 1970, pp. 82–3.

[3] Ahmed Zaki Yamani, Saudi Minister of Petroleum and Mineral Resources, in an address at the American University of Beirut, reproduced in *MEES Supplement*, 21 April 1967, p. 4.

Minister of Mines and Hydrocarbons, Pérez Alfonzo, and his Saudi colleague, Ahmad Zaki Yamani, have advocated direct contact between OPEC and EEC with a view to harmonizing oil interests and guaranteeing the flow of oil to the major market of Western Europe.[1] Pérez even called for a conference between OPEC members and the major oil importing countries in order to establish a new international price structure linking oil prices to a price index of internationally traded manufactured goods.[2] Another Venezuelan Minister of Mines and Hydrocarbons, José Antonio Mayobre, went further, and called for close producer–consumer co-operation along the lines of an international commodity agreement like the International Tin Agreement. Such co-operation should not involve replacing or displacing the private international oil companies by direct governmental deals between oil exporting and oil importing countries. It would aim for a general framework and a set of rules to regulate supply, demand, and price conditions in the international petroleum industry (whether trade is carried on by public or private agencies). The Venezuelan Minister stated in 1967 that the desire for co-operation was of long standing:

> The OPEC member countries have repeatedly stated that they have no desire to form a cartel that would exclude the consumers. They wish to enter into an agreement that would be favourable both to the producers and to the consumers.[3]

One suspects that OPEC countries have appeared to look favourably upon co-operation among oil importing countries only for the sake of 'good international relations'. OPEC countries, in fact, do fear the collective or individual policies of the powerful and sophisticated industrialized countries.[4] The policies of some 'tend to artificially depress petroleum prices in international markets,' as

[1] See OPEC, *OPEC and the Consuming Countries*, Vienna, May 1967. A similar attempt by OAPEC early in 1971 to establish direct links with EEC on oil and related matters might elicit a positive response. *MEES Supplement*, 2 April 1971, reproducing a talk by Suhail Sa'dawi, Secretary General of OAPEC; and *Petroleum and Economic Digest*, 30 April 1971.

[2] *The Financial Times*, 3 December 1962.

[3] José Antonio Mayobre's address to the Venezuelan Senate, Ministry of Mines and Hydrocarbons, *Monthly Bulletin*, May 1967, pp. 4–5. The author interviewed Mayobre on 9 August 1969 in Caracas.

[4] For example, Japan's threat to authorize its oil companies to form an 'oil import cartel' to resist the 1971 price increases started by OPEC countries: *Petroleum Intelligence Weekly* (*PIW*), New York, 22 February 1971, p. 3; and Statement of K. Miyazawa, Minister of International Trade and Industry, in *Japan Petroleum News*, Tokyo, 22 February 1971, pp. 1–2.

put by OPEC resolution XVIII.94 of November 1968. The Conference resolved then that 'Member countries should not grant any new oil rights of any nature whatsoever to companies whose home countries pursue such policies'.

The Italian state-owned ENI saw matters differently, and contended in 1966 that the interests of consuming countries had been subordinated to those of the international major oil companies and the group of producing countries. It alleged that both oil producer states and companies had always had the upper hand economically and politically in the oil trade as compared with consumer countries, which, it claimed, had never had any control:

> For a series of economic and political reasons consumer countries have always been in the hands of the producers [states and companies], accepting now better now worse terms of supply, thus contributing to an unequalled concentration of economic and political interests over which they have never had and have no control.[1]

ENI described this situation as 'dangerous to importing countries', and called on consumer countries 'to assert their bargaining power' with a view to exercising 'a check on producers' freedom of action'.[2] Early in 1971, ENI explicitly dissociated itself from the group of international oil companies which began joint negotiations with OPEC countries concerning crude oil prices. ENI considered itself 'committed to looking after different interests [consumers'] from those of the international oil companies'.[3] Under the leadership of the Italian Minister of State Participations, ENI favours direct EEC–OPEC delineation of special relationship, with EEC countries facilitating the industrialization of OPEC countries in return or secure oil supplies.[4]

Unlike ENI, ERAP, and other 100 per cent state-owned companies of major oil importing countries, international oil companies are not intimately linked to governmental policies of their parent countries. Nevertheless, parent-country influence looms large in their behaviour, to varying degrees of course. Penrose considers Jersey, the largest oil company in the world, 'very American in its outlook, with all that this implies for its foreign policy, for its

[1] ENI, *Energy and Petroleum in 1965* (Milan, 1966), p. 19.

[2] *Ibid.*, pp. 21–2, see also *Successo*, International Edition, Milan, April 1970, p. 114.

[3] *MEES*, 23 January 1971, p. 15.

[4] *PIW*, 12 April 1971, p. 2.

attitude toward government social and economic measures, and for its views of the relation between big business and government' – despite the international character of the company's operations.[1] Indeed, that company has chosen to be an apostle of American capitalism overseas. Its chairman in 1963, M. J. Rathbone, once declared:

> Our affiliates as corporate citizens communicate their ideas on sound business policy to the people and governments of the countries in which they operate. The public statements made by our management, our written communications, and our advertising seek to emphasize the benefits of free competitive enterprise and private international investment.[2]

Further, Jersey wants the American government to support and promote American business overseas with a view to furthering U.S. foreign policy. A vice-president of the company, addressing the U.S. Naval Academy in 1966, said, 'Our government has the interest, as well as the means, to promote U.S. investments abroad in furthering the objectives of our foreign policy'.[3] As for following U.S. government oil policies, a chairman of the Board of Jersey M. H. Haider once confidentially intimated, 'We're flexible. We can play the game any way you [the U.S. government] want – if somebody will just tell us what the rules are.'[4]

Jersey's claim that American business is dedicated to 'free competitive enterprise' is as open to doubt as any claim OPEC might make (but has not) that its oil pricing policy is differentiated in favour of the least developed countries. Historical evidence abounds with restrictive practices exercised or supported by U.S. firms. American oil companies have even welcomed governmental regulations and controls, so long as these tend to promote their long-term interests.[5] For example, the oil prorationing and import control systems have been established and maintained in the United States, with the active support of private producers.

Oil executives occasionally make contradictory statements on the subject of controls. For example, the chief executives of Texaco, J. H.

[1] Penrose, *op. cit.*, p. 101.
[2] *Annual Report, 1962*, p. 18.
[3] J. R. White, Annapolis, Maryland, 22 April 1966, p. 7 – typescript.
[4] Allan T. Demaree 'Our Crazy, Costly Life with Oil Quotas', *Fortune* (June 1969), p. 180.
[5] Paul Frankel calls the American oil companies' advocacy of 'free competitive enterprise' an idea 'strictly for export'. See *Platt's Oilgram News Service* (2 April 1968).

Rambin and M. J. Epley, support production and import controls in the United States (admittedly on grounds of national security), yet declare themselves for 'our competitive system of free enterprise', and oppose U.S. mandatory restrictions on the movement of private capital for direct investment abroad.[1] Jersey chairman Haider claims that he is 'basically a free trader', although he opposes free 'uncontrolled imports'. Moreover, though 'chief executive officer of a major international company, operating in more than 100 countries', he thinks primarily as a U.S. 'citizen' concerned about his 'country's security':

> As chief executive officer of a major international company, operating in more than 100 countries, I am well aware of the economic interrelationships in the free world. Being basically a free trader, I object to anything that impedes free trade among nations. Moreover, since Jersey has major reserves abroad, I am well aware of the potential market these reserves have in the United States. But as a citizen, I am opposed to anything that would jeopardize our country's security. And uncontrolled imports could do just that.[2]

These contradictory views regarding government regulations can best be reconciled by reference to the profit motive. In 1957, Jersey opposed U.S. import control lest it surrender the opportunity to make profits in the United States with its cheap overseas crude oil supplies. In 1969, when oil profits outside the United States were just normal (11·3 per cent for the seven majors), Jersey defended import controls, ostensibly on the grounds of security. In fact, Jersey wanted to protect the high profits then earned by its U.S. affiliate (Humble), amounting to 17 per cent of invested capital and 52 per cent of Jersey's total net income. One astute analyst commented thus on the recent protectionist stand of Jersey:

> If the [import control] program should be substantially changed, it would cut sharply into Humble's [Jersey's U.S. affiliate] earnings at a time when its favourable position in domestic crude oil could be expected to give Jersey an increasing profit edge over its major international rivals.[3]

[1] Texaco, *Annual Report* 1969, p. 3.
[2] At the 87th Annual Meeting of Shareholders in San Francisco on 14 May 1969.
[3] Dan Cordtz, 'They're Holding Feet to the Fire at Jersey Standard', *Fortune*, July 1970, p. 81.

The ethnocentric support offered by Jersey's chief executive to the interests of the United States is understandable in the context of his concern for maximizing the long-term prospects of the company as he sees it. This attitude is similar to that of the chief executive of British Petroleum (BP). The chairman of that company has unequivocally stated that his aim is to run BP (48·6 per cent owned by the British government) in support of the British national interest, and that he would be embarrassed by foreign nationals in positions of power at BP's headquarters.[1] The following interlocution[2] is revealing:

Jones: So that the only sort of effective promotion for the boss of a major subsidiary would be a seat on the board? And that is ruled out because your articles of association do not allow foreigners on the BP main board.

Drake: Well, that is true, but it is an historic situation which goes back to Churchill in the First World War. It does not mean we are shutting out people.

Jones: Do you think you might alter the articles in the future?

Drake: Could be, could be.

Jones: Do you have any present intentions?

Drake: Not immediate, no.

Major international oil companies, according to their spokesmen, often claim to seek the 'greatest good of the whole unit'. But the concept of 'good' is generally conceived in headquarters in New York, London, Paris, or The Hague. Some may attempt to achieve this objective even if the interests (for example, the profitability) of an affiliate or branch in any host (producer or consumer) country – and consequently the interests of that host government – must suffer. Such a conflict of interests is bound to produce clashes between international companies and host countries. This interpretation is questioned by one company executive. He claims that investment decisions of international oil companies 'will reflect economic considerations and comparative advantage', although he later admits that company decisions may not be consistent with the 'concept of economic man'.[3]

Major oil importing countries and their companies have, however, come to realize the necessity of recognizing OPEC as a legitimate

[1] See Barton William-Powlett, 'The Transnational Companies: British Petroleum', *The Times*, London, 5 January 1970, p. 21.

[2] Robert Jones talks to Eric Drake, Chairman of BP, *The Times*, 21 January 1970, p. 23.

[3] Chandler, 'The Myth of Oil Power', *op. cit.*, pp. 710-18.

manifestation of its members' collective aspirations (for example, see the reaction in 1966 of the Energy Commission of the European Parliament).[1]

It is possible that major oil importing countries, namely the rich industrial countries, might be willing to pay something extra to secure regular and reliable oil flows. But it is yet to be proved whether OPEC countries are able to guarantee such security to the consumers' satisfaction, as they have agreed to do in 1971. Consuming countries generally aim at achieving security through diversification; lesser dependence on OPEC oil, and the satisfaction of part of their oil needs with so-called dependable but admittedly higher cost energy. The possibility that OPEC might become a cartel and raise prices to excessive levels is one of the reasons they seek such diversification. The financial cost to certain major oil importing countries of the policy to subsidize, or generally to discriminate in favour of, dependable but higher priced domestic energy is therefore equivalent to a premium for security.[2]

F. OPEC and its Environment

The interrelatedness of protagonists in the world oil industry (and in other international industries as well) can be analytically depicted with a matrix model (see Table 2.3). In column A, the left side of the matrix, are listed, for any year, collective OPEC policies which aim at achieving the collective goal of benefits optimization – to be defined, if at all, by the OPEC Conference. On the top horizontal level of the matrix, major groups of protagonists are listed together with suggested key variables relevant to OPEC collective policies. These groups are (I) the expatriate companies; (II) the major consumer

[1] 'Sans perturber le role jusqu'ici entièrement satisfaisant de l'industrie du pétrole et du gaz naturel, il faudrait examiner comment un executif européen fusionné pourrait assurer, avec des groupements tels que l'O.P.E.P. et les compagnies pétrolières internationales un approvisionnement de la Communauté, deuxième puissance économique aprés les U.S.A., conforme aux principes formulés dans le memorandum commun sur la politique énergétique de Juin 1962 [Bulletin de la Communauté Européenne du Charbon et de l'Acier (ECSC), "Memorandum sur la politique énergétique" (25 Juin 1962) p. 15] et dans le protocole d'accord d'Avril 1964 [EEC, Journal Officiel, No. 69, 30 April 1964, p. 1009], ainsi qu'aux vœux du Parlement européen.'
Parlement Européen, Documents de Séance, 'Rapport sur la politique de la Communauté en matière de pétrole et de gaz naturel', 12 October 1966, p. 15.
[2] U.S. oil import controls over 1958–71 have shown an average of about $0.75 a barrel cost advantage in favour of imported oil as compared with domestic oil.

Table 2.3
OPEC POLICIES AND EXTERNAL CRITICAL VARIABLES, 1971

I. EXPATRIATE COMPANIES
(from the more developed world)

I. to V Critical Variables / A. Collective OPEC Policies	1. Number	2. Financial resources	3. Geographic diversification of oil activities	4. Balanced vertical integration	5. Relative dependence on OPEC countries for income	6. Equity participation by home government	7. Stringency of anti-trust legislation in consumer markets	8. Joint operations or co-operation among expatriate companies	9. Extent of support by home government	10. Diversification in non-oil activities
1. Raising government take										
2. Effectiveness of production programming										
3. Oil industrialization										
4. National ownership of domestic operations										
5. Participation overseas with expatriate companies										
6. Vertical integration of OPEC national companies										
7. Diversification in non-oil activities										
8. Reduction of fiscal and trade barriers by oil importers										
9. Greater dependence on OPEC oil										
10. Acquiring and using expertise in oil										
= Goal: Optimization of benefits										

63

Table 2.3 cont.
OPEC POLICIES AND EXTERNAL CRITICAL VARIABLES, 1971

II. MAJOR CONSUMER COUNTRIES
(the more developed)

I. to V. Critical Variables / A. Collective OPEC Policies	1. Number	2. Size of domestic energy demand	3. Domestic sources of commercial energy	4. Relative dependence on OPEC oil for energy requirements	5. Intercountry co-operation in energy	6. Trade barriers and fiscal burdens with respect to OPEC oil	7. Strength of balance of payments	8. Rate of economic growth	9. Friendliness of their foreign policy to OPEC countries	10. Concern for pollution	11. Economic influence on OPEC countries	12. Noneconomic influence on OPEC countries
1. Raising government take												
2. Effectiveness of production programming												
3. Oil industrialization												
4. National ownership of domestic operations												
5. Participation overseas with expatriate companies												
6. Vertical integration of OPEC national companies												
7. Diversification in non-oil activities												
8. Reduction of fiscal and trade barriers by oil importers												
9. Greater dependence on OPEC oil												
10. Acquiring and using expertise in oil												
= Goal: Optimization of benefits												

Table 2.3 cont.
OPEC POLICIES AND EXTERNAL CRITICAL VARIABLES, 1971

III. OTHER CONSUMER COUNTRIES
(the less developed)

A. Collective OPEC Policies \ I. to V Critical Variables	1. Number	2. Size of domestic energy demand	3. Domestic sources of commercial energy	4. Relative dependence on OPEC oil for energy requirements	5. Intercountry co-operation in energy	6. Trade barriers and fiscal burdens with respect to OPEC oil	7. Strength of balance of payments	8. Rate of economic growth	9. Friendliness of their foreign policy to OPEC countries	10. Concern for pollution	11. Economic influence on OPEC countries	12. Noneconomic influence on OPEC countries
1. Raising government take												
2. Effectiveness of production programming												
3. Oil industrialization												
4. National ownership of domestic operations												
5. Participation overseas with expatriate companies												
6. Vertical integration of OPEC national companies												
7. Diversification in non-oil activities												
8. Reduction of fiscal and trade barriers by oil importers												
9. Greater dependence on OPEC oil												
10. Acquiring and using expertise in oil												
= Goal: Optimization of benefits												

E

Table 2.3 cont.
OPEC POLICIES AND EXTERNAL CRITICAL VARIABLES, 1971

I. to V Critical Variables / A. Collective OPEC Policies	IV. NON-OPEC OIL EXPORTING COUNTRIES (mostly less developed)						V. INTERNATIONAL ENVIRONMENT					
	1. Number	2. Relative size of commercial oil reserves	3. Rate of economic growth	4. Friendliness of their foreign policy to OPEC countries	5. Size of domestic energy demand	6. Relative costliness of their oil delivered to major markets	1. Relaxation of East-West relations	2. Stability of Middle East politics	3. World economic prosperity	4. Availability of technical and managerial know-how	5. 'World-wide' inflation	6. Nuclear technological advancement
1. Raising government take												
2. Effectiveness of production programming												
3. Oil industrialization												
4. National ownership of domestic operations												
5. Participation overseas with expatriate companies												
6. Vertical integration of OPEC national companies												
7. Diversification in non-oil activities												
8. Reduction of fiscal and trade barriers by oil importers												
9. Greater dependence on OPEC oil												
10. Acquiring and using expertise in oil												
= Goal: Optimization of benefits												

countries (mostly the developed OECD countries); (III) other consumer countries (mostly the less developed countries); (IV) non-OPEC net oil exporting countries (mostly less developed countries); and (V) the general international politico-economic environment.

This matrix is useful for identifying major collective OPEC policies and key external variables of various groups which constrain or favour the OPEC goal of benefits optimization. The relative importance of OPEC policies and of various external constraints or incentives is not constant over time. For example, the relative importance to OPEC policies of, say, group II versus group III countries, varies with changes in the ratio of the oil imports requirements of these two groups.

The author conducted an experiment by sending a questionnaire of a preliminary version of the matrix to forty oil specialists: officials of OPEC and oil exporting countries, of consumer countries, of the international companies, and scholars. These persons were requested to (1) add any variable they deem relevant to the (A) column of OPEC collective policies, and to each of the (I) to (V) categories of external critical variables; and (2) fill each box in the matrix with any of the following symbols:

(0)   no significant relation-   (−W) weak inverse relationship
      ship or opposite effects   (−M) moderate inverse relation-
      cancelling out   ship
(+W) weak direct relationship   (−S) strong inverse relation-
(+M) moderate direct relation-   ship
      ship
(+S) strong direct relationship

Only eighteen persons and institutions (including OPEC) have answered this time-consuming questionnaire. Table 2.3 incorporates the feedback the author has received with respect to OPEC collective policies and external key variables. Nearly all the listed variables have been considered by most respondents to have a significant relationship (weak, moderate or strong) to OPEC collective policies.

For example, most respondents agree with the author's interpretation that between A_1 and I_5, the relationship can be indicated by (+S) signifying a direct positive relationship, namely, that the higher the relative dependence of expatriate companies on OPEC oil for income, the greater the scope for raising OPEC governments' take. By comparison, A_2 and IV_2 are likely to have a (−S) relationship signifying a negative strong relationship. This means that the larger the relative size of commercial oil reserves in non-OPEC oil exporting countries, the lower the prospects for OPEC's efficient programming of world production. It is not impossible to foresee that the interrelationships depicted in the matrix in Table 2.3 can conceivably be translated into a system of equations, once the size of variables and of parameters are estimated and their relationships established.

The matrix approach to OPEC collective policies in the context of its environment should assist the Secretariat, the Conference, and individual member countries in determining the scope and limitations of fulfilling collective benefits optimization. It will assist them in considering trade-offs and alternative strategies to evade or reduce the impact of constraints, and in making full use of favourable factors. The purpose of the matrix, therefore, is to ask, for each problem, the right kinds of questions in the most precise manner possible. The proper formulation of a question is a major step towards the proper formulation of a solution.

The matrix in Table 2.3 taxonomizes collective OPEC policies and broad groups of possible environmental factors. One can build a more complex matrix to relate OPEC policies to a whole array of constraints or incentives separated into subgroups with a view to solving problems peculiar to specific areas. Subgroups, for example, of expatriate companies are U.S. majors, U.S. independents, West European majors, West European independents, Japanese firms, and others; and subgroups of major consumer countries are United States, EEC, Japan, United Kingdom, and other Western Europe. Similarly, one can subdivide the category of other consumer countries, and that of non-OPEC oil exporting countries.

One can also focus on the policies of a single OPEC member country; these need not be identical – at least with respect to priorities – to the collective policies of the organization. That country's policies would then have to be related to key variables of constraints or incentives in the categories discussed above.

In constructing the matrix model, the author shares the view that 'the trick is to achieve something so simple that it can easily be understood and manipulated, and yet not so ingenious that it omits major influences or encourages a view professionally naive. It is always a matter of opinion whether one succeeds in a particular case – one can but try!'[1]

[1] Dudley Seers, 'The Mechanism of an Open Petroleum Economy', *Social and Economic Studies*, University of the West Indies, Jamaica, Vol. 13, No. 12, June 1964, p. 233.

Chapter 3

CO-OPERATION AMONG OIL
EXPORTING COUNTRIES

The premise which underlies the present analysis is that the greater the similarity, consistency, and complementarity (for short congruence) in key relevant conditions, policies, and goals – referred to hereafter as 'profile' – among OPEC countries, the better the prospects of voluntary functional co-operation. Conversely, the greater their profile incongruity, the greater the potential for conflict. Congruence is likely to reduce or eliminate the uncertainty and mistrust associated with the feeling that one party can take advantage of another; it is also likely to reduce, but not eliminate, the temptation of any member to violate collective agreements.

This chapter describes the construction of a partial profile for an oil exporting country and relates it to a question common to OPEC countries in order to ascertain the extent of co-operation on that question. While it may not be possible to produce a consensus on key variables and their relative weights, the process is valuable in defining the problem, and in identifying relevant key variables and systematizing them. Profiles are aids, however, not substitutes for judgment.

The remainder of the chapter describes the conditions affecting co-operation among OPEC countries and the OPEC subgroup, OAPEC. OPEC was established as a 'defensive' mechanism to form a common front *vis-à-vis* expatriate oil firms and major oil importing countries. OPEC's concern, therefore, is not regional integration of members' economies and societies, but mainly the co-ordination of members' policies in one commodity, petroleum, and solely in the export market. In contrast, the Organization of Arab Petroleum Exporting Countries (OAPEC) has, as its ultimate goal, the integration of its members' national economies into a single regional economy.

69

A. *Measuring Compatibility*

Among the large number of parameters and variables relevant to OPEC co-operation,[1] some have dominated discussions of the joint regulation of production; area, population, oil reserves, amount and growth of oil production, production costs, oil revenues, factor endowment (other than oil), and a country's dependence on the oil industry.

Other variables relevant to co-operation among OPEC countries include the education and expertise of elites and political leaders, and their values, goals, and priorities. Variations among OPEC countries in socioeconomic systems, in international economic relations, in foreign alliances, in ideology and degree of dogmatism, and in political stability will also affect these countries' views and actions on common problems. Among the latter variables, political stability may defy ready measurement, since it contains a high proportion of intangibles and unknowns. However, the chairman of The 'Shell' Transport and Trading Co. Ltd, the 40 per cent owner of Royal-Dutch Shell, has said that his company was 'quantifying' political risks, but he would not elaborate on the techniques used.[2]

In addition to identifying critical factors relevant to OPEC co-operation, there is also the question of ascertaining their relative weights. A number of the variables suggested above are interrelated. These, in turn, interact with other diverse variables in complex and subtle ways too difficult to predict.

Some analysts have attempted to quantify and operationalize variables in the comparative study and measurement of co-operation or integration.[3] Haas and Schmitter have contended that economic

[1] For some general conditions of successful co-operation and integration, see F. Kahnert, P. Richards, E. Stoutjesdijk and P. Thomopoulos, *Economic Integration Among Developing Countries* (Paris: Organization for Economic Co-operation and Development, 1969), Chapter II, pp. 31–49; see also R. N. Farmer and B. M. Richman, *Comparative Management and Economic Progess* (Homewood, Ill.: Irwin, 1965), pp. 19-22 and 28–31; also K. W. Deutsch, 'Toward an Inventory of Basic Trends and Patterns in Comparative and International Politics', in *International Politics and Foreign Policy*, ed. J. N. Rosenau (New York: The Free Press, 1969), pp. 506–10.

[2] David Barran, *How Shell Works, Management Techniques in a Large International Group of Companies:* a presentation to the British Institute of Management, 30 November 1967, p. 27. See also R. B. Stobaugh, 'How to Analyze Foreign Investment Climates – Four Techniques for Dealing with Tricky Questions of Economic and Political Stability', *Harvard Business Review*, September-October 1969, pp. 100–8.

[3] Mario Barrera and Ernst B. Haas, 'The Operationalization of Some Variables

advantage can actuate the economic integration process, and that success in economic integration can lead to political integration. Their thesis is that 'under modern conditions the relationship between economic and political union had best be treated as a continuum. ... The higher the scores, the more likely it is that an economic union will automatically be transformed into a form of political union'.[1] The corollary is that with lower scores for the selected variables, the less likelihood economic integration will produce political integration. Haas' deterministic interpretation is revealed in this excerpt:

> The superiority of step-by-step economic decisions over crucial political choices is assumed as permanent; the determinism implicit in the picture of the European social and economic structure is almost absolute. Given all these conditions, we said, the progression from a politically inspired common market to an economic union, and finally to a political union among states, is automatic.[2]

Not only is this determinism questionable in the case of Europe, as recent experience and events indicate, but its relevance to developing countries is in doubt. Possibly, the conditions for economic integration are not necessarily the same as for political; economic integration may happen among a group of countries for which political integration is unthinkable – for example, in the Central American Common Market. One critic contends 'that their [Haas et al.] recently acquired emphasis on the operationalization and quantification of variables (all viewed over relatively short time periods) gives a distorted understanding of the integration process'.[3]

Related to Regional Integration: Research Note', *International Organization*, Winter 1969 (Vol. 23, No. 1), pp. 150–60; Philippe C. Schmitter, 'Three Neo-Functional Hypotheses About International Integration', *ibid.*, pp. 161–6; Philippe C. Schmitter, 'Further Notes on Operationalizing Some Variables Related to Regional Integration', *International Organization*, Spring 1969 (Vol. 23, No. 2), pp. 327–36; Joseph S. Nye 'Comparative Regional Integration Concept and Measurement', *International Organization*, Autumn 1968 (Vol. 21, No. 2), p. 875; see also J. S. Nye, 'Central American Regional Integration', in *International Regionalism*, pp. 377–429.

[1] Haas and Schmitter, 'Economics and Differential Patterns of Political Integration: Projections about Unity in Latin America', in *International Political Communities: An Anthology* (New York, 1966), pp. 261 and 274.

[2] Ernst Haas, 'The "Uniting of Europe" and the Uniting of Latin America', *Journal of Common Market Studies*, V (June 1967), p. 327.

[3] K. A. Dahlberg, 'Regional Integration: The Neo-Functional versus a Configurative Approach', *International Organization*, Vol. 24, No. 1, p. 123.

See also Roger D. Hansen, 'Regional Integration: Reflections on a Decade of Theoretical Efforts', *World Politics*, XXI (January 1969), pp. 242–71; and

This author suggests that it is possible to construct a partial profile for an OPEC member country on a question common to all members in order to ascertain the extent of actual and potential scope of co-operation in dealing with that question. One example of such a question is that of production programming. It calls for agreeing collectively on the total amount of oil exports from the OPEC area (or subareas), and for splitting the total among the member countries concerned. Chart 3.1 offers the partial profiles of both Iran and Kuwait, assuming the two countries are haggling for the split of total oil exports assigned to their two countries.

On the horizontal axis are the six factors finally agreed upon in 1966 by national representatives of OPEC's Economic Commission in devising their production programming formulae.[1] These factors are listed cumulatively with their weights adding to 100 per cent. A majority of national representatives opted for offering them equal weight, since no agreement could be reached on weighing them differently. The horizontal axis is close-ended, in the sense that factors listed are presumed to comprise all the relevant and critical ones to the problem under study. The vertical axis is a scale of relative shares of the countries under consideration in the combined total value of each of the six factors varying between two limits, from 0 per cent to 100 per cent. The 100 per cent point represents the combined value of the factor obtaining for all the countries under consideration. Thus on the variable of population, Iran gets 98 per cent and Kuwait 2 per cent, whereas on the variable of the relative size of oil income in government revenue Kuwait gets 66 per cent and Iran 34 per cent.

The relative shares of combined exports to be assigned to the two OPEC countries depicted in Chart 3.1 would be identical in the special situations when their partial profiles are identical or when the cumulative weights of their key factors are the same for each country. The actual relative cumulative weights in Chart 3.1 show almost a two-to-one ratio in favour of Iran. According to the profile, Kuwait will oppose, as in fact it did, sole reliance by the OPEC production programming formulae on the factors of area or population, and Iran will oppose sole reliance on the variable of percentage of oil income in government revenue – in deciding on the split of production quotas between the two countries.

J. S. Nye 'Patterns and Catalysts in Regional Integration', in *International Regionalism*, ed. J. S. Nye (Boston: Little, Brown and Co., 1968), pp. 333–49.

[1] The author was in 1966–67 a member of the official Kuwait delegation to the OPEC Economic Commission meetings. For more details, see Chapter Five.

Chart 3.1
Partial profiles of Iran and Kuwait with respect to co-operation in the OPEC production programme of 1966/67

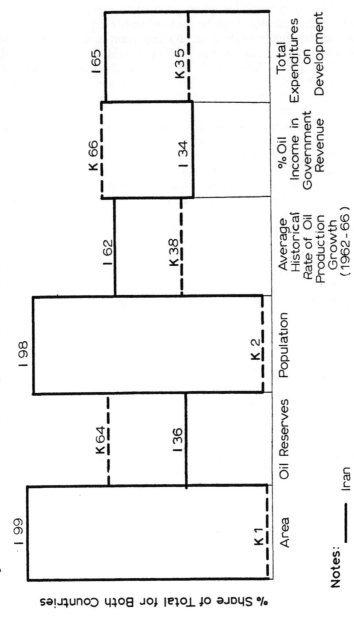

Notes: Iran
Kuwait

The figure submitted by Kuwait in 1966–67 to OPEC on its 'expenditures on development' ($360 million) does not tally with the significantly lower figure ($121 million) published for that year by the Central Bank of Kuwait in its *First Annual Report* of year ending 31 March 1971, p. 12.

73

In designing a workable OPEC production programme, the so-called Delphi Technique[1] can be used to identify key factors relevant to the problem under study, ascertain important functional relationships among them, and assign relative weights to variables and parameters. This is done on the basis of group opinion reached by experts in the field under study. The group opinion is not unanimity or consensus; it is simply a statistical average of the final opinions of experts in the group.

Experts consulted on any given problem should be generally acknowledged by serious students of the subject matter and appropriate international institutions to be highly qualified (have analytical ability), well-informed (have substantive knowledge), and to possess an independent and a perspicacious judgment.[2] Their past performance should vouch for their expertise. As far as the subject of this study is concerned they can come from the OPEC area or from outside. They may be government officials, industry officers, consultants, or scholars. Moreover, the larger their number, the more reliable the results. In this connection, one should note that national representatives to OPEC's Economic Commission are supposed to be experts as well.

The investigator should, according to the Delphi Technique, request each co-operating expert to answer a questionnaire independently in order to reduce the effect of psychological factors such as confrontation, specious persuasion, sway by eloquent dominant speakers, drift to a majority group for conformity's sake, and sticking to officially held positions regardless of one's personal reasoned judgment. Furthermore, the anonymity of experts should be fully protected. This is absolutely necessary if sensible answers

[1] The Technique strikes one as being pretentiously named. It has been developed in the writings of: Olaf Helmer and Nicholas Rescher, 'On the Epistemology of the Inexact Sciences', *Management Science*, Vol. VI, No. 1, October 1969; N. C. Dalkey and Olaf Helmer, 'An Experimental Application of the Delphi Method to the Use of Experts', *ibid.*, Vol. IX, No. 3, April 1963: T. J. Gordon and Olaf Helmer, *Report on Long-Range Forecasting Study* (Santa Monica, Calif.: The Rand Corporation, 1964), 65 pp. and appendix; Olaf Helmer, *Analysis of the Future: The Delphi Method* (The Rand Corp., March 1967), 11 pp.; Olaf Helmer, *New Developments in Early Forecasting of Public Problems: A New Intellectual Climate* (The Rand Corp., April 1967), 10 pp.; Olaf Helmer, *Systematic Use of Expert Opinions* (The Rand Corp., November 1967), 11 pp.; N. C. Dalkey, *Delphi* (The Rand Corp., October 1967), 11 pp.; Olaf Helmer, *Social Technology* (New York: Basic Books, Inc. 1966); and *Perspectives for the '70s and '80s*, ed. D. S. Morris, The National Industrial Conference Board, New York, 1970, pp. 2–3.

[2] The UN Secretariat in its choice of 'experts' has, for criteria, that the person should be recognized as such in his country and in his profession internationally.

are to be obtained and the expression of vested interests to be avoided. The investigator conducting such a study should command the respect and trust of experts.

The questionnaire should name one or more definite events or policies. In the case of OPEC production programming, events could be alternative quota distributions assigned to member countries. For each quota distribution, the experts would identify variables that tempt members to sell outside their production quota, and quantify the impact of these variables. Since OPEC aims at close observance of its production programme, the lower the cumulative size of estimated individual departures combining all member countries for any given distribution of quotas among these members, the better the distribution.

One index for the probability of a departure is that of commercial oil reserves available to each member country, since reserves are a measure, of a sort, of productive capacity, and ability to produce outside the production programme is a measure of ability to wreck the programme. The bigger a member's potential capacity, the more it can sell outside its production quota and thereby frustrate the OPEC production plan. Another likely index for the probability of a departure is the differential in treatment of member countries, assuming that a given nation's willingness to abide by its quota depends on whether its neighbour and rival has a similar or larger quota. A country's holdings of gold and foreign exchange could be added; the smaller these holdings, the greater the pressures for selling outside the plan. Experts could conceive other indices of departure. Once they have been identified, respondents will be asked to assign relative weights to them in order to form a composite probabilistic index for total departures from any set of quota distributions among members.

The first round of answers should be collated, summarized, and tabulated, to ascertain whether there is general agreement on key points. If such agreement exists, the experiment ends. If answers show dispersion, as they usually do, the investigator will reveal the points of disagreement to each expert, indicating the extent of dispersion (namely the median and the interquartile range containing the middle 50 per cent of the responses). One or more additional responses are sought, requesting justification for estimates falling outside the interquartile range. This new set of opinions will lead to a possible convergence in the answers – assuming that, as new evidence comes to light, individual biases are corrected, and due weight is given to variables which have been dismissed lightly or inadvertently. It is also possible for views to polarize in more than one direction. Under these circumstances, this author suggests that an arithmetic mean average of experts' opinions be taken for the variable(s) on which there is disagreement since it is difficult to differentiate among degrees of expertise. This mean can very well turn out to be a hypothetical intermediate view held by no one.

One can also resort to sensitivity analysis in profile building in order to ascertain the impact of small changes in weights assigned to key variables on the shape of profiles of individual countries. The greater the sensitivity of profiles to small changes in weights, the more cautious the analyst should be in interpreting results.

Compiling a master profile for OPEC and another for OAPEC would involve integrating partial profiles to cover all areas of co-operation, with proper weights assigned to each set of variables and with the interaction of various areas of co-operation taken into account. These master profiles should show the status and evolution of the whole range of areas of co-operation and integration among members of each group. Such an undertaking may well prove too ambitious, given the complexities of intercountry co-operation.

The profiles suggested should be considered dynamic; they are likely to vary over time along with the key variables chosen and the weights assigned to them. Accordingly, a series of profiles for various countries over different periods of time could be constructed in order to identify changes in congruence among the countries concerned in various areas of co-operation.

This approach to the study of co-operation or integration among OPEC and OAPEC countries should help to identify the relevant key variables; ascertain the nature and extent of differences among member countries with respect to these variables; ascertain changes over the years in the dispersion of profiles; and analyse and interpret the 'whys' of past and recent developments. In addition, such a study would assist the OPEC and OAPEC leaders in devising pragmatic policies and plans for influencing or manipulating controllable variables to obtain desirable results; set characteristics for eligible countries; and predict the behaviour of individual members on various subjects and their respective voting patterns.

This profile-building approach can also be usefully applied to the international oil companies and to major oil consuming countries already grouped in the EEC or OECD organizations. It will help to ascertain the extent of co-operation among members in each group with respect to energy questions and the prospects for functional coalitions. One could also compare the three collections of profiles (of oil exporting countries, oil importing countries, and international companies) in order to ascertain the relative degree of co-operation, actual or potential, of members in each group.

Moreover, the fewer the number of members, the greater the scope for agreement within the group – other things remaining constant. Size of membership in a group determines the possible number of relationships. With two members, A and B, there can be only one relationship; with three members, A, B, and C, there can be six relationships; with four members, there can be 18; with five, 44; with six, 100; with seven, 222; with eight, 490; with nine, 1,080; and with ten, 2,373. This surge is geometrical and illustrates the increasingly complex web of possible relationships, such as coalitions or confrontations, that can exist with an enlarged membership. Mathematically, the number of relationships faced by a single member of a group is equal to $n(2^n/2+n-1)$, where n is the number of the other members in the group.[1] In addition, parties with common interests in one or more areas may have conflicting interests in other areas, or be indifferent. Common interests may be congruent or overlap to a small or large degree.

One should guard against the deceptive glamour of indiscriminately using mathematical formulae in social studies. Complete faith in the figures underlying the profiles suggested above is unwarranted; the soundness of the approach in dealing with hitherto intractable problems and its reliable application are of greater significance. Profiles should act as aids, not as substitutes for judgment. Their function is comparable to that of computers which cannot perfectly match couples for marriage, nor children and foster parents. However, the method of testing and screening applicants delineates the 'correct' profile of each client that will obtain the requisite degree of compatibility in a partner.[2]

The profile model could also be used in connection with other schemes of co-operation outside the oil industry. For example, the Arab League Secretariat and its members might well stand to gain in knowledge and in effective action by attempting such an analysis. It will help certain members recognize and assess points of congruence and difference. Furthermore, it will indicate the scope and limitations of unified action.

[1] See H. Koontz and C. O'Donnel, *Principles of Management, an Analysis of Managerial Functions* (3rd ed.; New York: McGraw-Hill), pp. 219–22.

[2] A 65 per cent compatibility, according to one computer match service using sophisticated methods of interviews and tests, could lead to a workable match. See *The New York Times*, 25 December 1970, p. 31.

B. *The OPEC Group*

OPEC's only strength, as political leaders in member countries realize, lies in its solidarity, which can be analysed through the use of the profile and matrix models described previously. Has solidarity been demonstrated by effective collective action and mutual support, or have the members merely offered one another moral support and lip-service?

Some pronouncements made by government delegates in OPEC conferences appear to be 'suited to the occasion', and do not necessarily genuinely reflect attitudes, conditions, or pressures inside member countries. Therefore, a member may not get effective support from fellow members in an encounter with international companies. This was the fate of Iraq, when faced with a curtailment of the growth rate of its oil exports in 1960–70, in the course of a series of showdowns with international companies. The companies favoured raising the export rates of neighbouring countries (including Arab countries) at the expense of Iraq. Not one single country among the beneficiaries was interested in countering company actions which were damaging to Iraq. The Iraqi Oil Minister, addressing a small group of top Arab oil officials at the Fifth Arab Petroleum Congress, reflected sadly on intra-OPEC rivalry: 'Unfortunately, I don't think the other Arab states are ready to stand by Iraq against the cartels, even though it is their duty to do so in the common Arab interest.'[1]

OPEC countries did offer Iraq verbal support in several resolutions (II.16, III.18, XI.73, XIII.81, and XX.115). However, the Iraqi minister doubtless hoped that other oil exporting countries would force their concessionaires to cut down the expansion of oil production in their countries in favour of Iraq. Several governments were unwilling to co-operate with Iraq at the time, and, in fact, had little sympathy with General Kassem's emotional and high-handed unilateral actions.

On other occasions, OPEC offered a strong united front and was able to exert moral suasion influence over some companies. For example, Libya wanted to apply, by the Royal Decree of 20 November 1965, the terms of the OPEC settlement of 1964 with major companies regarding royalty expensing based on posted prices on all companies operating in the country, including a large number of independents. These independents, which were not a party of the OPEC royalty expensing settlement, used to pay income tax to the

[1] Abdul Aziz Wattari in *MEES Supplement*, 9 April 1965, p. 2.

Libyan government on the basis of prices bearing, according to one trade journal, 'notorious discounts'. These discounts varied between 40 and 60 cents per barrel below posted prices. Jersey, the only major company then exporting oil from Libya (some 575,000 barrels of crude per day) had been paying more income tax than the independents, based on posted prices used for transferring most of that oil to its affiliates.[1] One of the major companies with oil rights in Libya acknowledged that the cost of the Libyan legislation was only a few cents per barrel to majors, and as much as 45 cents per barrel to independents.[2] One of the independent companies commented acidly on the rivalry within the group of oil companies: 'In this case, the interests of a particular state in increasing taxes happened to coincide with the interests of some of the major companies in creating difficulties for other smaller companies.'[3]

The independents in Libya balked at the OPEC settlement, and rightly feared increased costs and loss of markets to the majors, who were not unhappy to see the independents' tax-paid costs go up and their share in international markets decline. To force the hand of the independents, the OPEC conference verbally threatened recalcitrant companies with collective boycott in the award of oil rights. A strongly worded resolution (Res. X.63) was apparently designed to induce the independents to comply with the new Libyan legislation. That resolution recommended (but did not require):

... that the Governments of Member Countries of OPEC, until such time when those title-holder companies operating in Libya undertake to comply with the obligations of Articles 11 and 12 of the Royal Decree of November 22, 1965, shall not grant any new oil rights of any nature whatsoever or enter into any new contracts concerning the exploration and/or exploitation of new areas to the parent companies of said title-holder companies, to the affiliated or subsidiary companies of any of them or to any other company in which one of the said title-holder companies has an interest of 10 per cent or more: nor shall any Government of Member Countries of OPEC enter into, or continue, negotiations with any of the above mentioned title-holder companies on any matter directly or indirectly concerning the grant of new oil rights.

[1] *PPS*, July 1965, p. 267; see also J. E. Hartshorn, *Oil Companies and Governments*, Faber and Faber (London, 1967), p. 21.
[2] Shell International Petroleum Co. Ltd., *Developments in Libya*, London, May 1966, p. 6.
[3] ENI, *Energy and Petroleum in 1965*, p. 12.

Collective support given to Libya in 1965 by fellow members was primarily prompted by self-interest. These countries were fearful of the keen competitiveness of Libyan oil, and consequently welcomed any increase in Libyan posted prices. One should not overemphasize OPEC's moral suasion; in fact, the Libyan government's success in getting company acceptance of its legislation should be attributed essentially to Libya's threat not to award any new concessions to recalcitrant companies, and possibly to stop the latter's exports.[1] Also, Venezuela was introducing at that time legislation that would raise its tax-reference prices, and Saudi Arabia was negotiating with its concessionaire, Aramco, the use of the posted price on sales to third parties for Saudi income tax purposes, instead of the lower (about 20 per cent) realized prices.[2]

Even unanimous resolutions at OPEC conferences have not been scrupulously observed. One illustration is Resolution XVII.94 of November 1969, inviting member countries to refrain from granting new oil rights to companies from the rich industrialized countries, such as Japan, whose governments espouse policies explicitly aimed at reducing oil import prices. This resolution was not honoured by Qatar and Abu Dhabi; soon afterwards, both countries granted oil rights to Japanese applicants. These countries' rulers claimed that they needed urgently additional oil revenues, and feared that Iran would go ahead and develop adjacent acreage at their expense. Need can be subjectively justified with the use of various criteria by those concerned; need for oil revenues may be related to the purpose for which resources will be used: development, defence, or even current consumption which often turns out to be on luxury items in several developing countries.

One top official of OPEC publicly admitted that 'formidable obstacles to smooth co-operation exist among Member Countries'.[3] This is probably the case in other plans for international co-operation, whether among developed or developing nations. Some of these short-lived or ineffective organizations have foundered on lesser difficulties, whether or not the countries concerned have a common cultural background.

To reach a fuller understanding of the formidable obstacles to

---

[1] See *Arab Oil Review*, Tripoli–Libya, January 1966, pp. 5–8, 17; *Petroleum Intelligence Weekly*, November–December 1965; and *PPS*, July 1965, p. 267.

[2] See OPEC, *Collective Influence in the Recent Trend Towards the Stabilization of International Crude and Product Prices*, VIth Arab Petroleum Congress, March 1967, pp. 6–9.

[3] Francisco R. Parra, *OPEC and the Oil Industry in the Middle East*, p. 10.

smooth co-operation and, consequently, to the growth of the OPEC organization, one should bear in mind the differences in the internal organization of the participating states, and the disparity of their economic and political interests. Indeed, oil is not solely an economic problem, and the student of international relations should investigate how far, given the vicissitudes of Middle East politics, oil increases or decreases solidarity among OPEC countries in non-oil fields.

Differences exist and will continue to exist between OPEC countries, for example, between Iran and its Arab neighbours. They pertain to domestic, regional, and international problems. The Iranian monarchy holds in repugnance regimes which call themselves 'progressive' or 'revolutionary' and which brand Iran's leadership and regime as 'traditionalist'. Iran's regime, according to the Shah, is 'revolutionary'; its purpose is to destroy the feudal and oppressive social foundations of Iranian society and replace them 'with the most progressive ones in this modern world'.[1]

Iran also has disputes with Iraq over land and water rights, and over the continental shelf with countries bordering the Arabian–Persian Gulf. Until 1970, Iran laid claim to Bahrain, a small Arab-ruled oil exporting sheikhdom. It seized on 30 November 1971 the islands of Abu Musa and Tumbs which belonged until then to neighbouring Arab sheikdoms.[2] Moreover, Iran has, since 1949, given *de facto* recognition to the State of Israel, recognition publicly reiterated by the Shah on 24 July 1960. Neighbouring Arab countries which have religious ties with Iran have been offended by this recognition and by the economic relations between the two countries, especially by the fact that Iran supplies oil to, and through, Israel.[3]

Differences between Iran and her Arab neighbours are not confined to regional politics; they also cover international politics. Iran is formally part of the Western alliance and is an active member of the Central Treaty Organization or CENTO (previously known as the Baghdad Pact), established in 1957 with the encouragement of the United States. CENTO now comprises – besides Iran – Turkey, Pakistan, the United Kingdom, and the United States.[4] Although

---

[1] The Shah's speech to the Majlis on 6 October 1967, published in *The Revolution: New Dimensions*, Transorient, London, 1967; see also an interview of the Shah by *L'Express*, Paris, 8 June 1960, p. 30; and S. Sanghvi, *Aryamehr, The Shah of Iran, A Political Biography* (London: Macmillan, 1968).
    The author interviewed in August 1968 Prime Minister Abbas Amir Hoveyda on the Shah's 'White Revolution'.
[2] *MEES*, 3 December 1971, pp. 1–9.
[3] See, for example, Hirst, *op. cit.*, p. 112.
[4] The United States is a member of several committees of CENTO. Since it did

Iran has developed economic co-operation in both oil and non-oil affairs with the U.S.S.R. since the 1960s,[1] and has played down the military aspects of the CENTO alliance, its formal alliance with Western powers is at variance with the official policy espoused by several Arab countries claiming to be neutralists. A Persian scholar commented on CENTO's eclipse as a military alliance in favour of an economic regional alliance and on Iran's clever handling of the Arab–Israeli conflict as follows:

> Iran has thrown full support behind the Regional Co-operation for Development (RCD)[2], which was created in 1964 in the wake of the crisis of confidence in CENTO marked by Iran's own growing disenchantment with the organization as well as the disillusionment of Turkey and Pakistan with the West over Cyprus and Kashmir respectively. And particularly since the Arab-Israeli war (1967), Iran has tactfully tried to perform a tightrope act between the Arab states and Israel, considering its guarded secret of technical, commercial and touristic ties with Tel Aviv on the one hand, and its overall sympathy with the Arabs, particularly the Palestinians, on the other.[3]

Boundary disputes, regional problems, dissimilar attitudes to East and West, and other political differences are not limited to Iran and certain Arab countries. These difficulties exist, in varing degrees, among Arab countries themselves. For example, General Kassem of Iraq laid sovereignty claim in 1961 to Kuwait, another Arab state; both Iraq and Kuwait are founding members of OPEC in September 1960. As a result of this dispute, Iraq boycotted OPEC's conference meetings in 1961, although it did not withdraw. Boundary disputes still exist between Saudi Arabia and Abu Dhabi with respect to potentially oil-rich areas, notably the Buraimi oasis.

Affinities or antagonisms among OPEC countries' leaders and systems of government have also been responsible, to some extent, for bloc politics in oil affairs, for example, the founding early in

not wish to become full member of the organization, it signed, in 1959, bilateral mutual security agreements separately with Iran, Turkey and Pakistan. See U.S. Department of State. *The Central Treaty Organization*, International Organizations Series, No. 1, Washington, March 1970.

[1] See *Petroleum and Economic Digest*, Dublin, 1–15 October 1970; and Rouhollah K. Ramazani, 'Iran's Changing Foreign Policy: A Preliminary Discussion', *Middle East Journal*, Washington D.C., Autumn 1970 (Vol. 24, No. 4), pp. 421–37.

[2] See Chapter Eight, Section A.

[3] Ramazani, *op. cit.*, p. 435.

1968 of OAPEC by three Arab OPEC countries: Kuwait, Libya, and Saudi Arabia. OAPEC, at its creation, cemented an alliance between members of a group of Arab conservative or traditionalist states, then politically more or less homogeneous. By joining forces, they deliberately parted company with Arab revolutionary states, such as Iraq and Algeria.

The student of international affairs can see that, in the rapidly changing conditions of the world, oil and non-oil interests may overlap or clash. It is also apparent that oil is a potent element of co-operation or discord among ten decidedly different countries. The great achievement of OPEC is that it has made some co-operation possible despite deeply rooted differences and serious conflicts among its member countries.

The financial negotiations of January–February 1971 are probably the best instance of solidarity shown so far by OPEC countries, and the first example of collective bargaining carried out by a Ministerial Committee appointed by the OPEC conference. The Arabian–Persian Gulf countries were able to win substantial financial gains from the international companies and consumer countries, thanks to their unity under the leaderhip and foresight of the Shah. He was ably supported by the dexterity of the Iranian Minister of Finance Jamshid Amouzegar, the leading OPEC negotiator, and the pragmatism and firmness of his colleagues, the Saudi Minister of Petroleum and Mineral Resources Ahmed Zaki Yamani, and the Iraqi Minister of Oil and Minerals Sa'doun Hammadi.

All OPEC countries' representatives, from revolutionary Iraq Minister Sa'doun Hammadi to traditionalist Kuwait Minister of Oil and Finance Abdel-Rahman al-Atiqi, had only praise for the role of Iran. All acknowledged that the key reason for the remarkable benefits realized was the solidarity shown by OPEC countries, which managed to put aside individual interests in order to serve the common good.[1] The psychological effect of having once united so profitably may develop their awareness of the benefits of collective action and weaken the tradition of intra-OPEC rivalry.

I. *The Conception of OAPEC*

OAPEC's creation can be viewed as a spillover process in so far as certain OPEC members – although agreeing on some goals for a variety of motives but not satisfied with their attainment of these goals – attempt to resolve their dissatisfaction either by collaborating in another related sector (expanding the *scope* of the mutual commit-

[1] See *Iran Oil Journal*, February 1971, pp. 9–10 and 37.

ment), or by intensifying their commitment in the original sector (increasing the *level* of mutual commitment), or by both.[1]

After the Middle East war of June 1967, and following Israel's occupation of over 26,000 square miles of Arab territories (in Egypt, Jordan, and Syria), some Arab states sought to balance their military setback by resorting to what a leading trade journal called the 'petroleum defence line.[2]' Defence consisted, in the compelling circumstances of that time, of a selective embargo on petroleum going to certain specified destinations, the United States, the United Kingdom, and, to some extent, West Germany. The object was to exert pressure on those Western governments friendly with the State of Israel, in the hope that they would, in turn, exert pressure on Israel to withdraw from the occupied territories. The embargo was also intended as a pre-emptive act to appease general discontent. Informed observers[3] note that the alternative to a selective embargo on oil exports would have been to allow anti-United States feeling among the Arab populace to explode, and probably lead to massive sabotage of oil installations.

The choice of the United States, Britain, and West Germany as targets for selective embargo was based on charges by Jordan and the U.A.R. that these countries offered Israel substantial direct military assistance in the June 1967 war. Cairo actually claimed that U.S. and British planes offered assistance in logistics and protective air cover to Israel in June 1967 to free its planes for invading neighbouring countries. The Saudi Minister of Petroleum and Mineral Resources said in 1968 that the embargo decision was originally prompted by political pressures overriding economic considerations; it was made, he added, in Baghdad by the hurriedly convening Arab Ministers of Finance, Economy, and Oil on the 3rd and 4th of June 1967 on the eve of the war, and was meant to deter an impending Israeli attack. 'In the heat of the moment' – during the invasion – the embargo decision was rushed into effect to prove its credibility as a deterrent.

Certain Arab leaders had the truth a few days after the Israeli attack of 6 June 1967, but allegations of direct Anglo-American involvement with Israel in military operations were not formally declared false until some nine months later. The first public record

[1] See Philippe C. Schmitter, 'Three Neo-Functional Hypotheses About International Integration', *International Organization* (Winter 1969), p. 162.

[2] *MEES*, 12 January 1968, p. 3.

[3] For example, Fuad W. Itayim in an unpublished address entitled 'Middle East Conflict and the Continuity of Oil Supplies', delivered on 7 May 1970 at Harvard University Center for Middle Eastern Studies.

admitting that neither the United States nor Britain participated directly in the Israeli attack was as follows:

> *Question:* It was you who broke diplomatic relations with us on the grounds that our planes participated in the Israeli attack last June. This unfounded accusation angered a lot of Americans. Why did you make it?
>
> *Nasser:* ... We said, The General High Command have indications that the U.S. and Britain are participating in Israeli aggression with carrier-based planes flying air cover over Israel to free Israeli planes for attacks. Jordanians say radar indicates U.S. and British planes were helping. King Hussein called to say U.S. and British planes involved. Later, Johnson called Kosygin to inform us, and he did.
>
> *Question:* In other words, your accusation resulted from a misunderstanding based on suspicion and faulty information?
>
> *Nasser:* You could say that, yes.[1]

The Saudi Minister, commenting in 1968, added that the embargo decision 'hurt the Arabs themselves more than anyone else, and the only ones to gain any benefit from it were the non-Arab [oil] producers'.[2] He was right. The embargo led to a vast wave of ill-feeling, not only in the United States but throughout the West toward the Arabs and their cause. Moreover, the resulting loss of revenues weighed heavily on Arab countries; consumer countries began to substitute oil from the United States, Venezuela, and Iran – although at higher costs – for Arab oil.

Not only did Arab governments become the victim of an economically self-defeating embargo, but they indirectly hurt consumer countries not involved in the Arab–Israeli conflict. These were countries that obtained their oil from U.S. and British controlled companies which had then about 60 and 20 per cent, respectively, of Arab oil production. This situation has spurred a number of major consuming countries in their search for direct access to oil production or supply rights outside the traditional Anglo-American

---

[1] Interview of William Attwood, Editor-in-Chief of *Look* with Gamal Abdel Nasser, late President of the U.A.R. (Egypt). See *Look*, New York, 19 March 1968, p. 63.

[2] Ahmad Zaki Yamani, 'Aspects of Oil Policy for the Arab Countries and the Relation of Arab Policy to that of OPEC', address at the American University of Beirut, 3 June 1968. Reproduced in *MEES Supplement*, 7 June 1968, p. 1.

channels, which have been subject to punitive actions in host countries.

The United States, a principal offender then in the eyes of most Arabs, was not hurt by the embargo. Its volume of imports from the Middle East was relatively small, about 300,000 barrels per day, thanks to its import control which was established partly to offset such a contingency. Moreover, several U.S. companies operating overseas derived additional profits as a result of the ensuing price increases in petroleum products, which more than counterbalanced increased transport costs.[1]

After the selective embargo failed, another Conference of Arab Ministers of Finance, Economy, and Oil was held from 15 to 20 August 1967 in Baghdad. Two diametrically opposed solutions were proposed. Iraq, supported by Algeria, advocated a three-month total stoppage of Arab oil exports, since a selective embargo for specified destinations could be circumvented by trans-shipments. It was hoped that a total ban on oil exports would deplete European oil stocks within three months, in time for the winter season. But according to one OECD calculation (possibly optimistic) communicated privately to the author, a total Arab oil stoppage would not cripple Western Europe for ten months, assuming that non-Arab oil sources remained open. Some Arab governments would find it hard to hold out so long without incurring grave domestic problems. Moreover, a total ban on oil shipments would hurt both foe and friend.

Another solution favoured by Saudi Arabia, Kuwait, and Libya was the positive policy of maximizing oil revenues. They urged the use of the oil proceeds to support the war-stricken Arab states in their efforts to regain and protect their territorial integrity. The Arab Summit Conference meeting in Khartum on 29 August 1967 opted for the positive approach and decided to lift the selective oil embargo:

> The Conference of Arab Ministers of Finance, Economy and Oil had recommended the possibility of employing the stoppage of the flow of oil as a weapon in the battle. However, after careful study of the matter, the Summit Conference concluded that oil flow could itself be used as a positive weapon in that Arab oil represents an Arab asset which could be used to strengthen the economies of those Arab states which were directly affected by the aggression, thereby enabling them to stand firm in the battle.

[1] See, for example, Ragaei El Mallakh, *Some Dimensions of Middle East Oil: The Producing Countries and the United States*, American–Arab Association for Commerce and Industry, New York, March 1970, pp. 13–15.

The Conference therefore decided to resume oil pumping operations on the grounds that this is an Arab asset which can be put to use in the service of Arab aims and in contributing towards enabling those Arab states which were subjected to aggression and a consequent loss of economic resources to stand firm in their resolve to eliminate the effects of the aggression.[1]

As a result of this decision, Kuwait, Saudi Arabia, and Libya offered financial assistance on an annual basis, to continue 'until the effects of the aggression are eliminated', – £55 million, £50 million, and £30 million, respectively, a total of £135 million or $378 million at the pre-November 1967 rate of sterling. The beneficiary states have been the U.A.R. (Egypt) and Jordan to the tune of $266 million and $112 million a year, respectively. Libya and Kuwait withdrew their aid to Jordan in 1971 on the grounds that the Jordanian regime was liquidating the Palestinian resistance.

By late 1967, the governments of the three major Arab oil exporting countries, Kuwait, Libya, and Saudi Arabia, which had suffered heavily from the oil embargo, thought it in their best interests to co-ordinate their policies outside the Arab League in order to exclude other Arab states from their affairs. In these dramatic circumstances, OAPEC was formed on 9 January 1968.

II. *The 'Revolutionary' Countermoves*

The Iraq government was invited in January 1968 to join OAPEC as a founding member. The offer was declined, however, primarily because the tripartite axis of conservative regimes interpreted OAPEC's charter in an unreasonably restrictive manner, precluding from membership, in effect, Arab countries which were politically at odds with the founders. Commenting on OAPEC's restrictive membership rules, the chairman of the Iraq National Oil Company (INOC) said:

We think this is wrong and unreasonable. According to the present rules, Algeria [a member of OPEC since July, 1969] – which is by any standards a substantial exporter of oil – would be excluded from membership; so would the UAR, which is also expected to become a significant oil exporter within the next few years. We are not against the establishment of an organization for Arab oil exporting countries as such, provided the conditions are reasonable. But we would apply the same membership rules to the Arab petroleum organization as are applicable in OPEC: namely

[1] Resolution 4: See *MEES Supplement*, 8 September 1967, p. 3.

that any (in this case Arab) country with a substantial net export of oil should be eligible to join.[1]

OAPEC's establishment as an organization outside the Arab League, the timing of its creation on 9 January 1968 (shortly after the Arab Summit Conference of August 1967), and its restrictive membership requirements constituted an act of defiance to certain other Arab oil exporting countries. Within twenty days of OAPEC's creation, Iraq and Algeria reacted forcefully. On 1 February 1968, their state-owned oil companies, INOC and Sonatrach, respectively, signed an agreement calling for utmost mutual co-operation in oil affairs to achieve 'an independent revolutionary oil policy for the benefit of the Arab nation'. The agreement is open to all Arab national oil companies, which are invited to 'adopt an independent national policy uninfluenced by the international monopolies and not subject to be used to increase imperialistic designs on, and domination of, Arab countries'.[2]

The revolutionary spokesmen may admit that their approach to the development of their oil resources may not, in the short- or medium-run, lead to economic benefits larger than those they would get by co-operating closely with the international oil companies. Therefore, they justify their stand on the grounds that they are speedily promoting national managerial talents and technical skills, oil-based industrialization, modernization, and economic independence, in the hope of larger ultimate economic benefits to their people.

The Iraq–Algeria communiqué was laconic about details of the February 1968 agreement. The communiqué referred to the creation of a joint technical committee and to periodic meetings – at least twice annually – between the parties concerned. A fortnight after the agreement was signed Iraq officially invited the national oil companies of the U.A.R. and Syria to join.[3] These countries were, according to Iraq, chosen explicitly for their revolutionary or independent policies in oil affairs.

Modest measures of co-operation in oil matters have been taking place among the national companies of revolutionary Arab states. Technicians are being exchanged, particularly between Algeria and Iraq,[4] and Sonatrach, the Algerian state oil agency, has undertaken to

[1] Adib al-Jader in *MEES Supplement*, 19 January 1968, p. 1.
[2] Text of Iraq–Algeria communiqué in *Arab Oil and Gas Journal* (in Arabic), January 1968, p. 19.
[3] *MEES*, 23 February 1968, p. 8.
[4] *Review of Arab Petroleum and Economics*, Beirut, 29 March 1968, p. 3.

carry out geophysical surveys in Syria and to assist in marketing Syrian oil abroad.[1]

Most revolutionary Arab countries (Syria, Algeria, U.A.R., Iraq, and, more recently, Libya) have sought the co-operation and assistance of the Soviet Union in oil affairs.[2] Specifically, Iraq and the U.S.S.R. signed in 1969–71 several loan investment agreements for a total of $364 million, and on 6 December 1969, three contracts providing for the supply of various types of Soviet equipment and the construction of oil plants, pipelines, and other facilities in Iraq.[3] In Algeria, Soviet co-operation is of long standing. The Soviet Union has established a Petroleum and Textile Centre in Algiers to graduate engineers and technicians, and has sent a large number of Soviet oil technicians (some 350 in 1967) under the terms of the Soviet–Algerian technical co-operation agreement signed on 4 August 1966.[4] Algeria, for its part, has avoided overt competition with Soviet oil in European markets, and has stated revolutionary and non-commercial reasons in an official document.[5]

With the overthrow of the Libyan monarchy[6] in September 1969 and the establishment of a revolutionary regime, the OAPEC group lost one important dimension of its uniformity, conservatism of

[1] *MEES*, 29 May 1970, p. 4.

[2] U.S.S.R. Delegation, *Oil Production Industry of the U.S.S.R. and Co-operation with the Arab Countries in Developing Their National Oil Industry*, Report to the VIIth Arab Petroleum Congress, Kuwait, March 1970, 13 pp.

[3] UN General Assembly, Report of the Secretary General, *Permanent Sovereignty over Natural Resources*, 14 September 1970, p. 106; and *MEES*, 12 December 1969, and 9 April 1971, pp. 4 and 5–6 respectively.

[4] *MEES*, October 1967, p. 7.
Press sources indicated that Algeria pays for Soviet 'aid' with exports of petroleum: *Platt's Oilgram News Service*, 26 July 1968, p. 1.

[5] Pour ce qui est des relations avec les pays socialistes d'Europe et en particulier l'U.R.S.S., l'Algérie considère qu'il eût été désirable d'éviter une concurrence qui ne serait pas dans l'intérêt des uns et des autres.
C'est pour cela que dès qu'elle a appris que l'Union Soviétique avait presenté des offres sur les marchés européens, l'Algérie s'est retirée de ces marchés, adoptant une attitude dictée par des considérations révolutionnaires et non commerciales.
République Algérienne, Ministère des Finances et du Plan, 'Caractéristiques de la Politique de l'Algérie en Matière d'Hydrocarbures', 30 June 1967, p. 9.

[6] The Libyan revolutionaries have accused the monarchists of corruption. According to an American reporter, 'Despite its tough stand against the West, Western observers to a man vouch for the honesty of the [revolutionary] Gadhafi government, at least so far'. That reporter quotes an old-time oilman in Libya thus: 'Yes, they are honest all right. If they were corrupt, they wouldn't give us so much trouble, then we would know how to handle them.'
David Pauly, staff reporter of *Forbes*, New York, 15 October 1970, p. 24.

political regimes. Nevertheless, the political defection of Libya to the revolutionary camp heralded the opening of OAPEC's membership to other eligible revolutionary Arab oil exporting countries, such as Algeria which joined early in 1970. Libya and Algeria have considered the formation of joint oil ventures,[1] and on 6 January 1970, a co-ordination agreement was signed between the national oil companies of Algeria, Iraq, Libya, and the U.A.R. The companies agreed to exchange information and technicians, to co-ordinate foreign marketing policy, to carry out joint projects, and to hold biannual meetings. They also pledged mutual support whenever any of them 'faces pressures from the foreign oil companies'.[2] Under this agreement, some 25 to 35 technicians of the Libyan National Oil Corporation (Linoco) are to receive training in 1971 with the Iraq National Oil Company.[3]

Of greater significance is the agreement of 23 May 1970 among the revolutionary major oil exporting countries – Algeria, Iraq, and Libya – which accounted among them for some 95 per cent of crude oil exports from Mediterranean terminals in 1970.[4] The purpose of the agreement is to respond collectively to problems with international companies operating in their countries. The ministers of the three countries, in order to get satisfaction on their demands, contemplated unilaterial action and legislative measures 'to set a limit to the lengthy and fruitless negotiations' they were having with concessionaires. Mutual support is advocated, and a joint co-operative fund will be established to aid any state which 'may suffer harm as a result of a confrontation with the exploiting oil companies.'[5] The latter is a potentially effective weapon of bargaining, and is probably novel in the annals of oil co-operation. It reflects an inclination to resist pressures which oil companies might exert if confronted by unfavourable measures.

Only time will tell whether the originally monarchical OAPEC and the revolutionary groups of national companies will, by the very nature of their different members and as a result of their political incompatibility, polarize differences or achieve some form of compromise. Both groups have in common the ultimate aim of unity among Arab countries; they also presume that oil can be a means to complete economic integration. Now that OAPEC has lost its

[1] *MEES*, 12 December 1969, p. 6.
[2] *MEES*, 16 January 1970, pp. 6–8.
[3] The *Baghdad Observer*, Baghdad, 21 October 1970, as reproduced in OPEC's *Weekly Bulletin*, Vol. 1, No. 34, 6 November 1970, p. 1.
[4] Text in *MEES*, 29 May 1970, pp. 2–3.   [5] *Ibid.*

original monarchical uniformity with revolutionary Algeria and Libya in both OAPEC and the revolutionary group, effective co-operation among Arab oil exporting states may cut across political differences.

It is, however, doubtful whether oil co-operation will lead to Arab unity. President Gadhafi of Libya was reported to oppose the inclusion of monarchies, such as Saudi Arabia, in a projected federation of Arab states, because, he asserted, 'monarchies had delayed the process of Arab unity'.[1] Similarly, monarchies are suspicious of revolutionary systems of government characterized by an approach to socio-economic matters that stresses state ownership and management of key sectors.

Although revolutionary governments in oil exporting countries are militarily based, they have had in their bids for power the inter-mittent support of labour and of some nationalist or reformist intelligentsia. Describing the Libyan revolutionary regime, an in-formed reporter remarked:

> Its government is reformist but not radical, nationalist but not communist, traditionally Islamic in some ways but determinedly modern in others. It is very much in the Nasserite[1] tradition. It is the kind of government many scholars expect to see win out eventually in the Arab lands – both over communist-leaning Arabs and over traditionalists like Kings Faisal [of Saudi Arabia] and Hussein [of Jordan].[2]

III. *Evaluation of Sectoral Integration in Oil*

The aspiration for unity is deeply rooted among Arab peoples. Nevertheless, past constitutional attempts at confederation (for example, the Arab League since 1945), at federation (the Federation of Jordan and Iraq in 1958), or at union (the U.A.R. in 1958–61), have been either short-lived or of little effect. The same has happened to the more modest co-operative or functional approaches, such as the Arab Common Market and the Arab Economic Union Conventions comprising Egypt, Iraq, Jordan, Kuwait, Sudan, Syria, and Yemen; and the specialized economic organs of the Arab League, including those dealing with oil matters.[3] It is true that, in modern times, 'the

---

[1] Referring to the regime of late President Nasser of Egypt. See *The New York Times*, 21 December 1970, p. 2.

[2] David Pauly, *Forbes, op. cit.*, p. 23.

[3] See, for example, Muhammad Diab, 'The Arab Common Market', *Journal of Common Market Studies*, Oxford, May 1966; 'Exposé of the Arab League' by Muhammad Hassanein Haykal in *Al-Ahram* (Arabic) Cairo, 9 February 1968;

Arab search for unity was often a source of division rather than a unifying force'.[1] But continued efforts and energies expanded in that direction might still pay off.

As a result of past failures, certain Arab leaders thought it more effective to begin the process of economic integration – which would lead, hopefully, to political integration – by agreeing on the integration of one industry or one sector of the economy in a selected number of Arab countries.[2] It was felt that a limited measure of economic integration would be politically realistic and administratively feasible. National governments, jealous of their sovereignty, are more amenable to undertaking precise commitments in a limited field than to integrating all sectors of their economies without a clear awareness of the extent and nature of the implications. Another reason is that success in one venture is likely to encourage integration in others until full integration is achieved. Arab unity, it is claimed by leaders known for their pragmatism and realism, cannot be achieved at one blow. Unity, in fact, requires certain propitious conditions and is the end result of an uninterrupted and gradual development. This development has a momentum of its own, and includes successive and successful joint ventures which establish among the members a *de facto* solidarity and a web of common interests and interrelatedness.

It is possible to think of a number of joint and mutually beneficial projects in the oil industry: the sharing of economic and technical information and personnel, the marketing of blended crudes, the transport of oil, the repair of tankers, and the erection of refining or petrochemical plants. These activities are more profitable if carried out jointly than separately in cut-throat competition. The participants can select the most economic locations, prevent needless duplication and follow the commercial and technological imperatives of economies of scale. The resulting rationalization of production and sales will open opportunities of specialization and avoid price or other types of competition.

Many economists, however, question the wisdom of seeking full economic integration by the sector-by-sector approach. They argue that sectoral integration leads to temporary equilibria of prices, inputs

Robert W. MacDonald, *The Arab League of Arab States, A Study in the Dynamics of Regional Organization*, Princeton, 1965; Alfred G. Musrey, *An Arab Common Market, A Study in Inter-Arab Trade Relations*, 1920–67 (New York: Praeger, 1969); and E. Kanovsky, 'Arab Economic Unity', *The Middle East Journal*, Spring 1967 (Vol. 21, No. 2).

[1] Knapp, *op. cit.*, pp. 159–60.
[2] This is also the point of view of neofunctionalists such as Haas.

and outputs; and that these equilibria are disturbed every time a new sector is integrated. The outcome is continuous dislocation or reallocation of resources with ensuing economic waste. This argument applies specifically to diversified economies, such as those of industrialized countries. It is not equally valid for countries overwhelmingly dependent upon one exportable resource, such as oil.

But integration in the oil sector, if it is to achieve efficiency and effectiveness, will require co-ordination of policies in related fields, such as transport, social affairs, foreign trade, and fiscal and monetary matters.[1] No clear provision on this score is to be found in OAPEC's charter, which states that the organization shall 'take measures to ensure the harmonization of the legal systems in force in the member countries to the extent necessary to enable the Organization to carry out its activities'. (Art. 2.)

Another obstacle to sectoral integration is the conflict between producers and users, a factor that has blocked close co-operation within the Association of Latin American state-owned oil companies, ARPEL.[2] In June 1961, less than a year after OPEC's inception, state-owned oil companies in Latin America convened in Caracas at the invitation of the Venezuelan Minister of Mines and Hydrocarbons, Pérez Alfonzo, himself an acknowledged father of OPEC. The meeting was attended by top executives of the national oil companies of Argentina, Bolivia, Brazil, Colombia, Ecuador, Mexico, Uruguay, and Venezuela. Peru joined in 1964, and Brazil in 1965.

The declared ultimate objective of ARPEL is the 'economic and technical integration' of Latin America, in close co-operation with other Latin American organizations.[3] But Venezuela is practically the sole sizeable net oil exporting country in Latin America, and understandably seeks the highest possible prices. The other members of ARPEL are mostly net importers of oil, and, naturally, want the lowest possible prices. This conflict of interest, of which Venezuela's national company (CVP) is well aware,[4] holds true for Arab League oil schemes which comprise the 'have' and the 'have-not' countries.

[1] For an analysis of sectoral integration, see Bela Balassa, *The Theory of Economic Integration* (London: Allen & Unwin, 1961), pp. 15–17; and UN-ECAFE, *Economic Survey of Asia and the Far East, 1969*, Part One, Bangkok, March 1970, pp. 131–6 and 167–70.

[2] Asociacion de Asistencia Reciproca Petrolera Estatal Latino Americana.

[3] See ARPEL's statutes in *Platt's Oilgram News Service*, Special Supplement, 25 February 1965, p. 1.

[4] CVP, *The National Oil Company and Public Opinion*, Caracas, May 1967, p. 66.

So far, ARPEL's achievements have been limited to the exchange of information among its members.

The recently formed Arab oil groupings – namely OAPEC and the revolutionary groups – are, by comparison with ARPEL, strictly confined to oil exporting countries, and the producer–consumer conflict does not exist. But other conflicts of interest exist; Algeria, Iraq, and Libya, for example, are direct competitors for the same European markets. Moreover, Arab oil coalitions suffer from the fact that there are no compensatory benefits in other sectors to make up for possible sacrifices incurred by a member country in the oil sector. For example, joint production programming may favour one country at the expense of another. The disfavoured country is likely to support the programme loyally if it expects compensatory benefits. If there were other integrated sectors besides the oil sector, compensatory measures could be evolved, although difficulties are bound to occur in assessing and administering compensations. It is still possible to devise a 'limited industrial community' in one single venture or field offering each participating country a share in the potential benefits of integration.[1] As yet, few inter-Arab joint projects have proved of much practical consequence. Most of the schemes are too ambitious, ill-prepared, or ill-timed, and a few represent token integration or lip-service to community building.

Other fields, notably agriculture, may offer an alternative basis for a take-off in economic integration among certain Arab countries. The agricultural sector offers a wide range of a variety of products, and individual countries may have a comparative economic advantage in one or more of these products, with the result that there is better scope for trade creation. Trade creation, in a common market, could lead to the expansion of trade among member countries resulting from low-cost producers replacing higher-cost producers within the region, thus improving the international division of labour and the efficient use of resources. Trade diversion, by comparison, refers to the expansion of trade in the common market by replacing trade that was carried prior to the formation of that market between members and non-members; the diversion of that trade worsens the efficient allocation of international resources to the extent that supplies external to the common market are lower cost than internal supplies.[2]

[1] See the model suggested by I. M. D. Little, 'Regional International Companies as an Approach to Economic Integration', in *Journal of Common Market Studies*, Vol. V, No. 2, pp. 181–6.

[2] See, for example, G. M. Meier, *Leading Issues in Economic Development, Studies in International Poverty*, Oxford University Press, 1970, p. 569.

Chapter 4
INSTITUTIONAL ASPECTS OF OPEC
AND OAPEC

This chapter analyses the administrative set-up and work of the OPEC and OAPEC institutions. It also compares OAPEC with the European Communities, and concludes that conditions are not currently conducive to co-operation along the lines of the Communities.

On the importance of institutions, Jean Monnet, whose ideas on European economic co-operation crystallized in the successful launching of the European Coal and Steel Community (ECSC) under the leadership of French Foreign Minister Robert Schuman, once wrote:

> Men pass, others will come and replace us. We cannot hand down to them our personal experience, which will vanish with us. What we can hand down to them is our Institutions. The life of institutions is longer than that of men, and institutions, if they are well constructed, can thus accumulate and transmit wisdom to successive generation.[1]

For an analysis of the OPEC and OAPEC institutions one could choose among several patterns of a community model for a frame of reference. The ECSC characterizes 'Community, Communauté, Gemeinschaft, Communita' as an original institution and realistic method of economic organization among states. This method takes into account both power relations (economic and non-economic) among states as well as the need to guarantee small states protection against big states, while opening the way to common, concrete, and dynamic acts.[2]

---

[1] Quoted by Derek Prag, 'Vision and Reality 20 Years on', in *European Community*, London, May 1970, p. 11.

[2] La pièce maîtresse du système institutionnel de la Communauté consiste dans l'organisation d'un *dialogue permanent* entre une institution qui dégage, défend et

THE COMMUNITY OF OIL EXPORTING COUNTRIES

A. *OPEC and its Secretariat*

In accordance with the ECSC definition, the OPEC Secretariat is supposed to represent the common interests of member states, while the Conference represents the individual interests of national governments. However, member governments have not endowed the OPEC Secretariat with sufficient power to enable it to engage in dialogue as an equal with the Conference.

There are other definitions of community. One of these stresses the socio-psychological community of common beliefs, values, attitudes, and loyalties. Another is the political community characterized by sole control by a single decision-making centre, thereby providing a focus of identification for members. To certain writers, community represents a pluralist model of society where competing interests coexist within a constitutional system.[1]

The OPEC countries are not a political community, and hardly form a socio-psychological community, although the Secretariat has endeavoured to promote co-operation, and community conscious-ness by propagating common beliefs and attitudes about oil and international trade. The Secretariat seems to resemble a trade union, especially as it has acted as a 'manager of discontent' for member governments in dispute with oil companies. In fact, two leading oil writers have labelled OPEC as a trade union – of sheiks[2] or oil-rich governments.[3]

Pérez Alfonzo, the Venezuelan Minister who is credited with conceiving the OPEC idea, informed this author that his model for OPEC was that of a cartel of governments. Its aim is to protect the public interest of the countries concerned, as opposed to a private cartel, which promotes the commercial interest of stockholders of the constituent firms.[4] Accordingly, he considered the backbone of OPEC to be the centralized regulation of production or exports with

représente l'interêt commun des Etats membres de la Communauté et une autre institution indépendante et distincte de la première, qui harmonise en permanence le dynamisme propre de la Communauté et les actions des gouvernements nationaux.

La C.E.C.A. Première Assise d'Une Communauté plus Large et plus Profonde, Luxembourg, June 1967, p. 10 – their italics.

[1] See Paul Taylor, 'The Concept of Community and the European Integration Process,' *Journal of Common Market Studies*, December 1968, pp. 85 and 87.

[2] Paul H. Frankel, 'Structure of World Oil Industry', lecture at Northwestern University, 28 March 1965, p. 39 – typescript.

[3] J. E. Hartshorn, 'OPEC and Newcomer Governments' in *Continuity and Change in the World Oil Industry*, p. 33.

[4] Interview in Caracas on 6 June 1970.

96

a view to stabilizing prices at a desirable level. This objective was stated in the first resolution approved by OPEC's Conference: 'Members shall study and formulate a system to ensure the stabilization of prices by, among other means, the regulation of production'.

OPEC's first Secretary-General informed the author that the persons concerned (including himself) did not have an organizational precedent to copy.[1] One of the primary concerns of the originators of the statutes was to ensure the continuance of OPEC by not limiting its functions to one goal which could turn obsolete, for example, restoring the pre-August 1960 posted prices. They emphasized the need for a continuous exchange of information, consultation, and co-operation in all matters relating to the international oil industry. Their concern was that several goals should be sought for the organization's self-interest, and new ones added or old goals replaced.[2]

OPEC statutes restrict membership to countries with 'a substantial' net export of crude petroleum; the exact export size is not defined. Moreover, every founding member has a veto power on any new applicant. In April 1965, an additional restriction was adopted on new applicants: they should have 'fundamentally similar interests to those of Member Countries' (Res. VIII.56). That restriction was probably politically motivated. It was intended to satisfy certain anti-Communist or anti-Socialist members, and to preclude the entry of the Soviet Union (a major oil exporter) and the possible entry of the U.A.R. (then a potential oil exporter, and in 1971 an actual exporter). These two countries' regimes have been suspect to some founding members. The countries which joined OPEC after its establishment are Qatar (January 1961), Libya and Indonesia (June 1962), Abu Dhabi (November 1967), Algeria (June 1969), and Nigeria (July 1971).

In January 1961, agreement was reached on the basic organizational structure of OPEC, and three main bodies were set up: the Conference, the Board of Governors, and the Secretariat. The *Conference* is the supreme authority of the organization. It is responsible for formulating general policy and for devising appropriate means for implementing that policy. It is composed of member countries' representatives, usually of ministerial rank. It works on the principles of unanimity and equal voting rights for members. Meetings are ordinarily held twice a year, one at the headquarters of the organization, and another in the capital of a member county. Consultative meetings of heads of delegations or their representatives may be called

[1] Interview with Fuad Rouhani, Tehran, 9 July 1968.
[2] This is a common concern among several organizations: See Amitai Etizioni, *Modern Organizations* (Englewood, N.J.: Prentice Hall, 1964), pp. 13–14.

at any time by the president of the Conference; decisions must be approved by the next Conference, unless otherwise authorized by a previous one. These meetings serve primarily to expedite discussions and consultations among member countries.

The *Board of Governors*, also with one representative from each member country, is responsible for implementing the decisions of the Conference and for overseeing the management of the Secretariat. Governors are appointed for a period of two years, and their board meets at least twice a year.

The organization set up its *Secretariat* in Geneva in 1961. The Swiss government was unwilling to grant diplomatic immunity and fiscal exemptions to the OPEC staff on the grounds that the organization's membership was 'closed' and that its objective was commercial. Better facilities were offered by Austria and, in 1965, OPEC moved to Vienna. The *Secretariat* comprises five departments: administration, economics, legal, information, and technical.

The Secretary-General is the legally authorized representative of the organization, and the chief officer of the Secretariat. He must be a national of one of the member countries. He was nominated, until 1970, by the country concerned (subject to the perfunctory approval of the Conference) on the basis of a rotation principle, and for a period of normally one year. The rotation principle allows each member country to feel that it is sharing leadership roles.

OPEC, during its twelve years of existence, has had several changes in its statutes and organization. Organizational changes have been instantaneous and static. Moreover, they have not produced fundamental mutations in the aims, quality, nature, powers, or responsibilities of the organization; for example, no planned progressive evolution or strengthening in the role assigned to the Secretariat is discernible. The lack of fundamental change has not, however, precluded the introduction of effective approaches, policies, strategies, or tactics with respect to the interpretation or implementation of objectives.

OPEC Secretariat has been faced by certain institutional limitations in serving the common objectives of member countries. For example, the statutory one-year term (occasionally extended; see Table 4.1) has not allowed the Secretary-General enough time to fully understand OPEC's problems, to win the co-operation of the staff, and to plan and carry out important work. Additional handicaps have included the absence of binding requirements for adequate technical knowledge of, or experience in, the international oil industry for a number of posts, including the all-important post of Secretary-

General, and the absence of a career system with tenure of office which gives officials security and enables them to resist national influences. OPEC staff members are appointed for a maximum period of four years, with a possible extension of two years, a factor responsible for their lack of independence of national governments.

It is true that there has been a statutory provision for a deputy Secretary-General with a three-year term subject to extensions (Art. 30). This position would give OPEC supportive continuity at the top management level; it has never been filled, however, largely

Table 4.1

SELECTED DATA ON OPEC'S SECRETARIES-GENERAL*

Name	Country Represented	Dates of Office	Age at Appointment
1. Fuad Rouhani	Iran	Jan. 1961–Dec. 1963	54
2. Abdul Radman Bazzaz	Iraq	Jan. 1964–April 1965	51
3. Ashraf Lutfi	Kuwait	May 1965–Dec. 1966	46
4. Mohammad Joukhdar	Saudi Arabia	Jan. 1967–Dec. 1967	36
5. Francisco Parra	Venezuela	Jan. 1968–Dec. 1968	40
6. Elrich Sanger	Indonesia	Jan. 1969–Dec. 1969	40
7. Omar El Badri	Libya	Jan. 1970–Dec. 1970	33
8. Nadim Pachachi	Abu Dhabi	Jan. 1971–Dec. 1972	54

* For biographical details see Appendix One.

because of rivalry among member governments, each eager to appoint a national.

By 1970, member governments realized that the absence of professional requirements and the one-year term for Secretary-General have failed to attract the requisite talent for effectively running the Secretariat. Consequently, the Conference agreed in June 1970 to increase the term to three years, subject to renewal for a similar period. The post, beginning in 1971, need not be rotated among member countries, and now requires the following qualifications: a minimum age of 35 years, an appropriate university degree, and some fifteen years of relevant experience. The nomination should receive the unanimous approval of all members. In the absence of such agreement, the post will then be rotated among member countries for two-year periods, while observing the requisite qualifications (Res. XX.117). As no agreement could be reached on the selection of a Secretary-General for three years, the rotation system has been maintained. The current (1971–72) Secretary-General, Nadim Pachachi, meets the requisite professional standards. (See biographical note in Appendix One.)

In this context, what has been the role of the Secretariat and its staff? OPEC's first Secretary-General, Fuad Rouhani (a former vice-president of the National Iranian Oil Co.) was appointed in January 1961, and his term was extended for a total period of three years. By mid-1963, he could claim that the Secretariat was adequately staffed and equipped for documentation and research to offer assistance to member countries. Moreover, he boasted that his personnel worked together 'with such complete harmony and understanding that differences of citizenship, language, religion, race and colour appear to them to be unreal'.[1]

To well-placed observers, his description is somewhat glowing, to say the least. The personnel of any international organization, including that of OPEC, is subject to national influences or interferences which militate against complete harmony, and may well be at variance with the over-all international objectives they are supposed to serve. Almost all OPEC officials are on assignment from their government posts in member countries for an average of four years. Concern for promotion and advancement at home precludes them from thinking independently of their governments. Moreover, pronounced national differences have impeded the development of OPEC loyalties and *esprit de corps*, and the high turnover of personnel has precluded the accumulation of expertise.

In 1967, another Secretary-General, Ashraf Lutfi, doubted the Secretariat's ability to carry out research and to offer advice, and considered the organization's employees lacking in independence and initiative:

The biggest problem of the Organization is the failure of its members to recognize what a formidable instrument the Organization Secretariat could become if its members would only take this Secretariat seriously, and built it up into a true research center to which they resort for consultation, advice and guidance. Yet the role of the Secretariat, despite the fairly numerous employees it has at its disposal, has been to obediently (and perhaps not very efficiently) implement certain directives from OPEC Conferences for the preparation of sets of data and figures to put them hurriedly in some sort of reports to be submitted at the

[1] Faud Rouhani, *op. cit.*, p. 5.

very last minute, if ready, to the consideration of the delegations to the next Conference. In fact, initiative has never been a virtue of the Secretariat, but the Secretariat should be the last to be blamed for this.[1]

Lutfi came to the rescue of the Secretariat when, by implication, he shifted the blame on to member governments. In fact, they must share the blame to the extent that they have been deliberately responsible for certain structural weaknesses in the OPEC organization. Nevertheless, a careful study of its statutes shows that the post of Secretary-General offers some scope for initiative. The official can initiate pertinent business with the Board of Governors or the Conference; he can refuse to carry out work hurriedly during his one-year term of office; he can, and normally should, require adequate time and appropriate staff work before submitting reports or studies.

Power and leadership have been exercised by the Secretary-General on the basis of both the authority offered by the position and the personal qualities inviting esteem, trust, and enthusiasm from his staff. The author estimates that the one-year term of Secretary-General does not provide him and the staff adequate time to develop mutual trust and appreciation, unless he has been long known to the staff, as was the case with Francisco Parra.

In one instance, a personal confrontation between a Secretary-General and the head of a department led the former to exercise the authority of his post, and dismiss the department head. The reason for the dismissal was not technical or professional competence, but failure of the Secretary-General to use the human relations approach. This approach assumes that the most efficient organization is the happy one, whereas the scientific management approach seeks efficiency in a highly specialized personnel motivated solely by economic rewards. A synthesis of these two approaches is known as the structuralist approach.[2] The first Secretary-General of OPEC, Fuad Rouhani, successfully emphasized the human relations aspect in building the Secretariat staff; others have tended to adopt the scientific management approach. OPEC needs a judicious blend of the two. Its prospective growth – for that matter of any international organization – calls also for imaginative leadership, statesmanship, and a sense of independence in respect to national governments.

Trained and experienced human resources are limited in the

1 Lutfi, *OPEC and its Problems*, p. 8.
2 Etzioni, *Modern Organization*, Chapters 3 and 4.

OPEC countries. Some of these countries can ill afford to loan such personnel to the organization, but a few member governments have made special efforts to provide highly competent officers. The organization does take second place, however, because most member governments are primarily concerned with staffing their petroleum departments and national companies with whatever managerially oriented and trained talent they possess.

As things now stand, OPEC countries have not yet built up a Secretariat with a permanent and highly qualified civil service endowed with an independent leadership and a momentum of its own. Therefore, the OPEC Secretariat is hardly suitable for the role of collective spokesman, policy maker, or negotiator. Other major reasons for its inability to fulfil this role are the unwillingness of member countries to delegate authority to it and the staff's lack of knowledge concerning special details and changing conditions in member countries. The Secretariat is best suited to act as a clearing house, a research and training centre, an advisor, and a co-ordinator for negotiations carried out directly by member governments individually or collectively. Therefore it cannot substitute for the petroleum departments in member countries. More generally, 'to be acceptable as a substitute for special-group facilities – local, national, or even segregated ones – *integrated* facilities must usually be *better* facilities'.[1]

Given the diversity or even incompatibility of certain member states' objectives and policies, the OPEC institution cannot be endowed with supranational authority. Moreover, the Secretariat has generally been put in the position of reacting to events, instead of controlling or influencing events reasonably well in advance of their occurrence – to the extent they can be controlled or influenced. The Secretariat has yet to map and analyse in detail the problems faced by the organization, delineate the alternatives, decide with realism on priorities, draw up consistent policies and plans for short and longer terms, and see to their implementation. Ashraf Lutfi, a former Secretary-General, has suggested that the OPEC Secretariat should:

> ... study and advise on the feasibility of unifying financial arrangements as applicable in member countries and draw up a list of priorities as far as implementation in concerned. It could also attempt to spell out in clear detail some of the ambiguities of

[1] K. W. Deutsch, *Nationalism and its Alternatives* (New York: Knopf, 1969), p. 171 – his *italics*.

such terms as 'safeguarding the common interests of member countries' or the demand for 'equitable prices'. After all what is in their best interest?[1]

More specifically, the OPEC Secretariat has yet to investigate thoroughly and candidly, though not necessarily publicly, such problems as the economic and non-economic implications of production programming, or the far-reaching impact on prices and government revenues of granting various types of oil production and supply rights to newcomer companies with or without marketing outlets. Nor has it studied the impact on international markets of launching national companies, or whether there are net economic (or non-economic) advantages to host countries in working for a disengagement of the international companies from the production stage – which means partially 'dis-integrating' their vertically integrated structure.

Fortunately, OPEC did not cling long to unrealizable objectives. Member countries, the Conference, and the Secretariat have begun to understand the complex problems of the world oil industry, and recent efforts in that respect have been, on balance, beneficial. For example, the OPEC Conference and individual OPEC countries now appreciate more fully the scope and limitations of raising posted prices than they did in 1960, and the pay-off was the round of increases in government takes in 1970–71. Moreover, the OPEC Secretariat has been attempting to study the purport and the mechanics of having national companies participate with international companies in joint ventures in various phases of the oil industry. It has advised member governments on important and difficult questions, particularly on the methods of participation of host governments and their agencies in the management and ownership of existing concessionary ventures, and assessed the expected cost and the likely benefits whether these are financial or otherwise, or of participation upstream and downstream.[2]

B. *OAPEC's Organizational Structure*

OAPEC's founding countries (Saudi Arabia, Kuwait, and Libya) wanted their organization to be restricted to Arab states in which oil

[1] Ashraf Lutfi, *OPEC and its Problems*, address at the Kuwait Institute of Economic and Social Planning in the Middle East, November 1967, p. 9.

[2] The author contributed to an OPEC study entitled *Economic Desirability and Feasibility of Participation Upstream and Downstream*, Vienna, May 1970 – not published.

constitutes 'the principal and basic source of its national income' (Art. 7). The degree of restriction has not been defined in the statutes; it has been interpreted to mean that only those Arab countries where the petroleum sector constitutes 'the number one source' of national income are eligible.[1] This is still a vague measure since 'number one' can be construed to mean any percentage of national income.

The only other independent Arab country which fitted this requirement in 1968 was Iraq; Algeria's petroleum industry replaced wine as the number one source of national income in 1970. The other Arab countries which meet the above requirement are the sheikhdoms of Abu Dhabi, Bahrain, Dubai, and Qatar, and the sultanate of Muscat and Oman. Even if eligible in principle, admission to OAPEC is not automatic. A majority of three-quarters of the votes of the founding members is required; since there are three this provision amounts to requiring unanimity, and any one member has veto power. The signers of the OAPEC charter, namely the major Arab oil producing countries, deliberately restricted membership to avoid being minority members as they are in the Arab League. This organization is dominated by a large number of non-oil producers or oil producers whose oil exports are not vital to their national economy.

In May 1970, Algeria, Abu Dhabi, Bahrain, Dubai, and Qatar were formally admitted to OAPEC. Iran, a principal oil exporter in the Middle East, is not an Arab country and is, therefore, ineligible for membership of OAPEC, which is designed to be a substitute for various oil activities of the Arab League. Members of the League are expected to shoulder certain political obligations. The Saudi Minister of Petroleum and Mineral Resources, Ahmad Zaki Yamani, explained this aspect of political obligations as follows:

> In so far as our OAPEC is concerned, we have to recognize that the Arab countries have a number of political obligations – including the Palestine problem, for example – regarding which the degree of Arab commitment is considerably heavier than that which Iran could reasonably be expected to bear. . . . Moreover, we regard OAPEC as to some extent a substitute for the various oil activities of the Arab League. And since Iran is not a member of the League, it would hardly be appropriate to have a non-Arab member in an organization conceived as a substitute for certain activities of the Arab League.[2]

[1] Interview of Suhail Sa'dawi, Secretary-General of OAPEC, in *MEES*, 27 March 1970, p. 1. This restriction was waived late in 1971.
[2] See *MEES* Supplement, 7 June 1968, p. 6.

At the time of OAPEC's establishment, all three founding members had monarchical sytems of government, though in varying degrees of conservatism. Saudi Arabia has a patriarchal system of government in which the head of the state is the focus of power. Popular representation in the Western sense of the word does not exist; religious precepts (*Shari'a*) and inherited traditions are the basis of law. Kuwait has some parliamentary representation and a semblance of a constitutional monarchy. Power in Kuwait is largely vested in the Amir and his family, and in the interested group or groups that support or serve them. The other OAPEC countries with patriarchal regimes are the sheikhdoms of Abu Dhabi, Bahrain, Dubai and Qatar.

OAPEC's charter decrees that its policies and actions must not conflict with those of OPEC. The charter also stipulates that OPEC decisions are binding on all members of the Arab organization 'even if they are not members of OPEC' (Art. 3); this applies to certain Arabian sheikhdoms such as Bahrain and Dubai. This provision was included to allay the fears of the non-Arab members of OPEC (Indonesia, Iran, and Venezuela), who might view OAPEC as a rival. OPEC thus remains the sole framework for policy co-ordination among the world's major oil exporting countries in such matters as prices, fiscal charges, and intergovernmental control. To quote a metaphor coined by the Saudi Minister of Petroleum and Mineral Resources, 'OPEC is the mother and our Arab Organization the child'.[1] But Iran does not conceal its dislike of an Arab bloc within OPEC. On the one hand, OAPEC might prove disruptive for OPEC; on the other, it may prove useful by applying OPEC's decisions to Arab countries which are members of OAPEC but not of OPEC.

The Saudi Minister wants OAPEC to extend its influence beyond policy co-ordination – which is OPEC's objective – and establish joint business ventures, ultimately integrating the oil and related sectors in its member countries. Certain joint projects – for example, international marketing – are likely to be more workable if carried out by a regional group, such as OAPEC, than by a loosely related international group, such as OPEC. In order to tighten intragroup relations, the Arab organization has been endowed with governing bodies commanding authority and responsibility. The supreme organ of the Arab organization is a Council of ministers representing member states. Unlike OPEC, where all decisions are taken by unanimous vote, OAPEC decisions differentiate between substantive and non-substantive matters. The latter require a simple majority of

[1] *MEES Supplement*, 7 June 1968, p. 6.

the Council members, and consequently can be expedited. Substantive matters require, by comparison, a majority of three-quarters of the total votes of the Council; nevertheless, this majority vote, if it is to be binding, must receive ratification by all the countries concerned (Arts. 11 and 12). This in fact means that there is no real difference between a unanimous vote and a three-fourths majority vote on substantive questions.

The OAPEC charter, unlike OPEC's, requires the sharing of damage, if any, incurred by any member country when enforcing a decision of the Council (Art. 12). This provision could prove helpful in promoting and developing certain common projects which might cause one member or more to incur loss or sacrifice.

Improving upon OPEC's original statutes, OAPEC gives its Secretary-General a three-year term renewable for a further period or periods, and its three Assistant Secretaries four-year terms, also renewable (Art. 19), to provide continuity. OAPEC requires its members to 'respect the neutrality of the Secretary-General, the Assistant Secretaries and all the Secretariat's employees and refrain from trying to influence any of them in any way whatever' (Art. 20).

A point of particular interest to the student of integration is the statutory provision for an OAPEC court. The court deals with disputes regarding the interpretation of the charter and those arising between member states regarding oil matters, or between member states and companies which, in the opinion of OAPEC's Council, fall within the jurisdiction of the court (Art. 23). It is hoped that the OAPEC court, like the EEC court, will promote supranational law in the organization to the extent member governments empower that court to supersede national courts in settling disputes between one member and its concessionaire companies, or between member countries.

In contrast, OPEC's December 1963 resolution to initiate studies for the establishment of an intra-OPEC High Court (Res. V.41) has been unproductive. The court was to have settled all disputes and differences within the OPEC area relating to petroleum matters; it was intended to serve in both an advisory and a judicial capacity. The failure of this project to materialize is eloquent proof of the reluctance of these countries to strengthen OPEC's role at the expense of freedom of individual action. Had the court come into being, it would have helped to cement the links between member states.

The OAPEC Secretariat was set up in Kuwait, and staffing began in 1968 under the leadership of Yamani, then OAPEC's acting Secretary-General. Since January 1970, the Secretariat has been headed by a Libyan national, Suhail Sa'dawi. As yet, no concrete projects have been launched. A few are under active consideration, notably the organization of a joint tanker company, the construction of a dry dock in the Arabian–Persian Gulf to service tankers, the establishment of a general petroleum service company, and the formation of a finance corporation. Although restrictive in membership requirements, OAPEC statutes can accommodate a pan-Arab approach. OAPEC's Secretary-General has stated that both Arab member and non-member states can participate in projects.[1] The decision, however, to launch these projects rests solely with OAPEC member states.

C. *OAPEC and the European Communities*

The initiator of OAPEC, the Saudi Minister of Petroleum and Mineral Resources, has claimed that the Arab organization is designed to become eventually 'the EEC of the Arab oil producers',[2] presumably in the same way the European Coal and Steel Community (ECSC) led to the European Economic Community (EEC). The Kuwait Minister of Oil and Finance also claimed on 4 June 1968, at a debate preceding the ratification of the OAPEC charter by the Kuwait National Assembly, that his country had proposed, at the Baghdad Conference of Arab Ministers of Finance, Economy and Oil in August 1967, the creation of 'an Arab bloc of oil producers akin to that of the European Economic Community'.[3]

It has been acknowledged that 'the founding of the European Common Market [EEC] had at first the impact of a threat [to developing countries], and only recently that of a positive inspiration'.[4] There are a number of similarities between OAPEC and the European Communities which include, in addition to the ECSC and the EEC, the European Atomic Energy Community (Euratom). One notable similarity is that OAPEC, like the European Communities, aims at regional co-operation. Another similarity is that OAPEC has a measure of administrative autonomy; it 'may conclude agreements with its member states, or with other countries, or with a federation of states or with an international organization, and especially agreements for establishing joint ventures in various phases of economic activity' (Art. 5).

Another point in common is that these entities owe their existence

---

[1] *MEES*, 27 March 1970, p. 2.
[2] *MEES*, 12 January 1968, p. 2.
[3] *MEES*, 14 June 1968, p. 8.
[4] *Economic Survey of Asia and the Far East, 1969*, Part One, p. 126.

primarily to political considerations. While OAPEC was created as a result of the June 1967 war in the Middle East, the ECSC was created to replace the ancient Franco-German antagonisms and bloody hostilities with loyal economic co-operation, subject to equal rights and obligations.[1]

In several other important respects, however, OAPEC and the ECSC/EEC communities are demonstrably different. First, the ECSC is a regional grouping of producer and consumer countries, whereas OAPEC members are producer countries selling in the export market. Second, OAPEC countries have much less in common in their socio-politico-economic systems than the ECSC countries. Third, the ECSC was formed by governments whose rights and responsibilities *vis-à-vis* their resident industries were not in any sense limited by the types of contractual agreements with expatriate operators that limit most host governments of OAPEC.

Fourth, the power and economic weight of the ECSC in relation to any single firm or industry within the European Community are greater than the power and economic weight of most OAPEC host governments in relation to the major international companies. Fifth, the ECSC is composed of modern industrialized countries with diversified economies, whereas OAPEC is a group of developing countries heavily dependent on the export of one primary commodity.

Sixth, the EEC treaty has a built-in dynamism that allows changes and mutations of relations among governments at agreed on deadlines, with a view to increasing the field of common interests. In the EEC, for example, it was originally agreed that national powers of veto are to be reduced with the passage of time,[2] so that EEC's functions will increase in responsibility and scope. One of the architects of European unity, commenting on the feature of planned evolution and dynamism in the EEC, remarked that 'the Common Market is a process, not a product'.[3] Unlike the EEC treaty, both OPEC and OAPEC charters are fixed arrangements, since they have to call *ad hoc* on their members when agreements on additional commitments are required.

Seventh, the European countries, furthermore, have endowed their community institutions with a remarkable degree of independence. In principle, these institutions are empowered to look at

[1] See Robert Schuman, 'Origine, objectif et élaboration de la Communauté du Charbon et de l'Acier' in *Pour l'Europe* (Paris: Nagel, 1963), p. 157; also the preamble of the ECSC treaty signed in Paris on 18 April 1951.

[2] This was, however, frustrated in 1965 by the opposition of the late President de Gaulle who feared political integration.

[3] Jean Monnet in *European Community*, Washington, March 1967, p. 3.

community interests and devise policies and plans accordingly. OAPEC's Secretariat (but not OPEC's) is likewise empowered to initiate and conclude all kinds of transactions and joint enterprises with regard to oil and other related economic topics,[1] but these actions are subject to the approval of the Council of ministers, representing individual national interests. By a stretch of imagination, one might compare the role of OAPEC's Secretariat to that of the High Authority in the ECSC or that of the Commission in the EEC. But the OAPEC charter has not given its Secretariat the same supranational powers as the ECSC gave to its High Authority, such as collection of levies, payment of compensations to operators, price scheduling, and policing departures from these schedules.[2] It is admitted, however, that the delimitation of competence as between national governments and the High Authority has, in practice, been a source of confusion and controversy. Moreover, the High Authority's supranational powers have not always been readily heeded by member countries; decisions have been enforced tardily, grudgingly, or not at all.[3]

In comparing OAPEC with the European Communities, care should be taken, in not identifying the contents of concepts, classifications, or processes which apply to developed communities (such as those of Europe) with the ones which apply to less developed communities (such as OAPEC). This has been brought to light by a distinguished scholar who also warned against the inadequacy of currently available concepts and tools for measuring schemes of co-operation or integration in both the developed and the less developed areas:

> Ten years after the formation of the EEC we are faced with a more difficult beast to analyse than many people expected at that time. Instead of a classical federation or neat supranational authority we have a complex web of interdependences between strengthened national-states. With the nature of the beast likely to remain ambiguous we need more refined concepts and measurements lest it slip through (or around) our traditional conceptual nets and we

[1] See Ahmad Zaki Yamani in *MEES*, 12 January 1968, p. 2.

[2] The High Authority was composed of nine members, each with a term of six years; eight of them appointed by national governments, the ninth is co-opted by the eight. Once appointed, they cannot be dismissed by national governments, although the Assembly of the Community (representing national parliaments) was empowered to dismiss the High Authority as a whole. Decisions are by majority vote. The executives of EEC, ECSC, and Euratom were merged in 1969.

[3] See, for example, M. A. G. van Meerhaeghe, *International Economic Institutions*, Longmans (London, 1966), p. 311.

make the mistake of thinking nothing has happened. At the same time we are faced with regional integration schemes in less developed areas which appear at times to resemble the European animal but in causal terms may turn out to be of a different genus or species. . . .

In conclusion, it is time for integration theorists to take a closer look at the concepts and measurements in our field. The fuzziness of our dependent variable has permitted the proliferation of causal theories of varying quality. It is the conviction of this author that after a decade of growth the plant of integration theory needs pruning. But for successful pruning we need sharper tools.[1]

[1] Nye, 'Comparative Regional Integration: Concept and Measurement', *op. cit.*, p. 880. Other recent critiques and commentaries include Roger D. Hansen, 'Regional Integration: Reflections on a Decade of Theoretical Efforts', *World Politics*, January 1969 (Vol. 21, No. 2), pp. 242–71, and Kenneth A. Dahlberg, 'Regional Integration: The Neo-Functional versus a Configurative Approach', *International Organization*, Winter 1970 (Vol. 24, No. 1), pp. 122–8.

Chapter 5

THE JOINT REGULATION OF PRODUCTION

OPEC's production programming has several objectives, among them the stabilization of prices at desirable levels, the ending of company leverage in manipulating exports from OPEC countries, and improvement of the member countries' bargaining position for larger government take. The major oil companies, which controlled in 1970 approximately 85 per cent of exports from the OPEC area, have opposed international production programming from the start.

This chapter describes the development of the OPEC's production programmes and its current status. It also outlines the requisite factors for success.

A. *Aims of Production Programming*

The primary aim of OPEC was and still is to replace the sagging oligopolistic control of international firms with its own control in order to resist sustained pressures on crude oil and product prices. At their first meeting in Baghdad in September 1960, OPEC countries agreed to 'study and formulate a system to ensure the stabilization of prices by, among other means, the regulation of production, with due regard to the interests of the producing and of the consuming nations and to the necessity of securing a steady income to the producing countries, an efficient and regular supply of this source of energy to consuming nations, and a fair return on their capital to those investing in the petroleum industry' (Res. I.1).

The OPEC Secretariat criticized in no uncertain terms the adverse impact of free pricing on member countries. Free pricing in a period of surplus availability, it contended, would drive prices to lower levels. This would hurt low cost producing countries (such as those of the Middle East) by depriving them of current economic rent, to the

111

same extent it would hurt high cost producers (such as Venezuela) by cutting down their production.[1]

In order 'to assist the Organization in promoting stability in international petroleum prices at equitable levels' (Res. VII.50), member countries agreed in November 1964 to form an intra-OPEC organ called the Economic Commission, comprising national representatives who meet twice a year. The crucial instrument for attaining price stability would be an international prorationing system, generally known as joint production programming. This entails limiting the OPEC area's total crude oil production to achieve the desired price level, and allocating that total among producing states, operating companies, and the various oil reservoirs in accordance with predetermined fractions of their total productive capacity. In July 1965, the Ninth Conference of OPEC meeting in Tripoli, Libya, adopted 'as a transitory measure' its first production programme. The programme called for 'rational increases in production from the OPEC area to meet estimated increases in world demand' at so-called 'equitable price levels', presumably at prices then current (Res. IV.61). OPEC hoped to achieve control by preventing the unrestricted competitive use of the substantial 'surplus' productive capacity available to oil companies, especially in the Middle East. Surplus capacity is defined as the potential low cost capacity readily available to a company in the intermediate run (by drilling and connecting wells in already discovered oil reservoirs) for a remunerative increase in its sales at existing or expected realized prices.[2] Realized prices have been held above the long-run marginal cost or supply price, essentially through restraints exercised by the small group of international oil companies. But at such prices, new firms find entry into the industry attractive, which leads to additional production pressing for market outlets – in the absence of any coercive power checking them. The outcome is further erosion in realized prices, ultimately reaching the point at which they become, under open competitive conditions, equal to the long-run economic cost or supply price.

[1] See OPEC, *Pricing Problems: Further Considerations*, p. 14; also, *OPEC and the Stabilization of Petroleum Prices*, p. 7.

[2] As expounded by M. A. Adelman in a speech delivered on 1 April 1965 at the 'Economics of Petroleum Distribution' Conference, The Transportation Center of Northwestern University – typescript.

Estimates of surplus capacity for the 1960s vary between 15 and 30 per cent of current production: see, for example, U.S. Cabinet Task Force on Oil Import Control, *The Oil Import Question, A Report on the Relationship of Oil Imports to the National Security* (Washington, February 1970), pp. 51–2.

Adelman estimated the economic cost of the Arabian–Persian crudes in the early 1960s at 20 cents per barrel, and in 1969 and 1970 at 12 and 10 cents per barrel, respectively (including a 20 to 21 per cent return on the necessary development investment), and their realized price at an average of 140 cents in the early 1960s, and at 120–125 cents in 1969. With some 89 cents going to host governments in the form of royalty and taxes in the early 1960s, the companies were left with earnings of 40 cents per barrel, a differential that enticed operators into entry and larger production. Price erosion and increased government take, rising to 85 cents per barrel, reduced that differential to 23–28 cents per barrel early in 1969;[1] nevertheless, oil exports from that area more than doubled in the 1961–70 period. Realized prices rose to an estimated 160–165 cents per barrel by mid-1971 as a result of general increases in host government revenues negotiated in 1970–71.

Another aim of OPEC's production programming is to prevent oil companies from exploiting their bargaining strength by using their producing capacity as a lever to switch off exports from a given host country – if they happen to want to exercise pressure. Bargaining strength may be taken to reflect the degree of dispensability of the object of bargain to a host government or a company.[2] Thus the less the diversification in economic resources or the fewer the number of opportunities available to one party, and the higher that party's dependence on income derived from the object of bargain, the lower its relative bargaining strength and the more vulnerable it is. Another criterion for bargaining strength is the ability of one party in the short run to absorb losses from its adversary and to inflict relatively heavier losses onto that adversary. A party's ability to absorb losses can be directly related to its existing and potential resources, including allies it can count on.

By instituting a joint production programme, OPEC hopes to deprive oil companies of the flexibility to 'play one country off

[1] Adelman's speech, op. cit.; M. A. Adelman, Oil Production Costs in Four Areas, paper delivered at the American Institute of Mining, Metallurgical, and Petroleum Engineers, 28 February–2 March 1966, p. 115; 'Statement of Professor M. A. Adelman' in Governmental Intervention in the Market Mechanism, Hearings before the Subcommittee on Antitrust and Monopoly of the Committee on the Judiciary, U.S. Senate, The Petroleum Industry Part 1, Economists' Views, Washington, March–April 1969, pp. 7 and 8; and M. A. Adelman, Oil Demand Supply, Cost and Prices in the World Market, paper submitted to the UN ad hoc Panel of Experts on Projections of Demand and Supply of Crude Petroleum and Products, 2 March 1971, New York, ESA/RT/Meeting II/6.

[2] Ref. the author's 'The Bargain', in A Financial Analysis of Middle Eastern Oil Concessions, pp. 264–72.

H   113

against another, by switching offtake volumes among them for non-commercial reasons'.[1] It is indeed true that major oil companies, thanks to their oil producing subsidiaries in various OPEC countries, have – within certain limits – been able to cut down their liftings of oil from subsidiaries in the country with which they happen to be in conflict and make it up by increased liftings from subsidiaries in other countries. Discounting short-run considerations of cost differentials, the purpose is to maximize their long-run benefits or to minimize their long-run costs in individual OPEC countries.

Other objectives were added in 1966 to OPEC's production programming. They included improvement of the bargaining position of member countries in their negotiation with companies for larger government takes, and facilitating the entry of host countries' national companies into the international market at more remunerative prices than would occur under an openly competitive situation.[2]

B. *Production Programming and Market Realities*

The first production programme covering the July 1965–June 1966 period estimated the over-all growth of demand for OPEC oil at stabilized current market prices at 10 per cent in relation to the previous year. The planned annual increase amounted therefore to 1,270 thousands barrels per day during the programme period. The actual total increase came at an annual rate of 7·7 per cent, or only 985·3 thousand barrels per day. The miscalculation can be attributed to the dearth of up-to-date and comprehensive statistics on worldwide demand, supply, and inventories, and to the problems of forecasting in a rapidly changing economic environment.[3] Also, allocations among member countries did not work out as planned (see Table 5.1), as several members did not exert any effort to keep within their quotas for reasons analysed below.

Still hopeful, the Eleventh OPEC Conference adopted in April 1966 a second production programme giving a 1966–67 production increment for the OPEC area almost identical in absolute terms with that devised a year earlier, also assuming current market price stabilization. That increment, estimated at 1,289 thousand barrels

[1] OPEC, *The Development of Petroleum Resources under the Concession System in Non-Industrialized Countries*, by F. R. Parra, 1964, p. 35; see also Ibnu Sutowo, *op. cit.*, p. 24.

[2] See Lutfi, *OPEC Oil*, pp. 53–65.

[3] These problems are outlined in a UN work *Projections of Demand and Supply of Crude Petroleum and Products*, prepared in March 1971 in New York by a group of 'Panel of Experts' of which this author has been a member.

114

per day, was then wishfully reported as 'conservative.' The distribution among member countries was the same as that of the year before except that Saudi Arabia's share was increased and that of Qatar reduced by 36,000 and 17,000 barrels per day, respectively. As with the first programme, member governments did not show any

Table 5.1

COMPARISON BETWEEN ACTUAL PRODUCTION INCREMENT
AND PLANNED PROGRAMME INCREMENT, OPEC AREA,
JULY 1956–JUNE 1966

Country	Programme Increment July 1965–June 1966		*Actual Increment Utilized*	
	TB/D†	% of total	TB/D†	% of total
Indonesia*	48	3·8	20·1	2·0
Iran	304	24·0	290·2	29·5
Iraq	125	9·8	56·9	5·8
Kuwait	147	11·6	(12·8)‡	(1·3)‡
Libya*	210	16·5	270·8	27·5
Qatar	67	5·3	39·4	4·0
Saudi Arabia	254	20·0	313·4	31·8
Venezuela	115	9·0	7·2	0·7
Total	1,270	100·0	985·3	100·0

* Partially estimated.
† TB/D = thousand barrels per day.
‡ Parentheses ( ) = decline.

Source: OPEC.

OPEC countries' share figures (proposed and realized) for the first production programme are also reproduced in a paper by W. J. Levy and Milton Lipton, 'The Organization of Petroleum Exporting Countries (OPEC) and World Oil', presented at the Petroleum Economic Symposium of Southwestern Legal Foundation, Dallas, Texas, 11 March 1966.

serious attempt to implement the second. OPEC production programming should therefore be evaluated with reference to the realism of its underlying assumptions and the mechanics of implementation.

First, OPEC production programming presumes political willingness on the part of member countries to reconcile competing objectives, to support it, and participate actively. This willingness has been demonstratively lacking. It presumes also the existence of an autonomous agency, able and equipped with sophisticated com-

115

puters, to match efficiently the complexities of crude oil supply with a still more complex pattern of demand for petroleum products.

Second, OPEC production programming assumes a general low over-all elasticity of demand in major consuming areas for crude oil at source within the price range envisioned.[1] Through a controlled reduction in the free growth of oil supplies, OPEC would expect additional financial gains from an increased per-barrel revenue (by staving off price erosion and reducing costs arising through a decline in excess capacity investments, if any), counterbalancing the impending loss of volume in favour of non-OPEC countries or other sources of energy.

The consumption of some petroleum products is little affected in the short run, other things remaining equal, by an over-all moderate change in crude oil prices at the source. But in an industry where the raw material yields several products, changes in the price of the raw material (or, for that matter, changes in the fixed costs of the whole production process) cannot be readily assigned to each of the products except by resorting to arbitrary assumptions. This implies that there is no direct relationship between changes in the price of crude and that of individual petroleum products, such as petrol or fuel oil.

Another problem pertains to ascertaining the short-run impact of changes in the price of each product on the amounts supplied. In fact, a change in the consumption of one product normally necessitates a parallel change in the supply of joint products. Accordingly, the supply of one product cannot be increased to the exclusion of the others unless the company concerned and the industry as a whole alter the product mix by changing the technological pattern of production.

It is recognized that the price elasticity of demand for petrol, in the short run, is generally low. Indeed petrol, although heavily taxed by governments in most major oil importing countries (in excess of one-half of the price to the consumer), is a relatively small fraction of

[1] Price elasticity of demand (or supply) for crude oil or products measures the percentage change in quantity demanded (or supplied) as a result of a small, for example 1 per cent, change in the price of the commodity under study. If the percentage change in quantity demanded is greater than the percentage change in the price, demand is said to be price elastic; if the percentage change is smaller, demand is price inelastic. The elasticity of demand (or supply) for a particular product can also be measured in relation to changes in consumers' income (income elasticity of demand) or in relation to changes in the price of a competing product (cross-elasticity of demand).

the cost of running a car. Accordingly, a small increase in the price of petrol is unlikely to dissuade the car owner from driving his car. Moreover, petrol has virtually no substitute. Empirical investigations in the U.S. market show that elasticity of demand for petrol can be as low as 0·13, assuming that the change in price is general in a particular market, and that buyers have no opportunity to buy petrol elsewhere.[1] In the long run, price elasticity is bound to be significantly higher; price increases in petrol would spur automobile manufacturers to design motor vehicles which will burn petrol more efficiently, and thus consume less of it per mile.

Comprehensive and detailed empirical evidence on elasticity of demand for most petroleum products in various consuming areas and over several years is lacking. Nevertheless, recent information suggests that the composite price elasticity of demand for petroleum products is low in the short run for the United Kingdom, which has exhibited along with other West European markets a vigorous growth in the demand for oil products averaging in the 1960s about 9 per cent, while the demand for higher cost coal was facing a declining trend. The London *Financial Times* estimated that the July–November 1970 price increases for various petroleum products (petrol, heating oil, kerosene, industrial fuel oil, and diesel fuel) initiated by major companies' affiliates in the United Kingdom should yield all marketing companies an incremental revenue approximating £100 million ($240 million) per full year.[2] In other words, the price increases were not expected to reduce quantities demanded and affect adversely sales receipts as one would expect under conditions of elastic demand; on the contrary, these receipts were expected to increase. Indeed, it seems that relatively small per unit cost increases, whether arising from freight, fiscal levies or inflation, can be passed in the short run to the consumer without loss of income to companies – or even with an increase as was the case in the fourth quarter of 1970 and the first quarter of 1971.[3]

The above interpretation regarding the low over-all combined elasticity of petroleum products is supported by government and company sources. One U.S. source said: 'Quantification is not easy, but we adopt as plausible the estimate of Standard Oil Co. (N.J.)

---

[1] See Weiss, *Case Studies in American Industry*, pp. 240–1.

[2] *Financial Times*, London, 4 November 1970.

[3] See, for example, statements of Jersey and of Continental Oil chief executives, J. K. Jamieson and John McLean, *The Wall Street Journal*, 13 May 1971, and 3 February 1971, respectively; also *PIW*, 3 May 1971, p. 6; and *Oil and Gas Journal*, 10 May 1971, pp. 29–31.

117

that a 10 per cent price decrease would increase demand 1 per cent'.[1] Japan, the second largest consumer of energy (about 70 per cent petroleum in 1970) in the non-Communist world, estimated that

Chart 5.1

U.K. wholesale price and wage indices

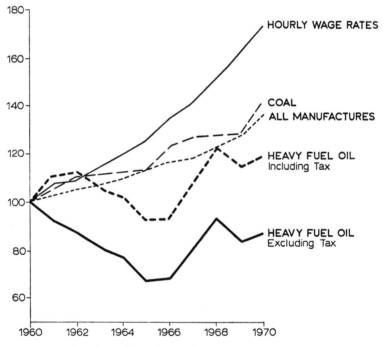

Source: Esso Petroleum Co. Ltd., London.

'the supply of and demand for energy is not sufficiently [price] elastic'.[2]

In the early 1960s, Adelman noted that the price elasticity of demand for crude oil as a whole was 'a composite of the moderate gasoline elasticity, the very great fuel oil elasticity, and the inter-

[1] *The Oil Import Question*, a Report on the Relationship of Oil Imports to the National Security, by the Cabinet Task Force on Oil Import Control, Washington, February 1970, p. 38.

[2] 'The Energy Policy of Japan' in *The OECD Observer*, No. 48, October 1970, p. 17.

118

mediate one for middle distillate'.[1] Prices of fuel oil and coal were then competitive, thus making for a very high cross-elasticity of demand. As the price of fuel oil dropped and that of coal moved up (see Chart 5.1), the price elasticity of demand for fuel oil declined. The price elasticity for fuel oil could increase, once nuclear energy or gas become more competitive. Under these circumstances, a change in relative prices of fuels may well lead to an immediate intensive operation of stations using the cheaper fuel, and a reduced operation of stations using the dearer fuel – to the extent this is feasible. The costly conversion from one type of power generation to another will not be made unless the relative change in fuel prices is expected to be permanent, and to yield users a net saving.[2]

Over and above price and cross-elasticities is the income elasticity of demand for energy, the percentage change in energy consumption associated with a 1 per cent change in per-capita national income. Estimates for 1968 show that the average elasticity coefficient has been 1 for developed private enterprise economies, 1·2 for centrally planned economies, and 1·6 for developing countries.[3]

For France, income elasticity of demand for petrol – according to one study – has been estimated at 1·6 in the short term (1-year period), and at 2·2 in the longer term (5-year period).[4] In Japan, per capita GNP grew in 1961–68 at an annual rate of 9·9 per cent, while the per capita demand for energy increased at a faster rate – over 11 per cent.[5]

Knowledge of income elasticity of demand for energy in major markets is necessary in devising OPEC long-term production plans. Table 5.2 and Chart 5.2 relate per capita gross national product to energy consumption over a number of years for several countries. The correlation coefficient 0·996 derived by the author is very high, and the functional relationship obtained is linear, $Y = 0·14X - 2·5$ where X is per capita GNP and Y per capita energy consumption.

[1] M. A. Adelman, 'The World Oil Outlook', *op. cit.*, p. 84.

[2] See, for example, J. A. van den Heuvel, 'Competition From Other Fuels: Natural Gas, Coal, Nuclear Energy', *International Oil*, pp. 61–76.

[3] UN Economic and Social Council, *Natural Resources Development and Policies, Including Environmental Considerations*, New York, 12 January 1971, pp. 5–6.

[4] P. Hatry, *Tendances et Perspectives de la Demande et de l'Offre de Pétrole Brut et de Produits Pétroliers dans les Pays Industrialisés à Economie de Marché, en Particulier durant la Période 1971–1980*, Brussels, January 1971, pp. 9–10 – quoting G. Vangrevelinghe, 'Modèles et Projections de la Consommation', in *Economie et Statistiques*, November 1969.

[5] See the Japanese National Committee of the World Petroleum Congresses, *The Petroleum Industry in Japan, 1969*, p. 5; and IBRD, *World Bank Atlas*, Population, Per Capita Product and Growth Rates, Washington, 1970.

119

Table 5.2

PER CAPITA GNP AND ENERGY, BY REGION, 1960–66

Region and Year	Per Capita GNP (1966 prices, $)	Per Capita Energy (barrel equivalents per year)
United States		
1960	3,071	43·6
1961	3,080	43·3
1962	3,228	44·3
1963	3,310	45·6
1964	3,442	46·8
1965	3,611	48·6
1966	3,796	50·6
Northern Europe*		
1960	1,687	19·5
1961	1,744	19·7
1962	1,791	20·7
1963	1,844	21·9
1964	1,941	22·5
1965	2,000	23·3
1966	2,038	23·4
Southern Europe and Japan†		
1960	647	6·1
1961	719	6·9
1962	763	7·3
1963	807	8·2
1964	873	8·8
1965	901	9·6
1966	969	10·5
Latin America‡		
1960	383	3·8
1961	393	3·8
1962	395	4·0
1963	393	4·0
1964	407	4·2
1965	415	4·2
1966	420	4·4

* Belgium, Luxembourg, France, Germany (West), Netherlands, Denmark, Norway, United Kingdom, Sweden, Switzerland.

† Greece, Italy, Portugal, Spain, Japan.

‡ Argentina, Bolivia, Brazil, Chile, Columbia, Ecuador, Mexico, Paraguay, Peru, Uruguay, Venezuela.

Chart 5.2

Per Capita GNP and Energy, by Region, 1960–66

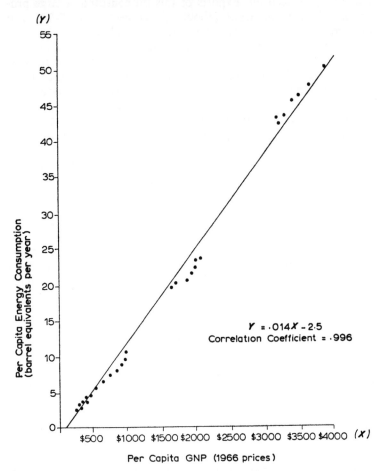

Source: Function derived by author from data in Table 5.2.

Source: Computed from data published by the United Nations and the U.S. Agency for International Development, and presented in the 'Statement of the American Petroleum Institute Submitted to the Cabinet Task Force on Oil Import Control', published in *Oil Import Control*, Hearings before the Subcommittee on Mines and Mining of the Committee on Interior and Insular Affairs, House of Representatives, 91st Congress, Washington D.C., March–April 1970, p. 465.

Third, OPEC production programming assumes that OPEC countries effectively control (and will continue to control) their domestically produced oil. Exports of this oil constitute a large proportion of world oil trade (about 85 per cent in 1962–70). But governmental control over oil production and exports has been hitherto generally nominal. These companies have refused, more or less successfully, to see their production targets and export requirements dictated by host countries. Governmental pressures have, however, begun to pay off, and OPEC countries may win in the coming few years from concessionaires the power to determine output.

The strength of a production programme is directly related to the amount of alternative supplies (including substitutes) that are available. Although OPEC oil represents a large share of the world oil trade, competitors are likely to show up if restrictive practices intolerable to companies or consuming countries are adopted by member countries. Alternative sources of oil or of substitute energy, over which OPEC has no control, have been and will continue to be developed by companies from the North Slope to the North Sea to Australia; these companies are motivated by their concern for protecting profits through diversification, and encouraged by consuming countries that seek to derive a large portion of their energy requirements from so-called reliable domestic and foreign sources where host governments are not likely to resort to restrictive practices to obtain economic or non-economic gain.

Fourth, OPEC production programming assumes that the international companies will be ready to co-operate on a voluntary basis.[1] Economic history shows, however, that no prorationing has been successful short of coercion or inducements – penalties to the recalcitrant and/or possible rewards to those complying. Even when a country agrees to observe a restrictive quota, the concessionaires in that country may resist, especially if they happen to have available equally attractive and non-restricted sources of supplies outside that country. In the absence of attractive alternatives, the concessionaire might well be forced to comply with the host government's measures.

The problem of co-operation includes devising the mechanics of allocation within a single country among several companies and

[1] Consent decrees between the U.S. Department of Justice on one hand, and Jersey (14 November 1960) and Texaco (4 June 1963) on the other permit American oil companies to enter into agreements with their competitors to put into effect a joint production programme which results either from legislation or official policy in OPEC countries. See *Platt's Oilgram Special Supplement*, 16 November 1960 and 24 June 1963, respectively.

among joint owners of these companies. This problem has become increasingly difficult as individual member countries have helped to undermine the concentration of the industry by offering oil rights to a large number of companies. Another difficult problem is that of programming allocations among countries and companies to meet the changing requirements of different types of refineries and markets which use various qualities of crude. OPEC formulae have not tackled these problems.

In an international openly competitive system of producing and trading in petroleum where prices are freely determined, the foregoing problems do not arise. This will lead to an automatic market-sharing mechanism for world oil supplies among oil producing centres and companies. Under these competitive conditions, the development of (or cut-back in) production from various oil reservoirs converges towards the equilibrium point where the incremental economic costs (including royalties) in each reservoir equate with those of every other reservoir – with due consideration for quality differentials and transport costs to major consuming centres. At that point, there are no economic incentives to develop (or cut back) production in any one centre to displace (or make room for) another.[1]

C. *Industry's Co-operation*

The major oil companies which control some 85 per cent of exports from the OPEC area have, throughout the life of OPEC, opposed international production programming.[2] They fear gradual loss of managerial freedom of action and control over their operations. Moreover, they doubt the success of programming since higher prices for OPEC oil would accelerate exploration and development activities in outside ventures.[3] Some of the majors even threatened in 1965 to invoke arbitration because production control was against the terms of their concession agreements (negotiated several years in the past), which provided for full managerial freedom in deciding volumes of exports.

The executive vice-president (now chairman) of Mobil believed the

[1] See M. A. Adelman, 'The World Oil Outlook', *op. cit.*, pp. 49–50.
[2] See statement by OPEC's Secretary-General, *MEES Supplement*, 15 March 1968, p. 2.
[3] See review of Lutfi's *OPEC Oil* by Henry C. Moses, vice-president for Middle East and Indonesian Affairs of Mobil, in *The Middle East Journal*, XXIII (Winter 1969), pp. 81–2.

attempts of OPEC countries to prorate crude production would be fundamentally bad for oil companies, 'since the industry would lose the flexibility and freedom of choice which it now enjoys'.[1] A former executive of Jersey, well-known for his outspoken opposition to production programming, conjectured in 1963 that an OPEC intergovernment cartel 'would in any event soon fall of its own weight'.[2] A senior official of BP (the largest crude oil producing company in the Middle East) at the Second Arab Petroleum Congress criticized international prorationing on the ground that Western consumers would oppose it: 'I think when our masters, the consumers, realize that the proposals [of international prorationing] put forward today [October 1960] really mean a control of world production, they will call it a producers' cartel; and you know in the West that is a very dirty word'.[3] A managing director of Shell offered a pessimistic outlook as to the workability and success of an OPEC production programme. He warned against the likely counter-reaction of consuming countries. His conclusions offered chilling prospects to OPEC's programmers:

> It is debatable whether programmed production will have much effect on prices. Even if this were the case in the short term – which I believe is unlikely – I would think that such effects would not be lasting in view of the new competitive pressures that would inevitably be generated, not only from alternative – that is non-OPEC – oil sources such as Russia, but from alternative fuels.
>
> The most unfortunate aspect of the OPEC plan, however, is that consuming countries cannot fail to regard it as being contrary to their interest. . . . I would accordingly expect the plan to result in counter pressure from the consuming countries. These would be all the more serious to the extent that the plan had any practical effects.
>
> However, it seems to me that the mechanics of the plan cannot guarantee success even in the short term. Long experience has taught us that it is practically impossible to estimate future growth in demand with precise accuracy – and yet it is on the

[1] Rawleigh Warner, Jr., 'Some Aspects of the International Oil Business', talk before the National Federation of Financial Analysts Societies, Richmond, Virginia, 1 May 1961, p. 5.

[2] Comments by H. E. Page on a paper entitled 'The Future Structure of the Market for International Oil' by Professor Wayne A. Leeman presented at the Princeton University Conference 'Arab Development in the Emerging International Economy', 25 April 1963 – typescript.

[3] Statement by M. E. Hubbard, quoted by *MEES*, 21 October 1969, pp. 9–10.

accuracy of the estimate of the OPEC countries' incremental production during any programme year that the whole success of the plan depends.[1]

The chairman of Texaco expressed qualified sympathy with OPEC objectives of international production prorationing. In particular, he praised their objective of keeping their oil revenues from falling, but insisted on the protection of free enterprise and the sanctity of contracts:

> In the international field, efforts are being made today by producing countries to find some method of prorationing that would in effect guarantee the continuation of their oil revenues at present or higher levels. This is a laudable objective, but in working out the methods of attainment, it is vital that those countries which have fared so well under the present arrangements retain the principles necessary to success in all international commerce. First and foremost of these, without which no nation or company can do business with others, are those which support free enterprise in the market place and the sanctity of contracts between the participating parties.[2]

It is virtually impossible to make a general statement about what companies think. Scholars shed doubts on executives' remarks made for public relation purposes, since executives are not free to express frankly all the objectives, policies, and practices of their companies; this can also be true of government officials. Nevertheless, it is ironic to contrast the overt opposition of U.S. major international companies to OPEC production programming at a time when they 'are all supporters' publicly of prorationing in the United States. They also supported United States 'oil import restrictions . . . despite the fact that these companies did not fare well under the import program having had to give up their imports to other companies. Furthermore, some of the internationals have an oil surplus overseas and an oil deficit at home, relative to their refining needs, and would therefore gain from freer imports'.[3] Companies invoke national security as their reason for supporting U.S. prorationing and imports

[1] Address by D. H. Barran, *Oil as a Source of Energy*, 14 April 1966, p. 10.
[2] Address by Augustus C. Long before the New York Society of Security Analysts, 14 December 1960, p. 15.
[3] U.S. Senate Subcommittee on Antitrust and Monopoly, 'The U.S. Oil Import Control Program – Costs, Benefits and Alternatives', statement by John H. Lichtblau, Executive Director, Petroleum Industry Research Foundation, Inc. (2 April 1969), p. 4.

programmes at a cost sacrifice to U.S. consumers as compared with free imports. The Cabinet Task Force on Oil Import Control put the long-run cost of the Import Control Program at $6.04 billion for 1969.[1] One company has contended – with no supporting evidence, however – that import controls, besides being vital to U.S. national security, are also in the long-run economic interest of U.S. consumers:

> Limitations on imports of foreign oil into the United States are vital to the nation's security. The United States cannot afford to become overly dependent on foreign sources for its petroleum supplies. Removal of import controls could virtually bring to a halt the discovery and development of new petroleum reserves, on which the nation's producing capacity so heavily depends. Moreover, removal of these limitations on imports, in all probability, would not result in savings for consumers of petroleum products over the long run.[2]

The president of the American Petroleum Institute explained that national security for the United States is not only defence capability. He referred to 'two other critical aspects of national security which are equally important. One is the strength of a nation's industrial and civilian economy; the other is its independence in international policy – its freedom from foreign coercion'.[3] Indeed, Arab governments, like the U.S. government, had also hoped to use oil for national security, or as a defence line to retain their territorial integrity after the Middle East war of June 1967. According to Ikard, the strength of the U.S. domestic oil industry enabled the U.S. government to protect its national security and that of its allies, and to thwart the aims of the Arab governments' oil boycott in 1967 in their endeavour to protect their own national security and territorial integrity.[4]

In the absence of full control over the size of oil exports of companies operating in the OPEC area, the effectiveness of international prorationing will depend on the support which major oil consuming countries might offer. This support can come through limiting purchases from non-member countries and by promoting the

---

[1] Higher figures were estimated by John M. Blair, and by Charles River Associates; a lower figure was offered by John H. Lichblau: *Oil Import Control*, pp. 166–7 and 398–9; and *The Oil Import Question*, February 1970, pp. 259–63.

[2] Texaco *Annual Report 1969*, p. 3.

[3] Statement of Frank N. Ikard, in *Tariff and Trade Proposals*, Hearings before the Committee on Ways and Means, House of Representative, 91st Congress, Washington, D.C., June 1970, Part 8, p. 2203.

[4] *Ibid.*, pp. 2206 and 2208–9.

companies' observance of quotas set by OPEC. Venezuela has long wanted major consuming countries to consult directly on this subject, so far without response.

D. *Disparities Among OPEC Countries: a 'Rational' Versus a 'Workable' Formula*

Among the factors contributing to the strength of international commodity control is the presence among the signatories of a single producer or consumer who controls a large share of the market and definitely intends to make the agreement work. In the case of OPEC, no single member country commands a predominant position, as compared with the International Tin Agreement which includes Malaysia, producer of some 40 per cent of the world's tin. Moreover, most OPEC countries have shown little willingness to see the production programme succeed. Mutual trust and some assurance that sacrifices they might make by limiting oil production would pay off in higher total revenues are prerequisites of success.

To argue that oil exporting countries (and, equally, oil importing countries or international companies) constitute a homogeneous group oversimplifies complex reality to the point of distortion. The growth of the OPEC organization, and the formulation and execution of production programmes, have suffered from differences in members' conditions and needs. Oil exporting countries, for example, have a considerable range of production costs and reserves. An oil exporting government includes in its calculation (with implicit or explicit use of a discount rate for the present valuation of expected future net receipts) the size of its reserves, the cost of producing and selling oil discovered, expected benefits from oil exports, as well as rising prices of commodities it imports.[1] A country with vast low cost proved reserves, say 75 times its annual production rate, is likely to be reluctant to defer production and tends to worry about the possibility that some of its oil will remain in the ground unwanted. Such a country fears the possible discovery of competing sources of hydrocarbons, progressive reductions in nuclear energy costs, or inflation that will reduce the attractiveness of oil and gas reserves as a store of value.

On the other hand, a country with proved reserves of say only 15 times its annual production rate will tend to worry about the wastage of its asset, and accordingly will be reluctant to quicken the pace of production in a period of depressed petroleum prices – unless it

[1] See discussion on terms of trade in Chapter Seven, and Chart 5.1.

127

expects prices to persist in their downward fall despite its own actions. A number of Middle East countries belong to the first type of country, while the United States and Venezuela belong to the second.

Venezuela has been foremost in proclaiming that open competition could lead to the squandering of depletable natural resources, notably oil. It has openly and repeatedly sought to impress upon its partners in OPEC the usefulness of instituting international pro-rationing. Its attitude is explained by its concern that cheaper Middle East oil will displace Venezuela's exports to major consuming markets. Moreover, Venezuela is fully aware that its proved reserves are now roughly equal to some 15 years of production at the current rates of exploration and production, as compared with reserves equivalent to several decades for some of the principal oil exporting countries in the Middle East.

Strains among OPEC countries in agreeing on a production programme do not arise solely from differences in their costs and reserves, and from their expectations about the future competitiveness of oil with other sources of energy. They may well arise from varying requirements for public expenditures on socio-economic development or on other activities, such as internal security and defence. In trying to maximize revenues, an oil exporting government will normally consider the element of time in its export plans, because a project (say a dam or a port) is worth more, if it can be built now, than a few years later. Large, populous, and politically stronger countries like Indonesia and Iran, where oil is crucial to their development plans,[1] are likely to press harder and probably successfully for larger oil exports, oil reserves permitting, than small Abu Dhabi – other things being equal. The weaker state might be willing to compromise by accepting a lower production quota than it would under strictly commercial circumstances.

The Economic Commission's attempts in 1965–66 to devise a so-called rational formula for allotting future increments among member countries are worth noting. It chose six variables for the intended formula: reserves, historical rate(s) of growth of oil pro-

[1] Iran's fourth plan envisages an annual rate of increase in oil production of 15·3 per cent over 1968–73. The actual rate of annual increase over the first two years of 1968 and 1969 averaged close to the target figure; this compares with a 9 per cent per annum expansion in world oil trade.

See UN–ECAFE, *Economic Survey of Asia and the Far East*, 1969, Part Two, *Current Economic Developments*, Bangkok, March 1970, pp. 149–50.

See also Marwan Iskandar, 'Economic Development Plans in Oil Exporting Countries and their Implications for Oil Production Targets' in *Continuity and Change in the World Oil Industry*, pp. 38–63.

duction (several ranges of periods were debated), population, area of country, government expenditures on certain development items, and proportion of oil income in government revenues.[1] Spare production capacity (which is related to size of reserves) was first included but later dropped at the request of some national representatives. Cost of production was considered but not retained. Costs, reserves, and, to some extent, recent rate(s) of growth in oil production capacity may represent commercial or economic indicators of attractiveness which normally influence the decisions of oil companies. The others may be euphemistically called social variables of little import to companies but of great significance to some host countries in so far as they reflect the magnitude of their needs.

Full agreement among OPEC governments on the six variables can not be reached easily. It would entail agreement on definitions, uniform methods of measurement, and a practical machinery for implementation. The problem, therefore, is greatly complicated by the fact that reserves estimates for the same country vary widely from one source to another; historical rates of growth for a single country vary with base year(s) chosen; reliable population censuses are lacking for some countries; and some boundaries are disputed. In addition, development and total governmental expenditures may vary in accordance with definitions and the degree of government participation in the country's economic life.

To agree on variables for the production formula is therefore largely a product of power politics and haggling among OPEC countries' representatives. Agreement is also needed on the weights to be assigned to these variables, and the functional relationships between them. Countries like Iran and Indonesia have insisted on giving more weight to certain social variables, such as area of the country and size of population; tiny Kuwait, of course, prefers to stick to the economic variable of reserves, and the socio-economic variable representing its almost total dependence on oil for state revenues.

Divergent views in the Economic Commission have made it impossible to devise a single formula. After lengthy discussion, two bases (one, roughly speaking, comprising economic variables, and the other socio-economic variables) were finally voted on by the

[1] See Z. Mikashi, 'Problems of a Common Production Policy among OPEC Member Countries' paper presented at OPEC's Seminar on *International Oil* and reproduced in the *Middle East Economic Papers*, 1969, American University of Beirut, pp. 53–68.

I

commission's national representatives in December 1966. These alternative bases were submitted to the XIIth Conference as representing majority and minority wishes. Moreover, representatives of the Arabian–Persian Gulf countries – Iran, Iraq, Kuwait, Saudi Arabia, and Qatar (Abu Dhabi was not yet in OPEC) – and the Secretariat staff considered in 1966 limiting production programming to this region of OPEC. Reasons invoked were: Venezuela's growth in oil exports was modest (3 per cent), populous Indonesia needed all the exports its reserves could sustain, and Libya was at an initial stage of its oil development and should be entitled to unrestrained exports for a period of time.

The production programme and its formulae proved unacceptable to the Conference. Several member countries had by then abandoned their pledge – already tenuous – to support the July 1966–June 1967 programme, and production programming in general. In fact, some not only failed to instruct their concessionaire companies concerning production limits, but pressed them to increase production to the utmost and to raise their share of world oil trade. Moreover, almost all OPEC countries have continued to open up new areas for exploration and development. All this is incompatible with OPEC's professed objective of containing production.

The Shah's speech of 14 March 1968 expounded on Iran's 'right' to decide on the size of its oil exports:

> We have no objection when the existing companies export Iran's oil and serve as a means of securing revenue for Iran while safeguarding the county's interests and respecting its needs. What we must emphasize is that these decisions cannot be taken unilaterally. We, as the owners of this oil and the master of this land, must have a say in the production of this wealth because the needs of this country are clear. No firm, no company, no organization can tell us, merely because it has an agreement with us, that we will produce and export so much of your national wealth but you cannot touch the rest because we do not wish to exploit it. What this means in fact is that they want to deprive Iran of this wealth which rightfully belongs to it.[1]

The Shah emphasized the needs of his country, thereby abstracting commercial factors which weigh with profit-seeking commercial concerns. The Iranian Prime Minister, Amir Abbas Hoveyda, reemphasized the Shah's oil policy and its key variables before the Iranian Parliament in December 1970:

[1] See *MEES*, 22 March 1968, p. 2a.

130

The government has also made clear to member companies of the Oil Consortium that Iran is determined to maintain her historical role as the biggest exporter of oil in the Middle East through exports of oil from the Agreement Area. Besides Iran's historical role, this position is regarded by the Government of Iran as an undeniable and a conclusive fact in view of the country's population, its size, the needs of its development plans, as well as the regional commitments of Iran, which serves as a factor of peace and stability in this part of the world. This principle forms the basis of the country's oil policy, and the Oil Consortium has recognized it and assured us that it will be reflected in Iran's oil revenues.[1]

Table 5.3 shows that, among OPEC countries, Iran has the largest population after Indonesia. Although available statistical information is scanty and not completely reliable, the table indicates that the contribution of oil revenues per head of population in 1969 was smallest in Indonesia (about $1.2), and highest for Abu Dhabi (close to $2,400), the richest oil land in the world on a per capita basis. To compare the dependence of OPEC countries on the petroleum industry, one would need national income and balance-of-payments figures. Moreover, comparisons dependent on exchange rates of these countries cannot be made readily since most have variously overvalued currencies; put differently, their exchange rates do not properly reflect scarcities of foreign exchange. One would have therefore to impute the opportunity costs of foreign exchange reflecting conditions of demand and supply in these countries, and use them in making inter-country comparisons.[2]

Available estimates show that countries with higher per capita income (Abu Dhabi, Kuwait, Qatar, and Libya) derive almost all their foreign exchange receipts and most of their national income from oil in contra-distinction with countries with lower per capita income. Moreover, income distribution within these countries varies widely, but reliable statistics are lacking here too.

A country's argument for larger oil exports and oil revenues can be expressed on the basis of social need, and supported by the fact that oil reserves may be ample enough to sustain an increase in oil exports – comparative cost considerations aside. But a country pressing for a larger share of oil exports at the expense of others can

[1] *MEES Supplement*, 18 December 1970, p. 2. The author was privileged with an interview with the Iranian Prime Minister in Tehran in July 1968.

[2] See I. M. D. Little, 'Cost–Benefit Analysis of Projects' reprinted in *Leading Issues in Economic Development*, pp. 381–2.

Table 5. SELECTED INFORMATION ON OPEC MEMBER COUNTRIES, 1969

Country	Abu Dhabi	Algeria	Indonesia	Iran	Iraq	Kuwait	Libya	Qatar	Saudi Arabia	Venezuela
Regime	Sheikhdom	Military	Military	Monarchical	Military	Principality	Military	Sheikhdom	Monarchical	Republican
Area ('000 sq. km.)	170	2,382	1,904	1,648	449	16	1,760	22	2,383	912
Population (million)	0·08*	13	116	28	9	0·6*	1·9	0·085*	7	10
Gov't revenues from oil (millions of U.S. $)	191	299	140	1,159	529	1,006	1,132	118	1,158	1,245
Per capita oil Revenues (U.S. $)	2,388	23	1·2†	41	59	1,677	596	1,388	165	125
GNP per capita† (U.S. $)	n.a.	220	100§	310	260	3,540	1,020	3,490	360	950
Oil production (million bbl.)	219	345	271	1,232	555	1,012	1,135	130	1,174	1,312
Oil reserves (billion bbl.)	16·00	8·00	9·00	55·00	27·50	68·00	35·00	9·50	140·00	14·75
Reserves/production	73	22	34	45	49	67	31	42	119	11

* About half the population are foreigners.
† Estimated.
‡ 1968
§ Excluding West Irian (estimated at $50).

Sources: OPEC; *Oil and Gas Journal*; *MEES*; Petroleum Information Foundation; International Bank for Reconstruction and Development, *World Atlas*, Population, Per Capita Product, and Growth Rates, Washington. September 1970.

132

invite immediate countermoves, especially from lower cost producers. Thus, soon after the Shah's speech of 1968, the Minister of Petroleum and Mineral Resources in Saudi Arabia (the country with the largest proved oil reserves in the world) reacted sharply. He stated that his government did not interfere with the export plans of concessionaire companies which responded to economic factors (such as commercial reserves and costs) favouring Saudi oil exports. He added, 'If, however, we see that the oil companies have allowed pressure from other host governments to interfere with the free play of these factors vis-à-vis Saudi offtake levels, we will at once move to safeguard our interests'.[1] In fact, production costs in Iran are reckoned to be higher than in a number of neighbouring countries. The cost of producing a barrel of oil in Iran was estimated in 1968 to average about 13 to 14 cents, compared with 8 to 9 cents for Saudi Arabia and 6 cents for Kuwait.[2]

These cost comparisons are approximate; accounting conventions employed in the various countries could well be different and no consideration is given to quality differentials and geographical advantages of oil sources. Furthermore, one should be careful of comparing average costs per barrel, because it is marginal costs which are relevant for short-run price competition. It is reasonable to assume that the lower-cost producer is always tempted to shade prices to increase exports. He may regard his sales as 'marginal' in relation to world oil trade, with little effect on prices; but the cumulative impact of a series of individual actions by several producers is bound to lead to significant price erosion – economic costs permitting.

Despite the failure of previous production programmes and OPEC's public admission regarding 'doubts felt by some member countries with respect to the system's efficacy',[3] OPEC's January 1968, June 1970, and December 1970 Conferences came out with three resolutions (XIV.84, XX.112 and XXI.121 respectively) which gave firm support to joint production programming.

Whether the member country delegates are genuinely convinced of the effectiveness of joint production programming, or whether they are only paying lip service to satisfy public opinion in one or more member countries, notably Venezuela, must await the test of time. The Head of the Venezuelan Delegation to OPEC's XIXth Conference of December 1969, Maurice Valery, declared: 'We are insisting on the implementation of a joint production program in

[1] MEES, 5 April 1958, p. 1.
[2] PPS, April 1968, p. 128.
[3] The Secretary-General in OPEC Bulletin, March 1967.

line with the OPEC Resolution on the subject issued two years ago.'[1] At any rate, it is unrealistic to claim that the considerations for the practicability of a production programme are strictly economic. There are political considerations as well, essentially the willingness and determination to reconcile the different policies of disparate member countries.

E. *A Historical Precedent*

OPEC's production programming was inspired partly by conditions and events in the U.S. oil industry in the late 1920s and early 1930s. During that period, unrestricted drilling and production, large oil discoveries, and cut-throat competition in the United States (particularly in Texas, the major oil producer in the United States, and Oklahoma) led to physical wastage and economic losses. With the discovery of the gigantic East Texas Field in 1930, prices bottomed out at 10 cents per barrel in 1931. To remedy this situation, state agencies (the Oklahoma Corporation Commission and the Texas Railroad Commission) instituted state-wide prorationing systems beginning in 1928 and 1932, respectively, in order to prevent the wasteful production of oil reservoirs and to support prices at the so-called market demand.[2] Louisiana, New Mexico, and Kansas later established their own prorationing systems. But other oil states, notably California and Wyoming, refused to adopt market demand prorationing, primarily because their production was small relative to domestic demand.[3] In 1970, the states with market demand prorationing (though they followed different rules) accounted for two-thirds of U.S. domestic production.

Prorationing in the United States has proved effective in stabilizing prices at higher than free-market levels. Stabilization has been possible thanks to the advanced technical and economic know-how among private operators and public regulators of the U.S. industry; to the relatively short period (one month) during which production is planned, thus avoiding the uncertainties of longer periods; and to the assistance of the Federal Bureau of Mines, which offers detailed up-to-date statistics and monthly estimates of market demand at

[1] See *MEES*, 19 December 1969, p. 4.

[2] W. F. Lovejoy and P. T. Homan, *Economic Aspects of Oil Conservation Regulation*, Resources for the Future, Inc. (Baltimore: Johns Hopkins Press, 1967) pp. 33–5.

[3] *Ibid.*, p. 129.
They abide by the maximum efficient rate (MER) production rule which represents the ceiling of producibility of oil reservoirs consistent with maximum recovery of reserves.

134

current prices. Stabilization has also been possible because prorationing is enforced and policed by state authorities and because of the federal ban since 1938 on interstate oil shipments in excess of state-authorized production (the Connally Act), and federal support through import control.

In Texas, the prorationing system distributes shares among operators in amounts varying in direct relationship to the number of wells drilled and the depth of these wells. Marginal or so-called stripper wells are exempt from production limitation. As Adelman says, this system protects stripper wells, 'the weeds at the expense of flowers'.[1] Moreover, many wells are drilled (subject to minimum spacing) on fully explored and developed fields with a view to getting quotas. Some are unnecessary for the optimum production of these fields,[2] and consequently economically wasteful. Efficiency is achieved when production from a single oil reservoir is 'unitized' or rationally distributed among the several operators in order to reduce the number of wells to the economical minimum.

Early in 1931, an attempt was made in the United States to adopt a centralized country-wide prorationing system. The Oil States Advisory Committee (or Governors' Committee) was set up to devise a plan of co-operative action to limit production in support of prices that would 'assure to all producers a fair and reasonable return on their necessary investments'.[3] However, individual states, particularly Texas, were unwilling to relinquish their autonomy in oil affairs to an interstate or federal agency, and were unable to agree on market sharing.

The U.S. Governors' Committee of 1931 – having failed to centralize prorationing – contributed later, in 1935, to the formation of the Interstate Oil Compact Committee with the sole object of agreeing on standard rules for conservation. Close personal contacts among oil officials from various states have helped to 'keep the states in step with one another in the loosely knit system of production control and market stabilization administered by the several states'.[4] Moreover, all of these states have welcomed Congressional legislative assistance in the form of a federal ban on interstate oil shipments in excess of state-authorized oil production.[5]

[1] M. A. Adelman, 'Efficiency of Resource Use in Crude Petroleum,' *op. cit.*, p. 104.

[2] Weiss, *op. cit.*, pp. 321–2.

[3] Lovejoy, *op. cit.*, p. 35.

[4] *Ibid.*, p. 46.

[5] Arthur M. Johnson, *Petroleum Pipelines and Public Policy, 1906–1959*, Harvard University Press, 1967, p. 468.

In comparing prorationing in the U.S. and OPEC production programmes, one cannot fail to observe at least two fundamental differences. First, although the federated states are autonomous with regard to oil production, the U.S. government regulates centrally and effectively interstate trade and import controls. The OPEC area, in contrast, is composed of ten independent and differing entities.[1] Second, OPEC production programmes would operate in open competition with other non-OPEC oil exporting countries; the internal market in the United States, in contrast, can be and is protected from foreign competition by tariffs and import quotas.

[1] Nigeria joined OPEC in July 1971, thereby raising membership to eleven countries.

Chapter 6
BARGAINING FOR ECONOMIC BENEFITS: GOVERNMENT REVENUES

Economic benefits accruing from the production and export of petroleum are of two kinds: those directly derived by the state, mostly in the form of fiscal revenues, and those derived by the nation, including income accruing to the state as well as to workers, suppliers, contractors, and others. This chapter reviews the role of OPEC in bargaining for state revenues.

Host countries have been able, thanks to the improvement in their bargaining position *vis-à-vis* international companies, to obtain larger government takes per unit of exports. In a market structure that is almost a bilateral oligopoly, the bargain does not have a determinate solution. The outcome depends largely on the bargaining strategy and tactics of each group, the cohesion of the members of each group, and the opportunities available to each negotiating party – factors that are constantly changing. Speaking generally about the bargaining power of international corporations, one scholar of international trade noted:

> One need not feel moved by the plight of the investing corporations. . . . Many of them are as big or bigger than the countries with which they deal in sales, assets, and skill of management, if not in sovereign power. . . . The corporations are too large and powerful to turn them loose in a partial laissez-faire for the less developed countries to exploit to the extent of their appetite and capacity.[1]

A. *Company Profitability*

OPEC countries' successes in obtaining larger revenues are the more remarkable in view of the fact that realized petroleum prices have

[1] C. P. Kindleberger, *American Business Abroad*, Yale University Press, New Haven, 1969, p. 205.

been eroded since 1957 while posted and tax-reference prices have been maintained at levels higher than realized prices. This is possible – and justifiable from the point of view of host countries – to the extent some concessionary oil companies derive excess profits, over and above normal return. The decline of market prices despite frozen or increased posted and tax-reference prices has contributed to some deterioration in company rates of return on invested capital.

To assess the commercial attractiveness of going concerns in oil exporting countries, one normally has access to three accounting indices: cost of production per unit, company earnings per unit of sale, and return on assets or on net worth. Assets should be taken to mean operating assets, net of depreciation. Net worth represents the equity of owners and includes paid-up capital, reserves, and retained earnings.

The cost of production per barrel or ton reflects largely the bounty of nature, the relative richness of oil reservoirs; this fact accounts for the relative costliness of oil extracted from a certain reservoir – assuming all companies are equally efficient in the extraction process. The per unit cost of production cannot, however, be relied on exclusively as an indicator of the attractiveness of an oil venture. In fact, low cost oil will be commercially unattractive if the deposit is far from a market; if the oil produced has a high sulphur content; or if its API gravity and other quality factors do not satisfy the pattern of demand in major consuming markets using conventional technology, thereby requiring additional investments (for example catalytic cracking) to get the required product mix.

The index of unit costs must, therefore, be supplanted by unit earnings. The profit margin earned on a barrel of oil produced and sold is a better indicator of profitability than unit costs. Nevertheless, the index of earnings derived from each unit of oil produced or exported, used alone, has an important shortcoming; it overlooks the relation between the total investment effort and the size of earnings derived from it.

To measure the historical reward to investment effort, one should rely on accounting records for both costs and earnings from sales. In the present state of financial practice, the two most widely used measures for assessing the profitability of an enterprise are the ratio of operating profits to operating assets, and the ratio of net earnings after tax to net worth.

Table 6.1 offers a set of figures for the operations of the seven major international oil companies in the Eastern Hemisphere, prepared by the First National City Bank of New York (FNCB) and

138

Table 6.1

PRODUCTION, EARNINGS AND GOVERNMENT PAYMENTS OF SEVEN INTERNATIONAL OIL COMPANIES*
EASTERN HEMISPHERE, 1957–70

	1957	1958	1959	1960	1961	1962	1963	1964	1965	1966	1967	1968	1969	1970
Gross production (million barrels)	1,370	1,598	1,710	1,950	2,077	2,310	2,540	2,882	3,235	3,627	3,928	4,422	5,034	5,832
Net earnings ($ millions)	1,069	963	999	1,101	1,128	1,227	1,429	1,245	1,353	1,491	1,446	1,748	1,785	1,907
Net worth on Jan. 1 ($ millions)	5,653	6,344	7,138	7,828	8,538	9,353	10,115	11,232	12,027	12,929	13,542	14,959	15,763	16,818
Return on net worth (%)	18·9	15·2	14·0	14·1	13·2	13·1	14·1	11·1	11·2	11·5	10·7	11·7	11·3	11·3
Earnings per barrel (cents)	78·0	60·3	58·4	56·5	54·3	53·1	56·3	43·2	41·8	41·1	36·8	39·5	35·4	32·7
Payments to producing governments ($ millions)	1,070	1,210	1,309	1,381	1,454	1,637	1,908	2,167	2,471	2,798	3,138	3,675	4,223	5,013
Payments per barrel (cents)	78·1	75·7	76·5	70·8	70·0	70·9	75·1	75·2	76·4	77·1	79·9	83·1	83·9	86·0

*Jersey, Shell, Texaco, Mobil, BP, Socal and Gulf.
Source: First National City Bank, New York.

often quoted by spokesmen of these companies.[1] The figures are derived from company sources and may involve differing methods of assessment, possible inaccuracies, and omissions. Factors which might distort comparisons include: lack of agreement among oil companies on what constitutes generally accepted accounting principles; absence of consolidated financial statements; arbitrary decisions in the allocation of company earnings or expenditures geographically, as admitted by FNCB,[2] and among periods; and inflation. In addition, company earnings on integrated operations are related to gross production; it is more proper to relate earnings to volume of products sold, since these earnings are derived mostly from the sale of products for the vertically integrated companies analysed by FNCB. The FNCB figures should, therefore, be taken as rough estimates of the size and direction of change.

Figures of Table 6.1 do not apply solely to OPEC countries. They cover the whole Eastern Hemisphere (outside the Communist countries), and include non-OPEC oil, gas, and petrochemical producing areas of Western Europe (notably the Netherlands and the North Sea); of Africa (notably Nigeria); and of Australia and Asia (notably Muscat and Oman, and Brunei). They also exclude one major OPEC country in the Western Hemisphere, Venezuela. Besides, these figures cover only the activities of the seven majors, thereby excluding CFP and the independents, whose combined share of oil production in the Eastern Hemisphere was about 20 per cent in the 1960s, and a larger percentage for downstream operations. Another limitation of these figures is the fact that, under the fiscal systems of oil exporting countries, an increase of government revenues per barrel need not necessarily result from an increase in the rate of taxation; it can also be caused by a decline in operating costs per unit of output (refer to sources in Table 7.3). Finally, the table fails to account for changes (usually increases) in the substantial levies charged by major oil importing countries on petroleum products. These levies, according to OPEC sources, reached in Western Europe six times the size of oil exporting governments' income per barrel.[3]

Despite these limitations, broad conclusions can still be drawn from Table 6.1. For example, both company earnings on integrated

---

[1] Another source often quoted is that of the Chase Manhattan Bank of New York, whose studies cover the domestic and international operations of 27 U.S.-based oil companies.

[2] FNCB, Energy Memo, *Risk-Bearing in the Eastern Hemisphere*, October 1970, p. 1.

[3] Reproduced by *Le Pétrole et le Gaz Arabes*, 1 February 1971, p. 37.

operations per barrel and over-all company rates of return on net worth declined steadily from 1957 to 1967. This trend was underway before OPEC's creation. Government revenues per barrel also declined from 78·1 cents in 1957 to 70 cents in 1961, though the decline for governments was relatively much smaller than that for companies. In 1963, when some of OPEC countries' policies for higher tax rates started paying off, government revenues per barrel started to rise in current dollar value, while company earnings per barrel persisted in their downward trend until 1970.

To ascertain whether host countries were justified in acquiring a higher share of company profits, OPEC commissioned in January 1961 a comprehensive study on 'the economics of investment in the oil industry by concession-holding companies' (Res. II.11). After allowing for discounts off posted prices current in major import markets at the time, the study estimated the 1956–60 average net earnings on net assets of major oil producing concessions as follows: Iran, 71 per cent; Iraq, 62 per cent; Qatar, 114 per cent; and Saudi Arabia, 61 per cent; no figures were then available for Kuwait. The total for the four countries combined averaged 66 per cent, compared with only 20 per cent for Venezuela.[1] This author's estimate for Kuwait over the same period, using the same assumptions, reveals an average in excess of 150 per cent, far above that in other Middle East countries.[2]

To distinguish between 'production/upstream' versus 'downstream' profits or losses for a vertically integrated oil company, special and/or arbitrary assumptions must be made concerning transfer prices among affiliates of the same parent company. Therefore, it is conceptually more correct to speak of the comparative economic attractiveness to a company of producing crude oil from various sources, given the presence of marketing outlets for that

[1] Made by Arthur D. Little, Inc., and entitled *Economic Aspects of the International Petroleum Industry, Report to the Organization of the Petroleum Exporting Countries*, Cambridge, Mass.: 15 January 1962, 2 vols., not published. Figures reproduced have, however, been widely quoted by spokesmen of host governments and of the international oil industry, and by petroleum consultants and the trade press. See, for example, J. E. Hartshorn, *Oil Companies and Governments, an Account of the International Oil Industry in its Political Environment*, Faber & Faber (London, 1967), p. 108; OPEC, *Pricing Problems: Further Considerations*, Geneva, 10 September 1963, pp. 6–10; Shell International Petroleum Co. Ltd., *Current International Oil Pricing Problems*, London, 29 August 1963, pp. 12–15; and *Petroleum Intelligence Weekly (PIW)*, ed. Wanda M. Jablonski, New York, 7 May 1962.

[2] Z. Mikdashi, *A Financial Analysis of Oil Companies' Performance in Kuwait*, Kuwait, February 1967, pp. 24 – not published.

141

company. Nevertheless, figures of costs, investments and imputed earnings calculated by OPEC, FNCB, and other parties[1] confirmed a general belief that concession-holding companies in the Middle East had been deriving, prior to 1960, relatively high economic rent from their operations; the figures tended to disprove company allegations that an increase in fiscal charges by Middle East governments would reduce company profits below 'reasonable' or 'normal' levels. Accordingly, the OPEC Conference resolved in June 1962 to ask companies to raise posted prices to their pre-August 1960 level, to expense royalty, and to eliminate marketing allowances (Res. IV. 32, 33 and 34.)

B. *Payment of Royalty*

Member governments in their 1962–64 negotiations asked for a separate payment of royalty by concessionaires before assessing their income tax obligations. Royalty would then be shown as an expense in the same way as other operating costs, such as salaries, supplies, and equipments, and deducted before arriving at taxable notional profits as defined by OPEC – namely, imputed sales proceeds on the basis of posted or tax-reference prices, less operating costs inclusive of royalty.

Total payments to these governments (income tax at 50 per cent plus royalty) would then come to more than 50 per cent of company notional profits. The following is a hypothetical illustration of company payments to host governments; (A) involves no royalty payment, whereas (B) provides for it:

	Cents per Barrel	
	(A)	(B)
	No Expensing	Full Expensing
If the posted price is . . .	200	200
If operating costs are . . .	20	20
and fully expensed royalty at 12½% of the posted price is . .		25
Then for host government tax purposes, profits are . . .	180	155
And host government tax at 50% is	90	77·5
Total host government take .	90	102·5

[1] For example, the U.S. Department of Commerce, *Survey of Current Business*, various issues; and the Chase Manhattan Bank's *Annual Analysis of a Group of Petroleum Companies*.

142

In 1962 member countries justified their claim for immediate payment or full expensing of royalty on the grounds that oil companies' profits were relatively high (as was apparent from the OPEC study), and that royalty was a legitimate reward to the 'landlord' (the state), owner of the natural resources. The reward was due as compensation to the landlord for using up his depletable asset, according to OPEC, regardless of whether any net profits were derived from the extraction of oil. OPEC went further and asked, in a position paper, to raise royalty payments from the rate current in 1962, namely 12·5 per cent of posted prices, to 20 per cent for the rich Middle East oil fields.[1]

After two years of drawn-out negotiations, which ended in 1964, OPEC failed to get satisfaction in its demand for raising royalty rates. Moreover, although major companies accepted the principle of royalty expensing, the advantages were partially offset by reducing taxable notional profits with discount allowances on current posted prices. The discount allowance on the posted price for income tax purposes was 8·5 per cent for 1964, 7·5 per cent for 1965, and 6·5 per cent for 1966 for heavy crudes of 27° API and below; reductions for lighter crudes in 1965–66 were slightly less.[2] This represents a progressive increase in per-barrel payments to host governments of about 3·5 to 5·5 cents, as compared with some 11 cents per barrel if immediate and full royalty expensing had taken place. OPEC's Secretary-General estimated that this compromise settlement brought Middle East OPEC governments some $311 million in additional revenues over the three years 1964–66.[3]

Claiming a general improvement in the 'competitive, economic and market situation of crude petroleum' (the quoted terms are contained in the OPEC-major companies' settlement of 1964), OPEC countries resumed in mid-1966 their strenuous negotiations with the oil companies. The countries sought to obtain the total and immediate elimination of discounts from posted prices in the royalty expensing operation (Res. XI.71). But the companies balked at such an arrangement. OPEC's Secretary-General, late in 1967, expressed the organization's disappointment, stating that 'eleventh-

[1] *Explanatory Memoranda on the OPEC Resolutions*, April–June 1962, p. 14.
[2] In 1965 and 1966, discount allowances off posted prices were increased by gravity correction for lighter crudes of U.S. cents 0·13235 and 0·2647, respectively, per barrel for each full API degree of crude above 27° API. This was aimed at reducing relative overpricing of higher-gravity lighter crudes, as changes in the pattern of consumer demand since 1960 had resulted in a decline in the commercial attractiveness of light crudes in relation to heavy crudes.
[3] *OPEC Bulletin*, May 1967.

hour company proposals containing slender and totally unacceptable offers are a waste of time and a tax on the producing countries' patience'. He even hinted that unilateral action might be taken by OPEC countries.[1]

Table 6.2

SUMMARY OF ROYALTY EXPENSING: PHASE-OUT OF PERCENTAGE AND GRAVITY ALLOWANCES, 1964–75*

	% Allowance Off Posted Price	Gravity Allowance Cents/bbl.
1964	8·5	—
1965	7·5	0·132350
1966	6·5	0·264700
1967	6·5	0·264700
1968	5·5	0·324259
1969	4·5	0·383818
1970	3·5	0·443377
1971	2·0	0·502936
1972	—	0·562495
1973	—	0·374997
1974	—	0·187499
1975	—	—

* Gravity allowance is expressed in terms of cents per barrel for each full degree API gravity in excess of 27° API, provided that all crudes with API gravity in excess of 37° API shall be treated as if they were 37° API gravity.

All allowances were eliminated towards the end of 1970 – see pp. 154–56 below.

Source: OPEC.

It is curious that a slightly more favourable last-minute version of the companies' proposals – already repudiated by OPEC's Secretary-General – was accepted by the XVth Conference on 8 January 1968. The acceptance, however, was made at the expense of unanimity; dissenting members were not bound by the resolution.[2]

The January 1968 agreement provided for phasing out the discount allowance on posted prices over a period of seven years (Table 6.2).

[1] OPEC Bulletin, January 1968.
[2] See MEES, Beirut, 12 January 1968, pp. 7–8.

For crudes of the 27° API or below, the companies offered a discount declining from 5·5 per cent in 1968 to 4·5 per cent in 1969, 3·5 per cent in 1970, 2·0 per cent in 1971, and phasing out completely in 1972. For lighter crudes, a gravity allowance postponed the full elimination of discount off posted prices until 1975.[1]

The net additional revenues ultimately accruing to member governments on the basis of the 1968 agreement range between 4·8 and 9·0 cents per barrel, depending on the gravity and the posted price of the particular crude oil, over and above the increases in revenues of 3·5 to 5·5 cents per barrel obtained by the end of 1966. Following the closure of the Suez Canal in June 1967, crudes from Mediterranean terminals became economically more attractive as compared with the Arabian–Persian Gulf crudes; oil companies agreed in September 1967 to waive all allowances on Mediterranean crudes 'for so long as the aforesaid improvement due to extraordinary circumstances continues to exist'.

Along with the expensing of royalty, OPEC countries sought to eliminate any contribution to the marketing expenses of the concessionaire companies previously allowable as deductible by the tax authorities of host countries (Res. IV.34). This allowance is considered fictitious by host governments since the bulk of the crude oil produced by concessionaire companies is marketed through their parents, no brokerage charges being incurred. OPEC also failed to obtain complete satisfaction on this score. In the original 50–50 profit sharing agreements, the so-called marketing expenses were set at about 2 per cent of posted prices; in 1958–63, they were reduced to 1 per cent of posted prices (averaging about 1·7 cents per barrel). The outcome of OPEC's 1962–64 negotiations with oil companies was a further reduction in the marketing allowance to half a cent per barrel effective 1964.

C. *Raising Posted Prices and Tax Rates*

Throughout the 1962–64 negotiations, major companies adamantly refused to restore, for income tax purposes, posted prices in the Middle East to their pre-August 1960 level. Just before the end of the talks, the largest international oil company, Jersey, argued that although it was within the administrative power of companies to raise posted prices, they would be reluctant to do so. They feared they would fail to recoup their extra tax payments to host countries from the consumer through higher prices, given the current market

[1] *Ibid.*, pp. 7–11.

K   145

conditions of excess availability of supplies and widespread price competition. The company argued:

> Although they have the power to increase the posted price of crude oil and thus add to their costs, the opportunity for recovering these higher costs through higher prices to the consumer is determined by the state of the market. Under present conditions of excess producing capacity world-wide, there is little prospect of recovering added costs. Any company that attempted to do so through higher prices would begin to lose market outlets, either to oil from other areas not affected by such higher costs or to such competing fuels as nuclear power or coal.[1]

It is understandable that one company alone cannot raise prices in a competitive industry lest it lose sales to rivals. But all firms can raise their prices and still not lose sales – assuming conditions of relatively inelastic demand.

Both posted prices and tax rates were first successfully negotiated to higher levels in 1970 – outside OPEC's framework. Libya assumed the role of leader in the assault. Libya's hand was strengthened because it was the leading oil supplier to Western Europe, filling close to 25 per cent of that area's oil requirements. In addition, Libya possessed official reserves that would finance two years' requirements of imported necessities. Western Europe, on the other hand, had only a two-month supply of oil stocks.

In January 1970, the Libyan government started negotiating an upward revision of its posted prices. For some seven months, all oil companies resisted staunchly. The government negotiating team at first consisted of officials of the Ministry of Petroleum, and later of a special Price Committee headed by the former Libyan Prime Minister, Mahmoud Maghrabi.[2] When negotiations proved inconclusive, the Revolutionary Command Council, the highest authority in the country, stepped in. The single-minded, audacious, and determined military leaders under Premier Mu'amar Gadhafi, who had the real power, could not tolerate failure to make satisfactory headway. Moreover, the military leaders were willing to prove that they meant what they said.

They threatened cuts or suspension of production, charging that companies were producing oil too fast and thus damaging the

---

[1] Jersey, *Middle East Oil Revenues in Relation to the Price of Imported Goods* (16 September 1964), p. 8 – not published.

[2] In 1971, Libyan ambassador at the UN: the author had the opportunity of interviewing him in New York on 15 March 1971.

efficient recovery of reserves. The power to conserve oil resources is legitimate; in Libya it derives from Regulation No. 8 passed in 1968 and modelled on OPEC's Pro-Forma Regulation for the Conservation of Petroleum Resources (Res. XVII.93). Company spokesmen questioned, however, the timing of applying conservation measures with the attempt to obtain larger oil revenues.

In carrying out its threats, the Libyan leadership first chose certain companies, the independents – specifically, Occidental. By a series of 'conservation measures' taken in June and August 1970, they ordered Occidental to cut back production by 360,000 barrels per day from a high of 797,000 in April – a reduction of over 45 per cent. The selection of Occidental for governmental action was prompted by the company's obvious economic vulnerability. Occidental, as indicated in its annual reports and statements by its chief executive (Armand Hammer), derived close to one-third of its earnings from the Libyan venture.[1] Moreover, unlike the majors, it had no alternative sources of supply. It could not, therefore, endure a drastic cut in its oil production – given its contractual commitments to buyers – without suffering heavy losses. Furthermore, its crude oil sales contracts contained provisions which enabled it to shift, totally or substantially, increased Libyan taxes onto the buyers of crude.

The timing of the Libyan move was most propitious to achieving its aims. The Suez Canal was closed; Tapline, capable of transporting 485,000 barrels of Saudi oil daily to the East Mediterranean, was cut off in Syria on 3 May 1970, presumably accidentally by a bulldozer engaged in a cable-laying project. Thereupon, the Syrian government refused to allow repairs before Tapline settled for higher transit dues. Some observers would like to link the financial aid offered by Libya to Syria late in 1970 to the puncture of Tapline in May 1970, and to the delay in repairs which could have been completed within 24 hours.[2] There is no evidence, however, to support the view that there was prior collusion between the two countries.

By August 1970, close to 800,000 barrels per day were cut from the oil output of Occidental and other oil companies operating in Libya, on the grounds of protecting the fields from premature exhaustion.

Libyan oil possesses two advantages for Western Europe. It is

[1] See *PPS*, January 1971, p. 10.

[2] *MEES* estimates that aid at $50 million: *MEES*, 25 December 1970, p. 2; by comparison Tapline's annual payment to the Syrian Government prior to the puncturing of the line was about $4 million. Repairs made late in January 1971 took in fact 12 hours to complete, and followed on the company's acceptance to double its payments to the Syrian Government: *MEES Supplement*, 19 February 1971.

147

almost free from sulphur, an important characteristic for pollution-conscious Europe. In addition, Tapline and Libyan oil are ideally situated to supply Western Europe at a relatively short haul. When oil supplies from Mediterranean terminals were drastically reduced, heavy pressures were exerted on the already tight tanker market facilities. Oil was in plentiful supply for Europe in the Arabian–Persian Gulf, but the haul required a fourfold increase in tanker requirements. Tanker freight rates soared from a level of Worldscale 95 at the beginning of May to a peak of 261 early in September. Expressed in monetary value, the freight charge of transporting one barrel of crude from the Arabian-Persian Gulf to Northwestern Europe rose from $1.10 to $3.00 over that period.[1]

The circumstances favoured Libya. Further cuts in supplies could be threatened; Occidental was feeling the pinch acutely; the winter season was getting close; freight rates were rocketing; and the demand for petroleum products in Western Europe was exceeding industry expectations. Libya's strong bargaining position was reinforced by disappointments in the development of the European nuclear energy programme. European coal and hydroelectric power are not, furthermore, so closely competitive with fuel oil to make up readily for shortages in oil imports, not to mention inelasticities of supply.

Consequently, Libyan leadership was able to obtain an increase in government take consistent with the comparative economic advantage of Libyan crude oil in relation to the Arabian–Persian Gulf crude. The terms of the settlement with Occidental were announced on 4 September 1970, and the company was authorized to get back to 700,000 barrels per day production.

Other independent companies (Amerada, Continental, and Marathon) – also largely dependent on Libyan crude – settled soon after, and the international majors followed suit lest their production be stopped. In fact Shell, the last major company to hold out, had its output share in the Oasis field (150,000 barrels per day) suspended in September 1970.[2] Caltex, jointly owned by Socal and Texaco, was first among the majors to fall into line after the independents settled. Both companies own 60 per cent of Tapline's throughput, and their rather tight tanker situation did not allow them much scope for manoeuvres. Losing Libyan output would have required them to lift oil from their concessions in the Arabian–Persian Gulf, a fourfold increase in the haul for their European markets. They had little spare

[1] *PPS*, October 1970, p. 358.
[2] See *PPS*, October 1970, p. 379.

tanker capacity of their own, and the cost of chartering new tonnage would be greatly in excess of the increase in revenues demanded by the Libyan government.

The 1970 agreements with the oil companies in Libya generally provide for, first, an increase of 30 cents per barrel in the posted price of 40° API crude oil to $2.53, effective from 1 September 1970 and rising further by 2 cents per barrel a year to reach $2.63 in 1975, and, second, an increase in the income tax rates, in lieu – so the agreements go – of payments retroactive to 1965 on the price revision. The 2 cents per barrel per year increase until 1975 – which is not matched by the Arabian–Persian Gulf countries – is explained by the sulphur differential in favour of Libyan crude. Libya made full use of this quality advantage, which is becoming increasingly important. Desulphurization costs range between 40 and 60 cents per barrel in the current state of technology. The increase in the tax rates was from 50 to 54–55·5 per cent for most companies. For Occidental, it was 58 per cent; the 'surcharge' was in exchange for relieving the company of a financial commitment it agreed to originally in its 1966 concession contract: the allocation of 5 per cent of its pretax net profits to agricultural development schemes in Libya.[1] These changes increased the Libyan government take by an average of 27 cents a barrel.

Following Libya's price increases in October 1970, the owner companies of IPC, on their own initiative, raised posted prices of Iraqi crudes at the East Mediterranean terminal by 20 cents a barrel. The Iraqis were not content with that increase, and asked for increases equal to those of Libya. The companies justified the smaller increase for Iraq by pointing out that Iraqi crude enjoys lower freight and quality advantages.[2] The companies agreed to pay 7 cents per barrel on oil exports from Southern Iraq, and 6 cents per barrel on oil exports from Mediterranean terminals beginning 1 January 1971, on account of back settlements, estimated at about $200 million, for the 1964–70 years on this item,[2] and other tax issues outstanding since 1956.[3]

The Libyan settlement was a watershed, not only for Mediterranean crudes, but for all oil exporting countries. International companies which had long balked at conceding Libya's demands for fear of

[1] For details, see *MEES*, 16 October 1970, p. 3; and *Arab Oil Review*, Tripoli–Libya, January–February 1971, pp. 7–13.

[2] *PPS*, January 1971, p. 2.

[3] *The Baghdad Observer*, Baghdad, 19 February 1971, reproduced in OPEC *Weekly Bulletin*, 26 February 1971, pp. 3–4.

setting a precedent for other countries where they had oil producing ventures, had to come to terms eventually with these countries.

Iran, which has been most articulate in clamouring for larger oil revenues, was next in line. The Shah's government has an ambitious development plan, and oil revenues are crucial to meet its targets. Iran, moreover, is an ally of the United States and the United Kingdom, is strategically located in the Middle East, and has recently expanded economic relations with the U.S.S.R. Not to have satisfied Iran would have endangered the socio-politico-economic stability of its regime. The oil companies, with vast interests in the Middle East, could not refuse to concede Iran terms comparable to those obtained by 'younger' and smaller Libya. The Shah described the negotiations with oil companies as 'talks of destiny',[1] and threatened the companies with partial nationalization of their reserves.

The oil companies took the initiative of negotiating first with Iran among the Arabian–Persian Gulf countries, because all the majors and several independents are represented in the Iranian Consortium. There is no opportunity for one company to follow an independent course or to bend prematurely to pressures a host country might exert, as Occidental did in the case of Libya. Whatever terms they may agree on in the Consortium will be heeded elsewhere by these firms. Thus, there is no fear of intercompany competition on tax issues, and no member of the oligopoly would offer more favourable or less favourable terms to another host government. In short, competition in offering financial frills to governments is reduced.

An executive of a major company confided to this author that larger volumes of exports to Iran were contemplated (at the expense, of course, of the growth of other Arabian–Persian Gulf countries' exports) if the Iranian government would accept lower fiscal levies per unit of exports. This might have appealed to some Iranians, but would have invited certain retaliation by other countries – notably Saudi Arabia, which has the largest oil reserves in the world. Some industry sources, furthermore, rightly fear the instability that would result should they encourage the development of a tax-cutting war – cutting down on government take in order to increase exports at the expense of another country.

The Iranian settlement provided for an increase in the tax rate by 5 per cent and an increase of 9 cents per barrel in the posted price of heavy crude, effective from 14 November 1970. This worked out,

[1] *MEES*, 6 November 1970, p. 7.

according to the Iranian Prime Minister Amir Abbas Hoveyda, as an extra payment of $125 million per annum.[1]

A similar offer was obtained by Kuwait. Almost all of Kuwait's crude is the heavy type, and assuming production costs at 6 cents per barrel, and bearing in mind the expensing of royalty, the net benefit to Kuwait works out at close to 12 cents per barrel.[2] Other countries won comparable hikes in their tax rates and their posted/tax-reference prices: Abu Dhabi, Dubai, Nigeria, Muscat and Oman, Saudi Arabia, and Venezuela.

In the hope of further improvements, the OPEC XXI Conference meeting in Caracas in December 1970 passed several important resolutions, notably one calling for an upward revision of posted prices, a minimum of 55 per cent income tax rate on concessionaire companies (already obtained by, or promised to, host governments), and the elimination for tax purposes of previous (royalty and marketing) allowances from posted prices, effective January 1971. OPEC governments agreed on a unified price strategy *vis-à-vis* the oil companies, and formed ministerial committees to negotiate uniform prices tied to 'the highest Posted Price applicable in the Member Countries, taking into consideration differences in gravity and geographic location and any appropriate escalation in the future years' (Res. XXI.120). The latter price, as of early 1971, would be that of Venezuelan oil.

Bargaining for oil revenues is not confined to OPEC *vis-à-vis* international companies. It is becoming increasingly a struggle between OPEC *vis-à-vis* the developed industrial countries acting through the international companies. Indeed, when OPEC countries' bargaining for larger oil revenues early in 1971 promised to pay off handsomely, both the developed industrial countries and the international companies owned and managed by nationals or governments of these countries saw themselves on the same side of the fence. The issue is one of terms of trade and of balance of payments between the two groups of countries.

Indeed, the industrial countries reacted promptly and forcefully to OPEC's attempt to effect to their detriment a further gain from the international oil trade. At the time company negotiators were in Tehran at the request of OPEC countries, government representatives of major oil consuming states met in Washington several times in January 1971 at the initiative of the U.S. government,[3] and also in

---

[1] *MEES Supplement*, 18 December 1970, p. 1.

[2] *MEES*, 27 November 1970, p. 1–2.

[3] See 'Nixon Moves to Aid Foreign Oil Talks', *The Oil and Gas Journal*, 25 January 1971.

Paris at OECD headquarters, where all the major industrial developed countries of North America, Western Europe, and Japan are represented. One oil industry official boasted then that 'discussions have been under way with officials of numerous countries in the last few days. All major Western industrialized nations are with us.'[1] Oil company representatives, it is pertinent to note, are retained as experts in OECD national delegations.

In giving support to the international oil companies, major industrial governments overcame their differences, notably France, known for its independent oil policy under President de Gaulle.[2] Moreover, the U.S. Justice Department offered an advisory opinion that it does not regard the joining of U.S. companies with other international companies to negotiate with OPEC countries a violation of antitrust laws, so long as 'the sole purpose of the oil companies' joint action is to resist unreasonable or unwarranted demands for higher revenues which raise the cost of petroleum and petroleum products to the consuming countries, principally in Europe and Japan'.[3] The chief of the U.S. Justice Department's Antitrust Division, Richard McLaren, explained that the antitrust clearances companies obtained in mid-January were intended to enable them to exert jointly 'a countervailing force to minimize the adverse price effects on consumers'.[4]

In mid-January 1971, President Nixon sent Under-Secretary of State John N. Irwin II on an emergency mission to Iran, Kuwait, and Saudi Arabia, 'to urge them to adopt a more temperate attitude', as one U.S. trade journal put it.[5] Henry Bellmon, a U.S. Republican senator from Oklahoma (an oil producing state) attacked, in a speech on the Senate floor early in February 1971, the role of the Nixon Administration (also Republican) in trying to use its influence to prevent an increase in the price of OPEC oil. He argued that the visit of U.S. officials to the Middle East at that time tended to prove 'the determination of our Government to force the governments of OPEC to sell their crude oil at the lowest possible price' and protested 'this unprecedented and holy involvement of our Government in a heavy-handed act of neo-colonialism which can only be resented by

[1] *The Wall Street Journal*, 18 January 1971, p. 4.
[2] Even the French state-owned company ERAP favoured the concerted action of international companies, although it refrained from joining formally that group: ERAP, *Bulletin Mensuel d'Informations Elf*, Paris, 25 January 1971, pp. 1–2 and 7.
[3] *The Wall Street Journal*, 28 January 1971, p. 4.
[4] *Ibid.*, 8 March 1971, p. 21; and *Oil & Gas Journal*, 15 March 1971, p. 28.
[5] 'Is a Cartel Next for Oilmen', *Business Week*, New York, 23 January 1971, p. 71.

and damaging to developing nations through the world. . . . Many of these countries are single resource countries and that single resource is oil. Through the sale of their oil to industrial nations many countries – Nigeria, Indonesia, Iran, Venezuela, Saudi Arabia, and many others – hope to earn the funds their governments need for better schools, better transportation facilities, better health programs, and more adequate diets for their people'. He stated that the U.S. State Department was 'working hand in glove with officers of the big international oil companies to force OPEC to sell their single resource for bargain basement prices', and concluded that the United States should 'help, not harm these nations' efforts to help themselves'.[1]

Most international oil companies agreed to join forces to negotiate as a unit with OPEC countries on various tax issues. The group, formed on 15 January 1971, originally comprised 15 leading companies; the number rose two weeks later to 22 companies. There were 16 U.S. companies (Jersey, Texaco, Mobil, Gulf, Socal, Continental, Occidental, Atlantic Richfield, Marathon, Amerada Hess, W. R. Grace, N. B. Hunt, Ashland, Aminoil, Sohio, and Signal); six West European (Shell, BP, CFP, Petrofina of Belgium, Gelsenberg of West Germany, and Hispanoil of Spain); and one Japanese (Arabian Oil Co.). In 1971, these companies produced about 85 per cent of OPEC oil. One U.S. trade source claimed that this group of companies 'issued an ultimatum of their own, outlining terms under which they would negotiate price increases and changes in operating procedures'.[2]

The Shah referred to the grouping of international companies and the support granted to them by their parent countries of the industrially advanced West as an example of 'economic imperialism and neocolonialism'. He warned that if Western governments intervene on the companies' side, and 'try to defend their interests, that would mean a terrible crisis between those countries, and the oil producing countries and the countries not yet fully developed. Then anything could happen, not only the stoppage of oil, but a much more dangerous crisis – a rebellion of the have-nots against the haves, and if this starts one day, it will be beyond my control'.[3]

Negotiations between the oil companies and an OPEC ministerial committee consisting of the representatives of Iran, Iraq, and Saudi Arabia – who also represented Abu Dhabi, Kuwait, and Qatar – first stalled on the subject of countries to be covered in the

[1] *Oil & Gas Journal*, 15 February 1971, p. 35.
[2] *Business Week*, 23 January 1971, p. 71.
[3] *The New York Times*, 25 January 1971, p. 12.

prospected agreement. OPEC wanted a regional agreement to cover crude oil exports from the Arabian–Persian Gulf; the companies wanted an agreement to cover all OPEC member countries. The companies demanded a global settlement in order to avoid a spiral of successive demands and on 16 January 1971 their terms were put to OPEC governments as follows:

It is therefore our proposal that an all-embracing negotiation should be commenced between representatives of ourselves, together with such other oil companies as wish to be associated with this proposal, on the one hand, and OPEC as representing all its Member Countries on the other hand, under which an overall and durable settlement would be achieved.

With a view to insuring the stability and mutual respect of contractual arrangements and to demonstrate our genuine desire to achieve such a settlement, we are for our part prepared now to offer, in good faith and in furtherance of our mutual interests, albeit in general terms, the broad lines of a settlement which we could envisage. This would contain:

(A) A revision to the posted prices of all crudes in all Member Countries of OPEC and with provision that the new levels should be subject to a moderate annual adjustment against the yardstick of 'worldwide inflation' or similar criterion.

(B) A further temporary transportation adjustment for Libyan crudes, with appropriate adjustments for other 'short haul' crudes, such adjustments to vary both up and down by reference to a freight escalator.

(C) No further increase in the tax rate percentage beyond current rates, no retroactive payments, and no obligatory re-investment.

(D) Foregoing all to be firm for a period of five years from the date of settlement, after which the foregoing terms would be subject to review.[1]

The financial terms were another difficulty in these negotiations. The OPEC Arabian–Persian Gulf governments asked on 19 January 1971 for increases in tax payments (through higher postings and elimination of allowances) on oil exports starting with an average 45 cents a barrel of 40° API gravity in 1971 and rising to 80 cents a barrel in 1975. The companies countered by offering 9·1 cents rising to 22 cents. The Extraordinary OPEC Conference that had been slated for 23–25 January was postponed to give the companies additional

[1] Text of Oil Companies' Message to OPEC States in *PIW*, 25 January 1971, p. 6.

time to reconsider their offer, and the companies came on 30 January with an improved offer of 16·4 cents for 1971 rising to 26 cents for 1975. The OPEC Committee, still unsatisfied, brought down on 2 January its demand to a so-called rock-bottom of 30 cents for 1971 rising to 53 cents in 1975[1].

The companies failed, however, to respond to OPEC's rock-bottom demand. Thereupon, the OPEC XXII Conference met on 3 February and issued one of the strongest resolutions OPEC countries have ever agreed on. The resolution was, for the first time, mandatory. It obligated all member countries concerned to deny concessionaire companies oil, should they refuse to comply with OPEC's minimum demands for the Gulf area. These demands were to be enforced by legislative measures starting 15 February 1971, if the companies would not accede by negotiation. The OPEC XXII Conference accordingly resolved:

... that each Member Country exporting from Gulf terminals shall introduce on the 15th of February the necessary legal and/or legislative measures for the implementation of the objectives embodied in Resolution XXI.120. In the event that any oil company concerned fails to comply with these legal and/or legislative measures within seven days from the date of their adoption in all the countries concerned, Member Countries Abu Dhabi, Algeria, Iran, Iraq, Kuwait, Libya, Qatar, Saudi Arabia and Venezuela shall take appropriate measures including total embargo on the shipment of crude oil and petroleum products by such company.

In case the oil companies operating in the Member Countries concerned express their willingness to comply with the minimum requirements agreed upon by the six Member Countries bordering the Gulf on the implementation of the objectives of Resolution XXI.120 before the expiry of the time limit set out above, then the Member Countries concerned shall refrain from resorting to the legal and/or legislative measures referred to above.

A day before the deadline, the companies agreed to Gulf countries' minimum financial terms, and accepted to raise government take from an average of 30 cents per barrel in 1971 (representing a 30 per cent increase over government income earlier in the year) to an average of 50 cents per barrel in 1975. In quid pro quo, the companies obtained 'security of supply and stability of financial arrangements' for a period of five years. This meant principally that there would be

[1] See details in *PIW*, 22 February 1971, p. 6; also *MEES Supplement*, 19 February 1971, and *PPS*, March 1971, pp. 82–3.

no leapfrogging among OPEC Gulf countries for better financial terms, and no production restrictions or suspensions aimed at obtaining better financial terms. Moreover, these countries agreed to the companies' wish to limit 'short-haul' premium payable by oil companies on Libyan crude to 21·5 cents per barrel. Libya and Algeria could not count, therefore, on the other OPEC countries if a showdown resulted from any demands outside the framework of OPEC resolutions XXI.120 and XXII.130, and the Tehran agreement of 14 February 1971. OPEC ministerial sources indicated that the Tehran agreement offered more than was provided in the OPEC XXI Conference in Caracas.[1]

Commenting on these price increases, one industry executive considers OPEC oil to remain commercially more attractive than other sources of energy: 'While a relatively stiff price has been paid, requiring substantial increases in product prices, oil continues to represent a highly attractive and competitive form of energy in relation to alternatives.'[2]

After the Tehran agreement, the Libyan government and the oil group carried strenuous negotiations. An agreement was reached on 2 April 1971. It offered Libya better terms than the companies agreed to pay that country in accordance with the Tehran settlement, but substantially less than Libya's set 'non-negotiable' terms. The upshot of the Libyan accord is a rise in government take from $1.378 a barrel on 1 January 1970 to $2.015 on 20 March 1971, gradually rising to $2.157 on 1 January 1975 – assuming the reopening of the Suez Canal by 1973.[3]

[1] *MEES*, 19 February 1971, pp. 3 and 10.
[2] Carl Burnett, Mobil Oil, 'Significance of New Trends in Crude Oil Pricing.' New York, 1 March 1971 – paper submitted to the UN Panel of Experts on Projections of Demand and Supply of Crude Petroleum and Products, New York, 9–18 March 1971 – not published.
[3] See *PIW Supplements*, 5 April 1971 and 12 April 1971; and *MEES Supplement*, 9 April 1971.

Chapter 7
BARGAINING FOR ECONOMIC BENEFITS: TERMS OF TRADE

The previous chapter has discussed OPEC's role in bargaining for larger government revenues. The second form of economic benefits accruing from the production and export of petroleum are those derived by the nation, including income accruing to the state as well as to workers, suppliers, contractors, and others. These global benefits derived from the oil industry and retained by individual oil exporting countries must be analysed in relation to the cost of commodities they import – the terms of trade.

For several developing countries, notably OPEC countries, large exports and favourable terms are necessary for economic development. Naturally, the terms of trade are of considerable concern to OPEC nations, and have often been dealt with as a first priority. OPEC and company methods for measurement differ, and the results vary. The author has found it necessary, for his analysis, to devise new concepts of terms of trade. Perfect accuracy and reliability in the statistical measurement of these concepts cannot be achieved, but a beginning must be ventured, no matter how imperfect. Subject to limitations, the author concludes this chapter with several inferences.

A. *The Significance of Terms of Trade*

The majority of the OPEC countries depend on the oil industry for large proportions of their national income, their balance-of-payments receipts (see Table 7.1), and their fiscal budget.[1] Their ability to increase their productive capacity, to diversify their domestic economic structure (specifically, to import capital goods) or borrow for developmental projects and repay debts, depends on the adequacy

[1] See, for example, L. E. Preston, *Trade Patterns in the Middle East* (Washington D.C.: American Enterprise Institute, October 1970), p. 6; and El Mallakh. *op. cit.*, pp. 7–13.

Table 7.1

VALUE OF PETROLEUM AS A PERCENTAGE OF EXPORTS FOR SELECTED COUNTRIES, 1961–70

	1961	1962	1963	1964	1965	1966	1967	1968	1969	1970
Iran	84·8	88·2	88·3	88·6	87·2	87·6	90·6	89·7	88·7	88·7
Nigeria	19·1	15·3	10·6	15·0	25·4	32·5	29·8	17·1	42·8	57·4
Iraq	94·4	90·5	92·9	94·0	93·3	92·0	91·9	92·6	93·1	93·7
Venezuela	92·1	92·7	92·6	93·4	93·0	92·4	92·3	92·8	91·3	90·2
Indonesia			38·6	36·8	38·4	30·0	36·0	38·9	44·9	34·8
Libya	51·0	93·1	97·5	97·7	98·4	98·7	99·0	99·6	99·7	99·6

Source: IMF, *International Financial Statistics.*

of their foreign exchange receipts, which are a function of both export prices and volumes. The significance of gain from international trade can be related to a country's economic welfare as measured by real per capita income.

The terms at which oil is internationally traded will not only reflect the relative performance of the two major parties concerned (the exporting and importing countries), but will also determine the size and composition of future international oil trade flows. If OPEC countries were to ask for excessively high prices (as compared with prices of competing sources of energy), the flow of international oil trade will be reduced (notwithstanding the low production cost of their vast reserves); conversely, if major consuming countries exact an excessively low price (as compared with prices OPEC countries may get in future years or prices they consider 'acceptable'), the OPEC countries would be unwilling to dispose of their oil. In a world where governmental policies and actions loom large in economic relations, the demand and supply for oil cannot be usefully analysed in the context of a competitive model; conditions of bilateral oligopoly are more relevant to the international petroleum industry. Under these conditions, governmental action, like that of individual large firms in highly concentrated industries, can have a marked impact on the flow of resources and commodities, compared to what would occur in a perfectly competitive model.

The concept of the 'terms of trade', according to one eminent economist, 'is perhaps the major contribution of economics to the total study of society'. Boulding defines terms of trade broadly as 'the ratio of inputs to outputs of any individual or group'. He admits, however, that 'when the inputs and outputs are heterogeneous aggregates of all sorts of things, as they usually are, the problem of measurement of necessity involves valuation, although the concept of improvement or worsening in the terms of trade does not necessarily depend on exact valuation'.[1]

Boulding argues that citizens have also terms of trade *vis-à-vis* their government. Should they feel that their terms of trade have turned unduly unfavourable, they may resort to civil disobedience and eventually change governments, either peacefully or by revolution.[2]

[1] Kenneth E. Boulding, *Economics as a Science* (New York: McGraw Hill, 1970), pp. 19 and 21. Boulding's concept of terms of trade refers to the ratio of payments made for inputs to payments received for outputs; the conventional 'net barter' or 'price' terms of trade concept refers to the ratio of price or value per unit of exports to the price or value per unit of imports.

[2] *Ibid.*, p. 21.

This interpretation can be extrapolated to the international level. Developing countries, if they feel their terms of trade are turning intolerably against them, may attempt to change the system and principles of international co-operation and partnership to their advantage.

The anxiety of the poor developing countries regarding their terms of trade *vis-à-vis* the rich industrial countries can therefore be a source of international political tension. Several economists have criticized the international trade system, and impute to it a general bias in favour of rich nations. Myrdal, among others, believes that the developed nations, with only a quarter of the world population, nevertheless possess the real economic and political power. It might be hoped they would be more yielding to the demands of less developed countries for 'distributional justice', but the governments of the developed countries are politically unwilling to call on their citizens to increase aid. Myrdal reflects sadly on the economic interrelations between the two groups, and on human solidarity:

> The richer nations, who are a tiny minority but exercise most of the real power in the non-Soviet world and are expected to make all the sacrifices, are not prepared to go along. The basis of human solidarity does not exist that would lead them to permit the extension to the poorer rest of the world of the solidarity principles of their own happy and progressive national welfare states. To most of their peoples the very idea is absurd.[1]

These so-called unbalanced international economic relations were largely responsible for the creation of OPEC in 1960, of the Inter-governmental Council of Copper Exporting Countries (CIPEC) in 1967, and, more important, of the United Nations Conference on Trade and Development (UNCTAD) in 1964. The first Secretary-General of UNCTAD pointed to the grave political significance of a deterioration in the terms of trade of developing *vis-à-vis* developed countries and referred to opportunities for remedying the situation:

> The starting point of this conference is a clear political concept which has apparently ceased to be a subject of controversy: that the prosperous countries of the world should not neglect the problems of the economic periphery, where two-thirds of the world's population live in very precarious conditions. But there is a basic difference between recognition of this concept and its translation

[1] Gunnar Myrdal, *An International Economy, Problems and Prospects* (New York: Harper, 1956), p. 237.

160

into a vigorous policy of international co-operation designed to bring about rapid development in this very vast part of the world. Never before has there been an opportunity like the present of quickly solving, thanks to the enormous potential of contemporary technology, the problem of poverty and its inherent evils in the developing countries. Yet never before have such distressing tensions, as those which beset the developing world, emerged on such a huge scale.[1]

As a result of the imbalance between rich and poor, and the consequent building up of 'distressing tensions', Prebisch contended that there was an imperative need for a fundamental change in the principles of international co-operation among the two groups of nations. He was, however, over-optimistic in his hope of quickly solving the world's problem of poverty. During the UNCTAD conference, heads of delegations from various developing countries, including oil exporting countries, joined Prebisch in expressing anxiety at the deterioration of their terms of trade, and concern for the adverse impact on their development programmes and stability.[2] This concern was also voiced at the International Monetary Fund, for example by the Iraqi Finance Minister, who observed that the rich industrial countries had pursued a deliberate policy of keeping raw material prices 'at their lowest levels'.[3]

The first Secretary-General of OPEC, Fuad Rouhani, considered that prior to OPEC's establishment, the destinies of the oil industry lay solely in the hands of concessionaire companies and major industrial oil consuming countries; the producing countries were merely collectors of such funds as the companies chose to pay.[4] He, like other spokesmen from OPEC countries, reflected on the rich

[1] Statement by Raùl Prebisch, Secretary-General of UNCTAD, published in *Proceedings of the United Nations Conference on Trade and Development*, Geneva, 23 March–16 June 1964, Vol. II, *Policy Statements* (New York, 1966), p. 76. For a discussion of the Prebisch–Singer–Myrdal view on the secular deterioration in the terms of trade of developing countries, see, for example: John Pincus, *Trade, Aid and Development, The Rich and Poor Nations* (New York: McGraw-Hill, 1967), pp. 131–4; and Gerald M. Meier and Robert E. Baldwin, *Economic Development, Theory, History, Policy* (New York: John Wiley & Sons, 1957), pp. 229–37.

[2] See statements on the deterioration of oil prices by heads of delegations from Algeria, Iran, Iraq, Kuwait, Saudi Arabia, and Venezuela; in UNCTAD *op. cit.*, respectively on pp. 94–101, 230–3, 233–5, 253–4, 331–2, and 405–7.

[3] International Monetary Fund, *Summary Proceedings 1960* (Washington, 1960), p. 73,

[4] This view is disputed by ENI, the state-owned oil company of Italy, a major oil consuming country. See p. 58 above.

L   161

industrial countries' denial of a fair price to OPEC countries in relation to import prices from industrial countries:

> This situation [the decline in primary commodity prices], which applies to petroleum too, is aggravated by the fact that the prices of manufactured goods which our countries have to buy from the industrialized countries continue to increase year after year. On the validity of this point, which has been questioned by the oil companies, we now have the authoritative words of no less a person than the President of the United States [J. F. Kennedy], who in the course of a visit to Bonn only a week ago said 'We can't help but be concerned by the fact that the price of raw materials of the underdeveloped world steadily declined relative to the price of manufactured goods, and therefore the economic position in some ways is worse in spite of all the aid we've given. So, unless we work hard and progressively and with imagination and idealism, we may find ourselves a rich area in a poor world which is subject to all the influences that poverty brings with it and ultimately we would be affected'.[1]

OPEC's IVth Conference held in April–June 1962 calls implicitly for the abandonment of all pretensions that competitive market forces prevail in the international oil industry, and recommends instead an administered price system. The OPEC Conference specified its 'rational price structure' as one linking 'crude oil prices to an index of prices of goods which the Member Countries need to import' (Res. IV.32).

This formulation, however, overlooks the fact that supply and demand conditions for various sources of energy in major consuming countries or areas are not constant in the long run; there can be significant cross-elasticities between oil and other sources of energy within certain price ranges. Therefore, 'better' price terms of trade can result in 'worse' income terms of trade for oil exporting countries, under conditions of high cross-elasticity between oil and other sources of energy.[2]

Probably the most eloquent expression of anxiety regarding the deterioration of the developing countries' terms of trade came from President Houari Boumedienne of Algeria upon opening OPEC's XXth Conference held in Algiers on 24 June 1970. He blamed the

[1] OPEC, *Speech Delivered by Fuad Rouhani, Secretary-General, at the IInd Consultative Meeting* (Geneva, 1 July 1963), pp. 3–4.
[2] For definition of terms of trade concepts, see section C below.

rich industrial nations for exploiting the poor primary producer countries:

The fact that the producer countries have been maintained as depositories of raw materials, that there has been a constant deterioration in what are known as the terms of trade, means that the major part of the benefits produced by this natural wealth goes to the rich countries because the mechanism which regulates prices and which, in a more general manner, establishes the form of present economic relations internationally, is such that the predominant feature of a colonial relationship still prevails in essence and in effect.

This serious imbalance harms our relations with the rich countries and poses an acute problem to all countries supplying raw materials. The one-sidedness of this relationship has reached such an extent that the conscience of the world has been awakened to it and the United Nations Organization, to which belong both the undeveloped countries and those which, until now, have been the beneficiaries of the system, ranks it among its preoccupations. By setting up specialized bodies, committees, commissions or working parties, the United Nations has been the forum for a debate that has lasted for some years in a number of international conferences.

In this debate, Algeria feels it useful to point out that in reality the problem cannot be dealt with solely within the framework of a theoretical, philosophical or economic debate and that, because of its very nature, it is in fact the continuation, albeit in another form, of the battle that formerly colonized peoples, or those economically exploited by another have had to wage for their freedom.

If we look at the problem from the viewpoint of the underdeveloped countries we see that it must be conceived of in terms of a struggle and that implies a commitment to a clear and consistent policy involving effort and sacrifice and directed towards revolutionary changes.[1]

These views[2] are quoted here not because they are necessarily valid, but because of the influence they have had in shaping public

[1] See *OPEC Bulletin*, No. 5, 13 August 1970.

[2] Similar views have been expounded by the Shah in his news conference of 24 January 1971 in Tehran: *MEES Supplement*, 29 January 1971. Also the Prime Minister of Iran, Amir Abbas Hoveyda, addressing the Iranian Parliament on 8 December 1970: *MEES Supplement*, 18 December 1970, pp. 2–3; the Secretary-General of OPEC, Nadim Pachachi, in *MEES*, 1 January 1971, p. 6; and President Rafael Caldera at OPEC's XXIst Conference in Caracas: *OPEC Bulletin*, 20 January 1971.

opinion and affecting inter-governmental action among oil exporting countries. Some Western economists share the fears expressed by spokesmen of developing countries exporting raw materials. One economist reproaches his country – the United States – for its obvious inconsistencies between the domestic and the international features of American commodity policies. He forthrightly exposes U.S. contradictions:

> Parity between prices paid and received by farmers remains the domestic standard, but at the water's edge we rightly renounce the terms of trade approach to stabilizing price relationships between primary products and manufactured goods. We endorse historical share of world markets as a rule applicable to our cotton exports, but would be considerably embarrassed if it were also applied to American exports of soybeans, corn, or inedible fats. International commodity agreements were long resisted for imported commodities subject to severe cyclical instability in industrial demand, but accepted and indeed promoted for an American export like wheat and also for an import like sugar, inasmuch as lower prices in world markets would have proved embarrassing to domestic commodity programs. Concern is expressed for the international competitive position of America's exports; but we forego the advantages of cheap raw materials, whether cotton, petroleum, or the non-ferrous metals.[1]

This interpretation is shared by other experts of international trade. Kindleberger, for example, has branded the U.S. position as 'inconsistent in the extreme', and claims that the government is following double standards of behaviour in the international and domestic fields, in response to conflicting pressures. He states:

> The United States' position on the international price question is hardly a consistent or easy one. All the devices so patronizingly dismissed as uneconomic in international trade are fully employed within the country. Although individuals may be consistent, opposing or supporting widespread interference with the price system at home and abroad, the net effect of the asymmetry in their success (the opponents of the price system winning in domestic, the supporters in foreign economic policy) has been to make the net position inconsistent in the extreme.[2]

[1] Boris C. Swerling, Princeton University Essays in International Finance, *Current Issues in Commodity Policy*, June 1962, p. 34.

[2] C. P. Kindleberger, *The Terms of Trade, A European Case Study*, The Technology Press and John Wiley, New York, 1956, p. 313.

The United States is not alone in this respect. The EEC agricultural policy also follows a similar pattern of policy objectives.

B. *OPEC and Industry Measures of Terms of Trade*

OPEC's studies have used throughout the concept of 'price terms of trade', and advocated that these terms have worsened for member countries. Whether this is true for major oil exporting countries deserves close scrutiny. Such an examination entails prior agreement, first, on a so-called normal or representative base year or period, and, second, on methods of computing export and import price or unit value indices. Agreement on these points is not always easy to reach, and differing results obtained by various researchers are not comparable. In its first analysis of terms of trade, OPEC took 1953 as a base year, and noted that 'posted crude oil prices in the Middle East are today [1962] lower than they have been at any time since mid-1953'.[1] It compared this decline with the increase in the UN unit value world export index of manufactured goods, which rose from a level of 100 in 1953 to 107 in 1962.

Shell, in an official comment on the OPEC memoranda, questioned the validity of figures quoted in the case of Iran: 'The prices of goods imported by Iran in 1961 were more than 10 per cent below the 1953 level.'[2] The Iranian Prime Minister, in December 1970, stated that the prices of manufactured goods imported by Iran from the developed countries rose by 20 per cent over the past decade.[3]

In 1970, the OPEC Secretariat maintained its use of indices of manufactured goods and of posted prices in computing OPEC countries' oil terms of trade, and adopted 1958 as base year (Table 7.2). It concluded that the terms of trade of Middle East OPEC countries fell from 100 in 1958 to 81 in 1968. But these import and export price or unit value indices are inadequate for measuring changes in OPEC countries' gains from international oil trade. The UN unit value world export index of manufactured goods does not measure variations in the actual cost of imports to OPEC countries, and the posted price index does not measure variations in economic benefits effectively derived by these countries from the export of crude oil.

In another more elaborate study, the OPEC Secretariat uses the

[1] OPEC, *Explanatory Memoranda on the OPEC Resolutions*, April–June 1962, p. 5.
[2] *MEES Supplement*, 24 August 1962, p. 1.
[3] *MEES Supplement*, 18 December 1970, p. 2.

actual c.i.f. prices OECD countries pay for importing crude from the OPEC area. Its statistics show a substantial decline from 1960 to 1967 in the cost of oil imports c.i.f. made by the rich developed countries of OECD. The decline was from $21.32 per ton in 1960 to $16.04 per ton in 1967, a drop of 24·8 per cent. The Secretariat then subtracts

Table 7.2

OPEC (MIDDLE EAST) TERMS OF TRADE
(Base Year 1958)

Year	*UN Unit Value World Export Index of Manufactured Goods*	*Index of Posted Prices*	*Terms of Trade of Crude Oil*
1958	100	100	100
1959	99	91	92
1960	101	89	88
1961	102	88	86
1962	102	88	86
1963	103	88	85
1964	104	88	85
1965	106	88	83
1966	109	88	81
1967	110	88	80
1968	109	88	81

Source: *OPEC: An Example of Sub-Regional Co-operation and Trade Expansion,* a study prepared by the OPEC Secretariat and submitted to UNCTAD's International Group on Trade Expansion, Economic Co-operation and Regional Integration among Developing Countries, July 1970 (not published).

from the OECD c.i.f. oil import prices imputed tanker freight charges to reach the f.o.b. export prices of OPEC oil. Its statistical findings show that the imputed f.o.b. export price of oil fell from $15.20 per ton in 1960 to $11.16 per ton in 1967, or by 27 per cent. It contrasts this decline with a rise of 5·6 per cent in the weighed unit cost of OPEC countries' composite imports from OECD over the same period of time.[1]

[1] Farouk Husseini, then Chief of OPEC's Economics Department, 'Some aspects of Trade Between OPEC and OECD Groups of Countries' delivered at OPEC's Petroleum Seminar held in Vienna, 30 June–6 July 1969, and reproduced as a *MEES Supplement,* 10 October 1969.

It is interesting that in this study the OPEC Secretariat has used, for the first time, imputed realized prices of oil exports from the OPEC area to the OECD countries, in preference to posted prices. This author holds that f.o.b. imputed realized prices, like posted prices, do not represent the value of oil exports to the exporting countries for reasons presented in the remaining sections of this chapter.

From the point of view of several oil importing countries, the realized price c.i.f. (not the posted price) represents effectively the per unit net expenditures made by them for imports. These countries are net oil importers which do not have international oil companies operating in the OPEC area and consequently do not gain from the repatriation of these companies' profits and salaries, or from other disbursements in the mother country – as is the case with countries with international oil companies (see pp. 54–6).

In contrast with OPEC's analyses, a study by the largest oil company in the world (Jersey) takes into account the limitations of using the posted price index and the UN world index of manufactured goods. Nevertheless, for the sake of defending its position, the company uses the same indices. The UN world index reports changes in the f.o.b. unit value of manufactured exports. Accordingly, these figures do not account for shipping and handling charges, freight, and insurance incurred by importers. Moreover, it is improper to use a world manufactured goods index to measure changes in the price level of imports by OPEC countries; these countries import substantial quantities of food and raw materials (close to one-fifth of total imports), and the composition of their manufactured imports may vary widely from that of the world index.[1]

Jersey chose 1952 as the base year, arguing its suitability on the grounds that it preceded the abnormally high increase in the price of raw materials toward the end of the Korean conflict in 1953. The company found that 'the prices of both crude oil and manufactured goods are today [1963–64] higher than in 1952; in 1963 the posted price of Arabian crude was about 5 per cent higher, while the index of manufactured goods' prices showed a gain of only 3 per cent'.[2]

It is curious that Jersey should choose 1952, which was also a year of war in Korea. But posted prices of Middle East crudes did not

[1] The author's conclusion derives from statistical computations for OPEC countries which report foreign trade data to the UN Secretariat. He also interviewed Mr Han-son Chu, chief of methodology at the UN International Trade Statistics Centre in New York on 21 December 1970.

[2] Jersey, *Middle East Oil Revenues in Relation to the Price of Imported Goods*, p. 1.

increase from 1950 to mid-1953 despite the outbreak of the Korean conflict and despite the industry's boycott of Iranian oil exports after nationalization in 1951. Jersey's selection of 1952 for comparison was tantamount to choosing crude oil prices for 1950, a year giving a relatively depressed base. By contrast, the UN index for manufactured goods rose sharply (by 20 per cent) from 1950 to 1952. So the base year of 1952 for manufactured goods is comparatively inflated.

As a result, we have two price bases, one for crude oil, which had been completely insensitive for some three years to the Korean war and the stoppage of Iranian oil exports, and one for manufactured products, which had been substantially affected by that war. The end result of comparing the two price indices with their peculiarly chosen bases has been to give for later years an apparently higher increase for crude oil prices, as compared with manufactured goods.

It is not the intention here to imply that Jersey's choice is more partisan than OPEC's. In reality, each party was trying to use base years and statistics to make the best possible case. Furthermore, there is no necessary relationship between whether one year or another is the 'right' base year yielding the 'proper' posted or tax-reference price to be used in computing a host government's revenues from an oil venture. This whole line of argument overlooks the basic economic variables underlying conditions of supply, demand, market structure and control, and relative bargaining strength of protagonists; all these variables affect prices and terms of trade, and, consequently, the benefits derived by host governments.

In explaining the 1950 to mid-1953 stability in crude oil prices in the Middle East, it is important to point out that, prior to 1960, posted prices were set and changed at the initiative, and, to a certain extent, discretion of the few vertically integrated international oil companies. Their method did not show ready sensitivity to competitive market forces. Indeed, one major oil company, Shell, implicitly conceded this point. It contended that posted prices were set by the international integrated groups – taking into account *inter alia* the availability of crude oil supplies, the activities of competitors, and the conflicts of interest between consuming countries and producing countries.[1]

Shell, along with other major international companies, did not change Middle East posted prices in 1950–53; however, as the largest buyer of Kuwait crude from Gulf, the company had to pay higher f.o.b. realized prices in 1952–53, as compared with 1951 (see Table 7.3).

[1] Shell, *International Oil Prices* (June 1968), pp. 4–5.

Table 7.3

SELECTED PRICE DATA WITH REFERENCE TO
KUWAIT CRUDE OIL EXPORTS, 1951–71*
(U.S. cents per barrel)

Year	Average Posted Prices	Average Imputed Tax Values†	Difference
1951	165·0‡	122·0	43·0
1952	165·0‡	131·5	34·5
1953	165·0‡	132·0	33·0
1954	172·0	127·5	44·5
1955	172·0	122·0	50·0
1956	172·0	160·5	11·5
1957	179·0	169·5	10·5
1958	185·0	174·0	11·0
1959	170·0	167·5	2·5
1960	164·0	162·5	1·5
1961–63	159·0	157·5	1·5
1964–69	159·0	158·5	0·5
1970	160·1	159·6	0·5
1971	182·4	182·4	0·0

* For a barrel of gravity of 31 to 31·9 American Petroleum Institute (API) specifications.

† Prior to December 1951, there was no income tax in Kuwait, and the owners of Kuwait Oil Co. Ltd paid a fixed tonnage royalty. In accordance with the agreement of 30 December 1951 with these companies, the 1951–55 imputed values of Kuwait crude oil exports for income tax purposes were equal to the weighted average of prices actually paid to Gulf (50% owner of Kuwait Oil Co. Ltd – the other owner being Anglo-Iranian Oil Co.) by all purchasers (excluding Gulf affiliates) under long-term contracts, short-term contracts, and spot cargoes. The major buyer from Gulf so far has been Shell, buying close to half of Gulf's share in Kuwait's production on a long-term contract. Imputed tax values in 1956–58 were equal to posted prices less authorized discounts (volume discounts, and selling charge allowances) in accordance with the agreement of 11 October 1955. This agreement provided for volume discounts of 8½% of posted prices on oil sales in excess of 20 million tons per annum valid until the end of 1958, and a selling charge allowance equal to 2% of posted prices. The selling charge was reduced to 1% effective

169

1 April 1957 in accordance with agreement dated 18 December 1958. It fell to ½ cent per barrel in 1964–70 in accordance with the OPEC royalty expensing agreement of 1964. Beginning 1964, royalty was expensed subject to certain tax allowances off the posted price (Table 6.2); these are not shown in the above figures. The definition of imputed tax value is therefore strictly related to the computation of Kuwait's income tax because there was another imputed value for the same crude in computing royalty payments to the Kuwait Government in 1964–70. Since 15 February 1971, the value of Kuwait's crude in computing royalty and income tax has been the same.

‡ Anglo-Iranian Oil Co. (later BP) first reported for publication on 1 April 1953 the price of $1.50/bbl. for Kuwait crude followed by Gulf on 10 July 1953 with a price of $1.75/bbl. The two companies had the same posting of $1.72/bbl. on 17 July 1953, and they effected changes thereafter almost simultaneously. For the years 1951–52, postings for Kuwait crude were made by Mobil, which had a long-term contract for the purchase of Kuwait crude from Anglo-Iranian Oil Co.

Sources and derivations: Posted Prices are published in various trade journals, and in particular in *Platt's Oil Price Handbook & Oilmanac*.

For 1951–58, the author's imputed tax values for Kuwait crude oil exports are equal to (1) per barrel income tax payments to the Kuwait Government derived from data published by OPEC's *Annual Statistical Bulletin*, by various agencies of the Kuwait Government and by Petroleum Information Foundation Inc. of New York; (2) the per barrel notional income of the 'trading companies' which export Kuwait oil, as derived (a) from their financial statements submitted to the Companies Registration Office in London and (b) in accordance with the methods and rates stipulated by various Kuwait Government agreements with these oil companies; and (3) accounting production costs published by the Central Bank of Kuwait in its *First Annual Report* for year ending 31 March 1970, p. 24: 12 U.S. cents per barrel in 1951, 11 in 1952–53, 10 in 1954–59, 8 in 1960, 7 in 1961–64, and 6 in 1965–68.

For 1959–71, the author's imputed tax values for Kuwait crude oil exports are equal to posted prices less the selling charge allowance which was discontinued in 1971.

Posted prices in the Middle East were not only set largely at the discretion of major companies, but were not always recognized by these companies as representing the value of their oil exports when computing their fiscal obligations in host countries, since discounts of varying sizes were obtained in assessing income tax and royalty payments. Moreover, posted prices cannot be used as an adequate measure of the price of crude oil sales to third parties, or even of the transfer price of crude oil among affiliates of the same parent company.

To illustrate this point, a series of financial data for Kuwait has been compiled by the author in Table 7.3. They show that imputed tax values, those used in assessing the concessionaire's income tax obligations, were significantly lower than contemporary posted prices in the years 1951–58. The difference peaked in 1955, when imputed tax value, then based on Gulf's realized prices from sales to third parties, fell short of the posted price by as much as 50 cents per barrel. In 1951–55, posted prices averaged about 168 cents per barrel as compared with about 127 cents for realized prices. Table 7.3 reveals, possibly for the first time, the fact that Gulf, a leading international oil company, sold the major part of its Kuwait crude in the first half of the 1950s at realized prices significantly lower than contemporary posted prices. One may speculate that realized prices would have been still lower if competition among oil companies were severe and unrestrained for extended periods of time, leading to possible deterioration in prevailing posted prices. Between 1956–60, posted prices and imputed tax values have differed, but imputed tax values moved closer to the former. Since 1971, they have become identical.

In a recent paper, the Petroleum Information Foundation refuted the approach and findings of the previously mentioned OPEC study entitled 'Some Aspects of Trade Between OPEC and OECD Groups of Countries'. It argued that export prices of oil from the OPEC area do not represent the economic benefits accruing to member countries, and that OPEC's terms-of-trade ratio

$$\frac{\text{Price of OPEC Oil Exports to OECD}}{\text{Price of OPEC Imports from OECD}}$$

is not meaningful. The industry paper offers a more 'realistic' definition:

$$\frac{\text{OPEC Government Take per Unit of Oil Export.[1]}}{\text{Aggregate Price of OPEC Imports from OECD}}$$

[1] Petroleum Information Foundation, Inc. (PIF), *Oil Producing Countries and Their Capacity to Import*, background information paper No. 9, by J. V. Whittlesey New York, October 1970, 4 pp. It is the author's understanding that PIF is supported by U.S. oil companies with major interests in the Middle East.

PIF's definition is an improvement, although the numerator does not account fully for 'the income generated by oil exports for the OPEC countries', as intended. There are other items, besides government take, which should be included as constituting income generated by oil exports, as explained below.

The PIF paper notes that changes in the quality and product mix were significant in OECD/OPEC trade during the 1960–67 period, and acknowledges that they 'cannot be satisfactorily quantified'. Nevertheless, the paper states unequivocally, with no supporting evidence, that if account is taken of change in mix, price increases in OPEC's imports from OECD over 1960–67 would be 1·9 per cent, using the 1960 weights by category of imports, and 0·5 per cent, using 1967 weights. PIF compares its 10 per cent estimated increase in OPEC governments' per barrel take between 1960–67 with the foregoing estimates of increases in the price of OPEC's imports from OECD; the result is a bold deduction, namely that the 'trend over the years 1960–67 has moved in favour of OPEC rather than the reverse'. Notwithstanding the need for devising relevant definitions and for ascertaining the accuracy of figures quoted, it is questionable to this author whether one can build a trend on the basis of a two-year calculation. In a later paper, PIF admits that corrected for inflation, the government per barrel take dropped by about 12 per cent from 1959 to 1969.[1]

Not only did the oil companies refute OPEC's methods and results in computing the terms of trade, but they argued until 1970 against the principle of income parity, or the stabilizing of oil countries' terms of trade. Jersey criticized the use of emotive and subjective standards of 'fairness' or 'equity', and refused bluntly in 1964 to respond to OPEC countries' fear of impoverishment and sense of insecurity. Furthermore, Jersey questioned OPEC's right for a guarantee of future income from oil in terms of the things that can be bought with that income:

> It is not the responsibility of the oil companies or the consumers of oil to provide the OPEC member countries with a guaranteed income level or standard of living. The land occupied by the Middle East countries contains a resource of much value to the rest of the world, but the value of that resource depends on today's technology which will use the most inexpensive source of energy available with reasonable security of supply. If a cheaper source of

[1] See PIF, *A Look at the International Petroleum Industry – Profitability*, paper No. 10, February 1971, p. 2.

energy should become available, then the value of oil would fall, perhaps to zero.[1]

The economic reasoning underlying Jersey's statement is that the long-run cross-elasticities of demand between oil and other sources of energy could well lead to a decline in the demand and value of oil in favour of, for example, solid fuels, nuclear power, or solar energy.[2] However, the time span for this argument is likely to extend over several decades, too long to warrant worry by host governments about dramatic shifts in demand. Moreover, statistical figures for 1960–70 show that the price of coal has had a higher rising trend compared with fuel oil in a major market (see Chart 5.1).

Certain OPEC spokesmen invoke a 'welfare' argument regarding price. They contend that since the countries that import the bulk of internationally traded oil are rich and developed, they will not suffer by paying a few extra cents per barrel of oil. This cost will be far outweighed by the benefits to be derived by nationals of some developing countries heavily dependent on oil exports for their standard of living and development, as are nationals of Algeria, Indonesia, Iraq, Iran, Nigeria, Saudi Arabia and Venezuela. This argument in political economy and international co-operation is occasionally raised by interested parties on the grounds of promoting 'international equity and harmony'. It is a fact that the consumers of industrial nations have been enjoying considerable consumer surplus (the differential between the maximum price a consumer would be willing to pay for a commodity rather than go without it, and the price he actually pays).[3] This surplus is, however, difficult to assess.

The terms of trade argument used by OPEC spokesmen has been prompted, as noted earlier, by their utmost concern for economic development. Several oil exporting countries would like to see their posted or tax-reference prices, on which oil revenues are assessed, linked to an index of goods they need to import for their development projects, which are financed by the oil revenues. The president

[1] Jersey, *Middle East Oil Revenues in Relation to the Price of Imported Goods.*
[2] Jersey considers all types of energies as falling within the scope of its interest. It has affiliates with natural gas, coal, shale, and uranium operations. See *1967 Annual Report*, p. 10.
Many other oil companies have gas, coal, or uranium operations, such as Gulf, Continental Oil, Occidental Petroleum, Atlantic Richfield, Getty, Union Oil, and ENI.
[3] This is similar to Paul Frankel's 'consumer rent' which he admits is 'considerable': see his 'Oil Prices: Causes and Prospects', in *Supplement to Platts Oilgram Price Service*, 29 January 1971.

173

of OPEC's XXth Conference (Belaid Abdesselam, Algerian Minister of Industry and Energy) in his opening statement at the XXIst Conference in Caracas in December 1970 pointed out that the goods needed for development are manufactured goods, particularly equipment. He said:

> We should act so that the prices of our oil may be related to those of manufactured products, and especially capital goods indispensable for economic take-off, to avoid not only a further deterioration of terms of exchange between our countries and industrialized nations, but also, and above all, to try to attempt to overtake the effects of inflation in the developed countries of which we are the victims.[1]

The novelty of the preceding formulation is that it asks for developmental terms of trade for oil, which can be put as Px/Pmd, where Px is the posted or tax reference price index and Pmd is the price index of developmental equipment. Statistical evidence for one OPEC country, Saudi Arabia, shows that the unit value index of imported capital goods has been rising at a much faster rate, from 100 in 1963–64 to 135·2 in 1968–69, than the general unit value import index, which rose to only 116·6 in 1968–69.[2]

The developmental terms of trade formulation may appeal to a number of developing countries exporting primary commodities; whether the principle is acceptable to industrial countries is open to doubt. It also raises a number of difficult questions: can a global index for equipment be designed to take into account changes in quality and efficiency? Will all industrial countries, regardless of their status in the production and export of this equipment, share equally in the price changes assigned to oil imports they need along with changes in the price index for equipment? Will these oil price changes (mostly increases) apply solely to the industrial developed countries, or will developing countries be equally affected by such changes (here increases)? What will be the impact of administrative escalation of the prices of individual primary commodities on the quantities demanded?

It was a momentous precedent-setting decision when a consortium of international oil companies, with the backing of their developed parent countries, offered on 16 January 1971 'a revision of the posted

---

[1] See *OPEC Bulletin*, No. 1, 1971, p. 2.
[2] Saudi Arabian Monetary Agency (SAMA), *Annual Report*, 1388–89 A.H. (1969), 8 August 1970, p. 92.

prices of all crudes in all member countries of OPEC, and with the provision that the new levels should be subject to a moderate annual adjustment against the yardstick of "world-wide inflation" or similar criterion'. The Shah of Iran, in a press conference on 24 January 1971, suggested measuring changes in the international 'cost of living' by reference to changes in 'the prices of such products as steel or five or six other commodities which influence the cost of living'.[1]

On 15 February 1971, OPEC Arabian–Persian Gulf governments, followed by Libya in April 1971, agreed with their concessionaires to a 2·5 per cent per annum escalation rate in posted prices on account of expected world-wide inflation between 1971 and 1975. This is equivalent to an effective annual increase in governmental oil revenues per barrel of oil exports of 1·5 per cent only, given the current fiscal arrangements obtaining in host countries.

Some OPEC sources claim that this is an inadequate guarantee against inflationary pressures in the industrial countries. They argue that price increases of equipment and materials bought by the oil producing companies and the oil exporting countries themselves are likely to be higher.[2] It is suspected that OPEC countries might see their hedge against inflation in industrial countries completely wiped out by inflation rates exceeding the fixed escalation rate of 2·5 per cent of posted prices or its equivalent of 1·5 per cent of governmental per-barrel revenues. Such a situation might incite OPEC countries to ask for still higher increases. This in turn might spark further inflationary pressures, and the vicious circle may continue, with a built-in structural inflation in world trade.[3]

OPEC countries are not concerned only about inflation and linking their prices to an escalation rate. Since their receipts are in U.S. dollars or computed on the basis of that currency, they are also concerned about the devaluation of the dollar, formally or effectively. Resolution XXI.122 of December 1970 states 'that in case of changes in the parity of monies of major industrialized countries which would have an adverse effect on the purchasing power of Member Countries' oil revenues, posted or tax-reference prices should be adjusted as to reflect such changes'.

---

[1] Quoted by OPEC *Weekly Bulletin*, 29 January 1971, p. 7; and *MEES Supplement*, 29 January 1971, p. 5.

[2] *The Libyan Times*, Tripoli, 16 February 1971 quoting the *El Mujahid*, Algiers, 15 February 1971 – as reproduced in OPEC *Weekly Bulletin*, 26 February 1971, p. 2. See also, *Le Pétrole et le Gaz Arabes*, Beirut, 16 1971, pp. 23–32.

[3] See *Le Monde*, weekly English edition, Paris, 17 January 1971.

OPEC countries' fears began to materialize in May 1971. The U.S. dollar lost value *vis-à-vis* the German mark, the Swiss franc, the Dutch guilder, the Japanese yen, and several other currencies. These countries, and notably Germany, are large suppliers to several OPEC countries (particularly Middle East and North African countries).[1] Shortly thereafter, OPEC countries sought price readjustments from the oil companies to compensate for the re-alignment of major currencies, and the companies eventually agreed.

C. *The Concepts and the Tools*

There are several concepts of terms of trade. It is important to find out which concept best serves the purpose at hand, namely the measurement of changes in the distribution of gain from international oil trade. Once the relevant concept is formulated, the problem to solve will be that of statistical measurement.

The commonly used concept is that known as commodity, net barter, or price terms of trade, and it refers to the ratio of price or unit value indices of exports to imports Px/Pm.[2] Another closely related concept, known as the gross barter terms of trade, refers to the relationship of the quantum indices of imports to exports Qm/Qx. The change in the terms of trade for a given country from period t_1 to period t_2 would be favourable if $(Px_{t2}/Pm_{t2}) \geqslant (Px_{t1}/Pm_{t1})$, which signifies that its price index of exports has increased (or decreased) by a larger (or smaller) amount than the increase (or decrease) in the price index of imports – using a representative base year for comparison. In other words, the country in question can import more goods with the same quantity of exports. The two concepts of price versus gross barter terms of trade would be equal if we assume that the country under study has a balanced international trade $(Px \cdot Qx = Pm \cdot Qm)$. When trade is not balanced, the price terms of trade alone can reflect the favourable or unfavourable developments in the relative price movements of exports and imports of a particular country, and consequently in the unit cost that country has to pay for imports with its exports.

A number of authors have found the price terms of trade an inadequate tool of analysis in the measurement of changes in the distribution of gain from international trade between countries. Despite a relative improvement in the price terms of trade resulting

[1] See 'West Germany Gains in Middle East Markets', *Middle East Economic Digest*, London, 30 April 1971, pp. 459–60.
[2] Used by OPEC and industry sources in section B above.

from an increase in the price of exports over that of imports, the country can still be worse off by selling less than before.

The price terms of trade, it is argued, cannot therefore effectively represent the distribution of gain from international trade. Certain authors recommend for an 'index of total gains from trade' the 'income' terms of trade, namely $(Px . Qx)/Pm$; this is considered a determinant of the purchasing power of exports.[1] Oil exporting countries, and other mineral countries exporting depletable and irreplaceable resources, could make use of the income terms of trade in devising their commercial policy. They should aim, in principle, at manipulating or influencing the price, volume, and timing of their exports in order to maximize their presently valued income.[2]

The income terms of trade, however, do not produce a satisfactory indicator of the magnitude and direction of change in the gain from international trade. Suppose, for example, that Px/Pm has fallen by 10 per cent and that Qx has risen by 10 per cent – assuming that the real cost of producing x remains unchanged, and that output, employment, and balance of payments conditions also remain unchanged.[3] In this situation, the income terms of trade remain unchanged, although the country is worse off; it has to export more goods to buy the same volume of imports. Or if Px/Pm has risen by 10 per cent and Qx has fallen by 10 per cent, the income terms of trade remains unchanged, but the country is better off; it has to export fewer goods to buy the same volume of imports. In these circumstances, the price terms of trade is a better indicator of change in the gain from international trade.

In order to improve further on the income terms of trade, international trade theorists recommend taking into account the impact of changes in efficiency on economic welfare. Thus a 5 per cent decrease in export prices relative to import prices can be more than compensated for by a simultaneous decrease of 10 per cent on the production costs of exports. This describes the single factoral terms

[1] See C. P. Kindleberger, *International Economics* (Homewood, Ill.: Richard D. Irwin, Inc., 1968), pp. 73–7.

[2] This would involve using a social discount rate to estimate the present value of future streams of income: See Mikdashi, *A Financial Analysis of Middle Eastern Oil Concessions*, pp. 244–5 and 280–1.

[3] The real cost of producing x and its impact on economic welfare is taken care of through the use of the factoral terms of trade concepts described in the next paragraph.

One can build more realistic and complex models with conditions of output, employment, and balance of payments changing, and assess the resulting impact on economic welfare.

of trade, and is represented by $(Px . Zx)/Pm$ where Zx is the productivity in the export sector. Exporting countries would like to see the benefits of technological change applying to production accruing totally to them.

The double factoral terms of trade is considered by some authors as more relevant to measuring the impact of change in the productivity of both the country's export sector Zx and the foreign industries' sector producing its imports Zm. This is represented as $(Px/Zx) \div (Pm/Zm)$. Measurement of changes in productivity is particularly difficult in less developed countries, and is complicated by the problem of deciding what measure of productivity to use (labour, capital, or labour+capital), and the problem of ascertaining changes in quality.

In the context of the debate on whether the terms of trade of developing countries have deteriorated *vis-à-vis* the developed countries, one should not overlook trade in services. It is possible that a country could be worse (or better) off in its price terms of trade, but that this deterioration (improvement) is outweighed by increased (decreased) profits in foreign investments, including international transport and insurance. 'What is needed for deeper analysis', according to Kindleberger, 'is the terms of trade on the current account of the balance of payments as a whole, not merely merchandise'.[1]

The author shares Kindleberger's view that trade in services as well as trade in goods should be included in the terms of trade calculations, because trade in services is often complementary to the trade in goods. Unfortunately, available historical statistical data in the international petroleum industry does not lend itself to such an analysis. The following approach is designed to attain a reasonable, though admittedly rough, measure of changes in the gain from international trade of mineral exporting countries, and in particular of the oil exporting countries.

The conventional price terms of trade applying to oil exporting

[1] Kindleberger, *op. cit.*, p. 76. For further description of terms of trade concepts, see: G. Haberler, *A Survey of International Trade Theory*, Princeton University Special Papers in International Economics, July 1961, pp. 24–9; G. Haberler, 'Terms of Trade and Economic Development', in *Economic Development for Latin America*, Proceedings of a Conference held by the International Economic Association, ed. H. S. Ellis (London: Macmillan, 1961), pp. 275–80; Gerald M. Meier and Robert E. Baldwin, *Economic Development, Theory, History, Policy* (New York: Wiley, 1962), p. 230; Gerlad M. Meier, *The International Economics of Development, Theory and Policy*, (New York: Harper & Row, 1968), pp. 41–65.

countries would be Px/Pm, where Px is the index of realized or market price of oil exports and Pm is the index of import prices for that country. It is practically impossible, however, to find complete or representative price data on crude oil or product sales in the open market, covering transactions among non-affiliated companies. The author has computed prices realized by Gulf on sales of Kuwait crude to non-affiliates for 1951–55 (see Table 7.3), but could not find reliable data for years beyond 1955. It is possible to extrapolate the realized prices beyond 1951–55, making them move proportionately with changes in posted prices until 1960, the years when oil companies were free to alter posted prices, ostensibly in response to market forces. However, 1951–55 changes in realized prices have not moved by the same proportion or even in the same direction as posted prices current during that same period.

Information on market prices is, unfortunately, not widely or systematically published. Newton gave one of the most comprehensive price reviews of open-market short and intermediate-term crude oil sales. The latter transactions are, however, limited to 5 to 10 per cent only of the volume of world oil trade. Prices listed by Newton for Kuwait show a decline in realized prices of a barrel of crude oil from 165 cents in 1958 to 147 in 1959, 134 in 1960–61, 131·5 in 1962, 129 in 1963, and 126·5 in 1964–67.[1] Newton's realized prices for 1958 and 1959 appear too high as compared with this author's figures for 1951–55. This is so assuming that the mid-1950s imputed realized f.o.b. prices were higher than those in the later 1950s – after accounting for explicit or implicit discounts such as freight absorption, technical and financial aid to the buying refinery, and purchase-back agreement of unsold products by said refinery.[2]

The difficulties outlined above for computing, imputing, estimating, or even 'guess-estimating' representative realized prices of Kuwait oil for long periods of time also apply to other oil exporting countries. Researchers have admitted that 'the ambiguity of the price of oil might often present a statistical problem in assessing the net barter terms of trade'.[3]

The author has found it more meaningful for his analysis to devise new concepts of terms of trade. More specifically, two concepts are

[1] W. L. Newton, in *Governmental Intervention in the Market Mechanism*, pp. 41–77.

[2] See also M. Suzuki, *op. cit.*

[3] See, for example, T. Wilson, R. P. Sinha and J. R. Castree, 'The Income Terms of Trade of Developed and Developing Countries', *The Economic Journal*, LXXIX (December 1969), p. 817.

recommended as a contribution to the study of measuring relative gains from international trade in the context of OPEC countries: a 'retained' unit value terms of trade, and a 'retained' income terms of trade. The first concept is defined as the measure of changes in the index of per unit payments actually disbursed in a country and resulting from the export of its goods (let us call it RVx) in relation to changes in the unit value index of imports Pm made by that country, thus giving RVx/Pm.

The retained income terms of trade becomes then $(RVx . Qx)/Pm$, where Qx is the quantity of exports. The latter index takes into consideration the volume of exports of a given country, and consequently offers a measure of that country's 'capacity to import'.

The term RVx covers two categories of disbursements made by expatriate concessionaire companies to host countries. The *first* category comprises payments to governments, and contributions to society – for example with respect to housing, education, medical care, and development projects. The latter are not an anomaly in business practices; they are common in industrial countries where businesses are required to contribute to local education and welfare services.[1] Such payments by companies are therefore sometimes considered as expenditures on inputs necessary to carrying out their business activities.

The *second* category of disbursements comprises expenditures of oil companies locally for wages, contracting services, and domestically produced supplies. Some of the contract services represent only imported goods, and such concessionaire expenditures are not effectively disbursed in the domestic economy, except for a relatively small portion representing remuneration to local contractors and other domestic factors of production. These local payments, in return for services rendered, represent the use of national labour and capital which would otherwise be employed in some other way. It is not, accordingly, a simple transfer of income. But these services are occasionally hired at a rate higher than that paid in the open market, which represents a measure of subsidization to the local factors. In addition, large proportions of the local labour force in a number of Middle Eastern countries (notably in the Arabian peninsula states) are not citizens or permanent residents. Many of them are Pakistani or Iranian, or from some other Arab country. In that case, their savings will be remitted.

The concept of retained income terms of trade measures the

[1] See, for example, P. W. Cook and G. von Peterfly, *Problems of Corporate Power* (Homewood, Ill.: Irwin), 1966, p. 5.

purchasing power of oil countries' exports in terms of imports. It can be adjusted for changes in population in order to get a per capita retained income terms of trade, thus relating the purchasing power of exports to changes in population. This is considered another index of progress,[1] especially for countries where the foreign trade sector represents a relatively large portion of gross national product, as is the case with most OPEC countries.

The choice of the concept RVx as defined above is consistent with views submitted by some international trade economists writing on developing countries. Singer, for example, presents his case as follows:

> Can it be possible that we economists have become slaves to the geographers? Could it not be that in many cases the productive facilities for export from underdeveloped countries, which were so largely a result of foreign investment, never became a part of the internal economic structure of those underdeveloped countries themselves except in the purely geographical and physical sense? Economically speaking, they were really an outpost of the economies of the more developed investing countries. The main secondary multiplier effects, which the textbooks tell us to expect from investment, took place not where the investment was physically or geographically located but (to the extent that the results of these investments returned directly home) where the investment came from. I would suggest that if the proper economic test of investment is the multiplier effect in the form of cumulative additions to income, employment, capital, technical knowledge, and growth of external economies, then a good deal of the investment in underdeveloped countries which we used to consider as 'foreign' should in fact be considered as domestic investment on the part of the industrialized countries.[2]

Singer is thinking essentially of mineral exporting countries, notably oil exporting countries.[3] Myint has similar views with respect to the role of foreign investments in developing countries. He argues that it is improper to use conventional price or income terms of trade without qualification to measure the gains accruing from international trade to the people of a developing country. The earnings from export proceeds, he points out, do not go *in toto* to the

[1] See T. Wilson, *op. cit.*, p. 830.
[2] H. W. Singer, *International Development: Growth and Change* (McGraw Hill, New York, 1964), p. 163.
[3] See his footnote referring to Iran: *ibid*, p. 162.

people of that country to the extent expatriate firms and non-resident labour remit their earnings abroad. He says:

> For the terms of trade (whether we take the 'price' or the 'income' version) are a satisfactory measure of the gains from international trade accruing to the people of a country only in so far as they receive the whole of the earnings from the exports of that country as a territorial unit. In the backward countries, however, due to foreign investment and immigrant labour, a substantial part of these earnings has had to be remitted abroad in the form of export surpluses on the trade account.[1]

Singer's and Myint's views are shared by other economists, notably Prebisch and Onitri. The latter suggests that:

> In cases where foreign enterprises play an important role in the international economy, it may be useful to make a distinction between the terms of trade of the country as a geographical entity (which may be referred to as the 'domestic' or 'territorial' terms of trade) and the terms of trade of the nationals of the country (which may be called the 'national' terms of trade). It is not unlikely that changes in the two terms of trade may diverge widely.[2]

The first reference known to the author regarding the possibility of a divergence between 'national' and the 'territorial' terms of trade for several developing countries exporting primary commodities is made by an UN report, although it did not use these terms. The report states:

> It is at least theoretically possible that when the terms of trade show an improvement, such improvement will mainly benefit foreign companies operating within the under-developed country. ... How much of the benefits to foreign companies, through the increase in their profit margins and wage-paying capacity, have subsequently been transferred to the under-developed country itself, can only be determined by separate economic analysis in particular cases.[3]

[1] H. Myint, 'The Gains from International Trade and the Backward Countries', in *The Review of Economic Studies*, 1954–55, London, Vol. XXII (2), No. 58, p. 131.
[2] H. M. A. Onitri, 'The Terms of Trade', in *Problems in Economic Development*, Proceedings of a Conference held by the International Economic Association, ed. E. A. G. Robinson (New York: Macmillan, 1966), pp. 516–17.
[3] United Nations, *Relative Prices of Exports and Imports of Underdeveloped Countries*, a study of postwar terms of trade between underdeveloped and industrialized countries, New York, December 1949, p. 123.

D. *Statistical Limitations and Measurement*

The use of retained unit value and retained income terms of trade are meaningful for countries whose foreign exchange receipts depend solely or largely on exports made by expatriate firms to affiliated companies outside host countries, using transfer pricing. This is the case with a number of oil countries such as Abu Dhabi, Iran, Iraq, Kuwait, Qatar, and Saudi Arabia in the Middle East; Algeria and Libya in North Africa; and Venezuela in Latin America.

Onitri warns that 'the difficulties of measuring the "national" terms of trade would, of course, be immense'.[1] The author, in suggesting an approach for a statistical measurement of his conceptual versions, is probably breaking new and uncertain ground. Any pioneering attempt, however, must be judged by its conceptual soundness and by the eventual cumulative impact on other research. The author admits the crudeness of data and of statistical measurement available for the concepts but emphasizes that a beginning must be ventured, no matter how imperfect.

Statistical information is readily available in a complete form for most OPEC countries on governmental revenues, which constitute the bulk of benefits host countries derive from oil exports. In the absence of accurate statistical data on the other elements of RVx (for example, local purchases and labour), estimates have to be made. It is the author's informed opinion that these have generally followed a declining trend. They may reach a high figure of 40 per cent or more of retained value of oil exports during the early period of developing and producing newly discovered fields, which call for relatively large expenditures in infrastructure. Once oil fields are fully developed, company domestic expenditures related to producing and exporting oil are bound to decline, probably to a figure around 2 to 3 per cent of retained value.

These figures vary from one country to another, from one oil field to another, and from one period of time to another. In a country with several operators and/or oil fields, domestic wage payments and purchases may 'bulge' in years of intense exploration and developmental activities, and dwindle in other years. The author has not estimated domestic wage payments and purchases for each OPEC country, largely because of the absence of reliable data on a year-to-year basis. The author estimates that the proportion of these payments has amounted by 1971 on a cumulative basis, taking the

---

[1] *Op. cit.*

whole group of OPEC countries, to approximately 10 per cent of retained value from oil exports.[1]

To measure or approximate the cost of imports to oil exporting countries, two types of indices can be used: national indices whenever available and UN import price indices for developing regions. In using the latter, one should be aware that the relative importance of different commodities in imports (also exports) of OPEC countries is not constant over time.

The check made by the author for a selected number of Middle East oil exporting countries and in selected years shows that the discrepancies between the commodity and origin composition of the average regional imports (as represented in the UN Asian Middle East index)[2] and the national ones for individual oil exporting countries are large enough to invalidate calculations. Moreover, the UN index has shown consistently lower price increases than the national ones (see Table 7.4).

Ideally, of course, one should use unit value import indices applying to the individual oil exporting countries. These indices are, unfortunately, not always available. Foreign trade statistics of developing (including OPEC) countries do not cover long periods of time. Also, import figures are not comprehensive in coverage of items, and commodity classifications have not been uniform over the years. Moreover, businesses tend to understate import values in order to evade their full *ad valorem* tariff liabilities, and overstate export values as a way to get hard currency to be held abroad, or reduce the

[1] Information from several sources, and notably from government publications and oil companies' reports or from those of their affiliated concessionaires. Also Arabian American Oil Company, *Aramco's Participation in Saudi Arabian Development*, by A. R. Khatib, H. M. Munif and F. A. Ruwayha, presented at the Fourth Arab Petroleum Congress, Beirut, November 1963, 12 pp.; Z. Mikdashi, *Economic Benefits to Host Governments from Major Oil Concessions in the Middle East*, Report prepared for OPEC, December 1964, not published; Z. Mikdashi, 'The Profitability of Middle Eastern Oil Ventures: A Historical Approach', in *Studies in the Economic History of the Middle East from the Rise of Islam to the Present Day*, ed. M. A. Cook, Oxford University Press, London, 1970, pp. 468–84; Petroleum Information Foundation Inc., *The International Oil Companies and Host Country Development outside the Oil Industry*, director J. V. Whittlesey, New York, 9 October 1969 – a mimeographed report; Bank Markazi Iran, *Annual Reports and Balance Sheets;* Bank of Libya, *Economic Bulletins;* Saudi Arabian Monetary Agency, *Annual Reports*; and R. F. Mikesell *et al.*, *Foreign Investment in the Petroleum and Mineral Industries*, Case Studies of Investor–Host Country Relations, The John Hopkins Press, Baltimore, 1971.

[2] The countries included are Bahrain, Cyprus, Iran, Iraq, Israel, Jordan, Kuwait, Lebanon, Muscat and Oman, Trucial Oman, Neutral Zone, Saudi Arabia, Southern Yemen, Syria, and Yemen.

taxable income 'assigned' to an affiliate in an importing country where tax rates are relatively high. Such practices reduce the reliability of figures declared to customs authorities, and affect the value of indices used in this analysis.

Furthermore, the construction and use over a period of time of the appropriate price indices raise several technical problems. These

Table 7.4

INDICES OF UNIT VALUES OF IMPORTS FOR SELECTED OPEC COUNTRIES AND YEARS
(1964 = 100)

	Iran	Libya	Saudi Arabia	Venezuela	UN Asian Middle East
1969	106·3		116·6	120·4	103·9
1968	102·2		109·9	117·5	100·0
1967	102·3		107·1	115·5	102·0
1966	101·4	111·1	105·5	111·7	101·0
1965	100·2	104·4	101·5	106·8	100·0
1964	100·0	100·0	100·0	100·0	100·0
1963	98·6	103·3		97·1	97·1
1962		97·2			96·1

Sources:
Iran and Venezuela: International Monetary Fund, *International Financial Statistics*, January 1971.
Libya: Kingdom of Libya, Ministry of Planning and Development, Census and Statistical Department, *External Trade Indices, 1962-1966*, Table 9, Tripoli, April 1968.
Saudi Arabia: SAMA, *op. cit.*, p. 92; all years are Hijri years with about three-quarters, in the corresponding Gregorian year and about one quarter in the following one.
UN Asian Middle East: UN *Monthly Bulletin of Statistics*.

include differences in definitions, in the adequacy of samples used, and in the comprehensiveness of coverage; errors of measurement and omissions which go undetected or uncorrected; changes in the design, quality, functional convenience, efficiency, or nature of manufactured goods (for example, vehicles and machinery), and the introduction of new goods; and changes in the mix and weights assigned to different commodities. The longer the period, the greater the changes which have occurred – thereby diminishing the value of an index over the years.

The criterion of choice among various possible indices using

185

different statistical methods is the precision with which any index approximates changes in value of the cost of imports of OPEC member countries. A UN report states that a 'true' index number for import or for export prices cannot be calculated, and consequently no 'true' figures can be derived for changes in the terms of trade:

> There can be no single 'true' index number of export or import prices. The impossibility of finding and presenting a single 'true' index number and therefore a single 'true' figure for changing terms of trade is not due to any deficiency in the statistical data used or the statistical technique employed. It is a logical impossibility. . . . The only case where a single 'true' index number could be calculated would occur where either the relative weights of the various commodities combined in an index remained completely unchanged or where the prices of individual articles included in the index changed in the same direction and in exactly the same degree. Such a case is so improbable as to border on the impossible.[1]

Although the 'true' changes in terms of trade of a given country cannot be identified, two related indices may be determined: first, how much more or less it costs in period 2 relative to period 1 to import the basket of goods purchased in period 1 (known as a Laspeyres index), and second, how much more it costs in period 2 to buy the basket of goods imported in period 2 compared to what it would have cost to import this basket in period 1 (known as a Paasche index). The foregoing indices may be integrated by the use of the so-called Fisher ideal, which is the square root of the product of the Laspeyres and Paasche indices. These indices could be used with fixed weights assigned to individual commodities which enter into each index, or with moving current weights. There are no good criteria for choosing among the three above indices or for the use of fixed versus moving weights.[2]

The year 1964 is the base period in Tables 7.4, 7.5, 7.6, 7.7, and 7.8. The author chose this year in order to base the time series on a 'normal' business year to the extent this is possible; to select the year when OPEC's collective bargaining started paying off; and to account for the fact that statistics on import prices and other factors (for

---

[1] *Relative Prices of Exports and Imports of Underdeveloped Countries*, p. 137.
[2] A survey reproduced in the UN 1959 Supplement to the *Monthly Bulletin of Statistics* showed that out of 43 countries surveyed, 22 used the Paasche fixed weight base, 11 Laspeyres fixed base, two the Paasche chained weight base and one the Laspeyres chained base. For Fisher's ideal, the countries which used a chained base were 6, while 1 used a fixed base.

Table 7.5

INDICES OF GOVERNMENT TAKE PER UNIT OF EXPORT FOR SELECTED OPEC
COUNTRIES UNDER THE PROFIT SHARING AGREEMENTS, 1952–69*
(1964 = 100)

	Iran	Iraq	Kuwait	Qatar	Libya	Saudi Arabia	Venezuela
1952		89·1	83·6	49·7		62·8	83·8
1953		99·8	79·8	74·3		91·8	84·0
1954	109·8	107·7	81·8	102·6		103·2	81·7
1955	101·2	107·6	99·7	104·5		100·1	84·6
1956	104·3	111·7	99·5	102·4		101·1	91·4
1957	107·4	116·2	103·5	113·7		107·6	108·0
1958	110·1	111·0	106·2	115·4		99·6	117·0
1959	103·5	102·9	101·2	109·9		92·4	103·1
1960	99·1	98·1	99·3	108·7		91·5	93·5
1961	93·8	95·5	96·7	106·8	99·7	92·1	97·4
1962	92·2	95·8	97·3	105·9	102·9	93·3	101·9
1963	98·6	100·7	96·6	110·2	103·3	96·0	103·4
1964	100·0	100·0	100·0	100·0	100·0	100·0	100·0
1965	100·4	102·0	102·6	99·2	133·2	101·5	100·2
1966	100·7	101·5	102·0	108·7	138·3	101·7	100·4
1967	102·1	106·4	103·1	110·4	161·5	103·4	107·1
1968	103·6	113·2	104·6	115·7	160·1	107·1	106·3
1969	100·1	114·1	105·1	116·6	159·0	106·2	108·6

* Abu Dhabi was still on the royalty method in 1956; no comprehensive and exact figures obtain for Algeria and Indonesia; and all government take figures are on an accrual basis.
Sources: Derived by author from data published in OPEC, *Annual Statistical Bulletins* and Petroleum Information Foundation, New York.

Table 7.6

QUANTUM INDICES OF OIL EXPORTS FOR SELECTED OPEC COUNTRIES, 1952–69
(1964 = 100)

	Iran	Iraq	Kuwait	Qatar	Libya	Saudi Arabia	Venezuela
1952		30·4	32·0	32·1		43·1	53·2
1953		46·4	36·7	39·3		44·2	51·6
1954	1·7	50·3	40·9	46·3		50·7	55·7
1955	19·1	54·4	47·0	53·3		51·2	62·0
1956	31·3	48·9	47·6	57·5		52·8	72·0
1957	42·3	33·3	49·9	64·2		53·5	80·0
1958	47·9	57·1	61·0	81·1		55·4	75·7
1959	54·1	66·8	61·0	78·9		60·7	80·0
1960	61·4	76·9	71·3	81·1		69·2	83·6
1961	68·5	78·8	73·3	82·1	1·6	77·5	85·8
1962	77·2	78·9	82·6	86·3	19·0	86·1	93·7
1963	86·1	91·4	88·0	88·8	53·3	93·2	95·4
1964	100·0	100·0	100·0	100·0	100·0	100·0	100·0
1965	111·0	104·1	99·8	107·7	141·1	115·0	101·0
1966	125·6	110·1	105·9	134·9	174·5	136·1	98·8
1967	153·9	96·2	106·4	149·9	198·0	146·8	104·3
1968	168·1	119·2	111·7	157·7	301·2	160·6	105·1
1969	199·6	120·1	118·0	164·6	360·7	169·1	105·9

Sources: Derived by author from data published by OPEC *Annual Statistical Bulletins* and Petroleum Information Foundation, New York.

Table 7.7

INDICES OF MID-YEAR POPULATION FOR SELECTED OPEC COUNTRIES, 1952–69*
(1964 = 100)

	Iran	Iraq	Kuwait	Libya	Qatar	Saudi Arabia	Venezuela
1952	71·4	70·9			33·3		62·7
1953	73·2	73·1			—		64·6
1954	74·9	79·4			50·0		66·5
1955	76·7	77·8			58·3		68·6
1956	78·5	80·2			60·0		70·6
1957	80·4	82·7	48·4		61·7		72·8
1958	82·3	83·3			66·7		75·0
1959	87·9	85·0	58·7		66·7		84·1
1960	90·0	87·8	65·3		75·0		87·2
1961	92·5	90·7	75·6		91·7		90·3
1962	95·0	93·7	82·9	93·1	91·7		93·4
1963	97·5	96·8	91·1	96·5	91·7	98·3	96·6
1964	100·0	100·0	100·0	100·0	100·0	100·0	100·0
1965	102·7	103·4	111·5	103·7	116·7	101·7	103·5
1966	105·8	105·9	115·3	107·6	118·3	103·5	107·2
1967	110·0	106·7	122·1	111·5	125·0	105·3	111·0
1968	112·9	109·2	126·8	115·7	133·3	106·9	114·9
1969	116·7	118·2	133·8	119·9	166·7	108·4	119·1

* All figures are estimates

Source: Derived by author from data published by the UN *Monthly Bulletin of Statistics*.

example, population) are not available for a number of OPEC countries in earlier years or gradually become unreliable. Certain years are notable for highly dramatic movements in international relations, for war, crisis, depression, and suspension or curtailment of oil exports for reasons not connected with market forces – all should be deliberately avoided as base periods in computing terms of trade. If 1955 (another normal year) were to be used as base year, indices of government take would be higher in 1969 for Kuwait and Venezuela, and lower for Iran, Iraq, Qatar, and Saudi Arabia. Using 1964 as a base, all countries presented in Table 7.5. had by 1969 gained increases in government take per unit of export (in current monetary value) except Iran. Libya's gain came to 159, followed by Qatar with 116; Iraq, 114; Venezuela, 108; Saudi Arabia, 106; and Kuwait, 105.

For terminal year, the author uses 1969, the year which has complete data. It precedes tax changes in OPEC countries leading to substantial increases in government revenues, and the formal use of a terms of trade clause. Boosts in government take amounted in 1971 to as much as 45 per cent over 1969.

Another problem in measuring changes in gain from international trade for a country is the problem of timing its foreign exchange receipts and of its disbursements of these receipts. Suppose some countries, such as many oil countries, have accumulated foreign exchange balances of several currencies as a result of exports made in a certain period of time, but that they have not made or could not make full use of them during the same period. If these countries later use these balances for imports, they are likely to derive lower benefits as compared with imports made in the original period, to the extent that the composite price index of their imports has had a generally rising trend (Table 7.4). This means that accumulated foreign exchange balances by an OPEC country (assuming it is not a debtor country) depreciate in real buying power as a result of the time lag between exports and the date when that country is able to make its imports, unless the earned return on these balances compensates for the depreciation in real buying power.[1] One should note that an investment decision has, in a sense, been taken when the country decides to spend or not to spend the proceeds of exports. Whether the return is relatively high or low is a commentary on the success of the investment decision. This depreciation (appreciation when world market prices fall) makes the country concerned worse

[1] See also UN, *Measures for the Economic Development of Under-Developed Countries*, New York, May 1951, p. 74.

off (or better off), and is not accounted for in the statistical measurement of terms of trade.

E. *Inferences*

Given the limitations of the computation of price indices, no significance should be attached to relatively small changes as the results may have a considerable margin of error. Available evidence, nevertheless, supports the following inferences.

First, unadjusted government takes per unit of oil exports have had a generally rising trend for all countries concerned with small dips in the late 1950s and early 1960s; available evidence for individual OPEC countries suggests that unit values of imports were rising at a faster rate until the end of the 1960s (Tables 7.4 and 7.5).

Second, the large increases in oil exports, except for Venezuela, have produced substantial gains in the income terms of trade of these countries.[1] These gains have come, however, at widely different rates of growth varying over the years (see Tables 7.6 and 7.8). The significant improvement in the retained income terms of trade reflects a vigorous expansion of world consumption of energy (about 9 per cent per annum) mostly in industrial countries; this expansion is related to increases in per capita income and to an income elastic demand for energy. The improved retained income terms of trade also reflects an improvement in the competitive advantage of oil in relation to other sources of energy (notably coal). Thereby, a significant cross-elasticity of demand in favour of oil is shown within price ranges like those in the 1950s and most of the 1960s. What most oil exporting countries could have lost over certain periods with respect to RVx/Pm would have been compensated for by larger volumes of exports, with the result that the $(RVx \cdot Qx)/Pm$ has been rising almost throughout the period under study for most countries. In Venezuela, both indicators have deteriorated between 1962 and 1969 (see Table 7.8).

In the price range of the latter 1960s and early 1970s, an increase in oil exports (for example, by competitive cuts in their levies), in the face of a largely price-inelastic and not upward-shifting demand schedule for petroleum, would lead to an income transfer from the OPEC countries to the more developed countries of OECD, the consumers of the bulk of world oil trade.

Third, one can see the impact of a general improvement in host

[1] For estimates of income terms of trade for developed and developing (non-oil) countries, see T. Wilson, *op. cit.*, pp. 819–20.

Table 7.8

INDICES OF GAIN FROM OIL FOR SELECTED OPEC COUNTRIES, 1962–69*

(1964 = 100)

	Iran			Libya			Saudi Arabia			Venezuela		
	(1) RVx	(2) $RVx.Qx$	(3) $RVx.Qx$	(1) RVx	(2) $RVx.Qx$	(3) $RVx.Qx$	(1) RVx	(2) $RVx.Qx$	(3) $RVx.Qx$	(1) RVx	(2) $RVx.Qx$	(3) $RVx.Qx$
	Pm	Pm	$Pm.L$	Pm	Pm	$Pm.L$	Pm	Pm	$Pm.L$	Pm	Pm	$Pm.L$
1962				105·9	20·1	21·6						
1963	100·0	86·1	88·3	100·0	53·3	55·2				105·2	101·6	105·1
1964	100·0	100·0	100·0	100·0	100·0	100·0	100·0	100·0	100·0	100·0	100·0	100·0
1965	100·2	111·2	108·3	127·6	180·0	173·5	100·0	115·0	113·1	91·6	94·7	91·5
1966	99·3	124·7	117·9	124·5	217·3	202·0	96·4	131·2	126·8	82·8	88·8	82·9
1967	99·8	153·6	139·7				96·5	141·7	134·6	87·1	101·4	91·4
1968	101·4	170·5	151·0				97·5	156·6	146·5	82·8	95·1	82·7
1969	94·2	188·0	161·1				91·2	154·2	142·2	80·2	95·5	80·2

* All figures are indices; RVx is exclusively composed of government take in these statistics.

Source: Data derived from Tables 4.4, 4.5, 4.6, and 4.7.

192

countries' bargaining power in the 1950s, 1960s, and the early 1970s, either through the individual efforts of host countries or through collective action via OPEC. The effect of the impact shows in larger governmental take per unit of export (Table 7.5 and pp. 149–56).

Fourth, technological developments in the international oil industry since the turn of the century have had beneficial effects. These include more efficient and less costly exploration and production; higher rates of recovery of reserves; more efficient means of transport and refining; and wider and more efficient uses of oil products and derivatives. How producer countries, consumer countries, and international companies have shared the benefits of these technological developments is, however, difficult to ascertain from the figures available. However, a managing director of Shell has stated that the benefits of improved techniques have been passed on to the consumer.[1]

Fifth, the fact that oil is a depletable resource is bound to lead, as oil production declines and if there are no discoveries, to a deterioration in the income terms of trade for countries that depend almost totally on that resource. As Nurkse said, 'the export of minerals involves in an obvious sense an element of living on capital'.[2] Several countries have seen their oil reserves depleted (notably Austria and Rumania), and OPEC countries could experience a decline in the growth rate of their oil production with a probable deterioration in the income terms of trade in the absence of new oil or non-oil resources. However, one should not overemphasize the depletable nature of mineral production. Certain agricultural commodities are subject to obsolescence with consequences similar to the depletion of mineral commodities. Japan's silk exports, for example, were heavily damaged in the late 1940s by technological change in favour of synthetics. There is no general rule regarding which is the more dangerous, the obsolescence of a commodity or the depletion of a mineral. Moreover, any sensible owner of a depletable resource should provide depletion allowances to maintain or reconstitute the value of his wasting resource by investing in other capital assets.

Sixth, the vulnerability of oil exporting countries is not the result only of the depleting nature of oil deposits, but also of four other

[1] L. E. J. Brouwer, in Royal Dutch *Annual Report 1970*, p. 1.
[2] Ragnar Nurkse, 'International Trade Theory and Development Policy', in *Economic Development for Latin America*, Proceedings of a Conference held by the International Economic Association, ed. H. S. Ellis, (Macmillan, London, 1961), p. 240.

N

interrelated factors: possible price increases in host countries' imports coupled with reductions in their government take; a decline in the external demand for energy, mostly that of the large oil importing industrial countries; the economic obsolescence or replacement of oil by other sources of energy or raw materials; and unpredictable political conflicts or instability. Since the beginning of oil production in the Middle East, oil exports and consequently oil incomes for individual countries were curtailed or stopped on several occasions, for economic or non-economic reasons; for example, during World War II, the Palestine war of 1948, the Iranian nationalization of oil in 1951–54, the Suez war of 1956, and the Middle East War of 1967 – to mention a few.

The vulnerability of oil exporting countries calls, therefore, for greater flexibility and diversification in the allocation of national resources. Such flexibility will enable the country concerned to take advantage of the benefits of working in the international market and to reduce losses should its supply of oil, or the demand for it, shrink. Mobility of resources and diversification of economic activities would permit these countries to shift productive resources rather quickly from declining industries to others with more promising prospects.

Seventh, the growth in OPEC countries' global oil revenues and in their retained income terms of trade have been remarkable. This, in turn, has had a favourable impact on the growth of gross national product. If, however, the growth in the retained income terms of trade is adjusted to the growth of population L in these countries, the growth of per capita retained income terms of trade $(RVx \cdot Qx)/(Pm \cdot L)$ will appear substantially more moderate (see Table 7.8). Population figures are, unfortunately, of questionable reliability, and conclusions have to be guarded. Available data (Tables 7.8 and 7.9) suggest that countries with growth rates in population larger than in GNP have had their GNP per capita adversely affected.

The general improvement in oil exporting countries retained income terms of trade does not mean that this improvement has been at the expense of their trading partners, mostly the industrial developed countries. The latter countries have also had in recent years very large increases in their income terms of trade, rising from 100 in 1950–53 to 236·5 in 1962–63.[1] This is to be expected under conditions of buoyant international trade, where both exporting and importing countries stand to gain in income terms. In contradistinction with income terms of trade, the conventional price terms of

[1] T. Wilson, *op. cit.*, p. 819.

trade must show that the gain of one party is at the expense of the other.[1]

[1] *Ibid.*, p. 832.

Table 7.9

OPEC COUNTRIES' POPULATION (MID-1964 AND MID-1969),
GNP PER CAPITA (1968) AND AVERAGE ANNUAL GROWTH RATES
(1961–68)

	Population (million)		GNP Per Capita (US $)	Growth Rates	
	1964	1969		Population (%)	GNP Per Capita (%)
Indonesia*	102·4	116·0	100	2·4	0·8
Iran	23·9	27·9	310	3·0	5·0
Iraq	7·9	9·4	260	2·8	2·9
Kuwait	0·4	0·6	3,540	8·7	−3·3
Qatar†	0·06	0·1	3,490	7·5	1·8
Saudi Arabia	6·6	7·2	360	1·7	7·2
Abu Dhabi	0·02‡	0·08	1,920§	3·9§	37·3§
Libya	1·6	1·9	1,020	3·7	19·4
Algeria	n.a.	13·3	220	2·3	−3·5
Venezuela	8·4	10·0	950	3·5	1·4

* Excluding West Irian.
† Estimates of GNP per capita and its growth rate are tentative.
‡ Mid-1967.
§ Figures apply to Trucial Oman sheikhdoms of which Abu Dhabi is the largest in area, and in population (about half). This author's estimate of GNP per capita for Abu Dhabi comes about the same as Kuwait's.

Source: *World Bank Atlas, op. cit.*
UN *Monthly Bulletin of Statistics*, January 1971.

Chapter 8

THE FUTURE OF CO-OPERATIVE EFFORT

An institution's achievements are pertinent to its future; successes are likely to win support of its membership, while failures may discourage the delegation of authority or continuance of the institution itself. Reliable indices for measuring success do not exist, and informed opinions do not always agree. Despite its limitations and shortcomings, OPEC has been useful to its members; all would be worse off without it.

OPEC's survival does not seem in doubt, but its functions may change. There are various possibilities. Given the multiple pressures it will face from within and without, the organization must remain flexibly knit if it is to maintain its growth, exerting its influence judiciously at propitious moments, and sustaining solidarity whenever possible.

A. *The Achievements*

OPEC's achievements over its twelve years of existence should be judged in terms of the net rewards member governments have received and perceived, whether these are economic or non-economic, measurable or non-measurable. The author shares the view that 'low effectiveness is a general characteristic of organizations. Since goals, as symbolic units, are ideals which are more attractive than the reality which the organization attains, the organization can always be reported to be a failure'.[1] For the purpose of this analysis, to judge the success of an organization only in terms of the complete or substantial realization of goals and resolutions appears too exacting. Performance and accomplishment of tasks must be considered and evaluated with reference to what the organization can reasonably do in the light of constraints imposed by member countries, by market

[1] Etzioni, *Modern Organizations*, p. 16.

196

conditions, and by other interested groups. In the case of OPEC, these other groups are essentially the consuming countries, non-OPEC oil exporting countries, and the companies supplying oil and other sources of energy.

Alternatively, evaluation can be made by comparing OPEC's accomplishments with those of other organizations grouping developing countries, for example OAPEC or RCD. The evaluation analysis should also ascertain the reasons for success or failure, and possibly analyse alternatives to avoid the latter. In this evaluation exercise, one may not escape a measure of subjectivity and value judgment; criteria for success are not uniform among the interested parties or even among third parties, such as scholars, and measures of success need not apply uniformly across all organizations.[1]

The ten OPEC member countries have made direct equal contributions to finance their organization, averaging about $1·25 million annually for the whole group. Complementary expenditures incurred separately by member governments for functions connected with OPEC are estimated by the author to add up to about the same amount. Accordingly, the sum of $2·5 million can be roughly considered as members' total inputs to the organization per year.

With respect to OPEC's output, some appear readily measurable in quantity, though not in quality. These include the frequency of meetings of various OPEC organs; the number of resolutions passed or acted on, and the time lag involved; the number of trainees or researching students and scholars the Secretariat has had; the size of communications and exchanges between OPEC officials on one hand, and member countries, and other consumer countries (notably major consumer countries) on the other; the number of studies commissioned or publications issued; the number of congresses, conventions, colloquia, public lectures, and so on sponsored or attended by OPEC.

But these as well as similar indicators are inadequate measures of output or success. Better indicators would be OPEC's contribution to its member countries' gross national product and balance of payments. However, it is very difficult to ascertain, for example, what proportion, if any, of the increase in revenue gained by these countries can be attributed to OPEC. Other types of output are not measurable, notably that of growth in solidarity in oil or non-oil affairs among members, although one could use professional public

[1] See, for example, B. S. Georgopoulos and A. S. Tannenbaum, 'A study of Organization Effectiveness', in *Readings in Modern Organization*, ed. Amitai Etzioni (Englewood, N.J.: Prentice-Hall, 1969), pp. 80–8.

197

opinion polling agencies for reaching estimates. Moreover, there is the problem of attributing too much weight to some indicators of output and too little to others; distortions may well arise in the evaluation exercise.

The evaluation of OPEC's success necessarily rests substantially on personal judgments; therefore, even informed persons do not agree with each other or may even change their opinions with the passage of time. For example, Tariki, a co-founder of OPEC in 1960 while Saudi Arabia's Director General of Petroleum and Mineral Resources, sharply criticized the organization's achievements in 1965.[1] Member countries should not, he said, follow the 'soft' path of negotiation and compromise; they should assume the prerogatives of sovereignty by legislating simultaneously if positive results are to be obtained, and expectations to be fully realized. In an impassioned speech at the Fifth Arab Petroleum Congress, he argued:

> The OPEC delegates had better fasten their seat belts: for the fact is that OPEC deserves little or no credit.... In the [1964] negotiations with OPEC member governments, the companies agreed to the principle of royalty expensing but only on condition that they were given an 8·5 per cent discount off posted prices. What a humiliation for the companies to dictate to a group of sovereign governments in this way – particularly considering that OPEC's main aim was the restoration of posted prices to the pre-August 1960 level![2]

But in 1971, Tariki praised OPEC for the substantial gains it had won for member countries in the Tehran agreement. He attributed these successes to 'the solidarity of its members and their awareness that despite their being independent states they were nevertheless being exploited'.[3]

Another Arab oil writer, Nicola Sarkis (currently advisor to the Algerian government, and previously an associate of Tariki), saw matters differently. He criticized the low gains accepted in Tehran by the OPEC Arabian–Persian Gulf countries with respect to posted prices, and the escalation rate used on account of world inflation. He argued that the freight premium of 21·5 cents per barrel that the Tehran agreement assigned to Libyan oil was too low and regretted that the signatory countries should withhold their support from

---

[1] Since 1962, a consultant and editor of *Naft al-Arab*, prior to 1969 called *The Arab Oil and Gas Journal* (Arabic), published in Beirut.

[2] *MEES*, 26 March 1965, p. 25.

[3] *MEES*, 12 March 1971, p. 7.

Libya, if the latter asked for a larger premium. He further deplored the renunciation by these countries of their 'most-favoured-nation' clauses which enabled them to ask the companies to match better terms other OPEC countries could obtain at later dates. Finally, he claimed that the Tehran agreement failed to enforce earlier OPEC resolutions recommending the participation of host governments in the management and ownership of their major concessions, and the creation of oil-based industries in the OPEC countries.[1]

Another informed observer, Ashraf Lutfi, a former Secretary-General, has cast doubts on OPEC's achievements in its first seven years of existence. In his view, it failed in three major areas: in 'unifying the policies of the Members', in deciding on priorities, and in devising ways and means for stabilizing petroleum prices. He commented as follows:

> An examination of the avowed objectives of OPEC, however, raises a big question as to whether the Organization has really succeeded in settling, or even in seriously tackling, such questions as the 'unification of the petroleum policies of member countries', determination of what their best interests are, or devising ways and means of ensuring the stabilization of world market prices.[2]

It is true that OPEC's attempts to unify the policies of the Members (Res. I.2) and compile a Code of Uniform Petroleum Laws (Res. V.41) have not yet borne fruit. Nevertheless, a beginning was made in June 1968, when the Conference recommended ten identical principles to be included in member countries' hydrocarbon laws (Res. XVI.90). Understandably, these principles were drafted in very general terms, with the intention of accommodating and encompassing the wide differences and the particular circumstances of each member in order to obtain a consensus. But by so doing, the Conference produced plausible principles with no binding element to really warrant much publicity. This may well be considered a failure on the part of the integrationists in the organization who wanted to offer member countries an effective additional dimension of unity in the legislative field through the introduction of a Uniform Petroleum Code and mandatory uniform policy directives.

It is noteworthy that OPEC's resolution of June 1968 *recommends* and does not prescribe. Moreover, the so-called chart for the future it offers does not envisage means for implementation, and does not have a built-in timetable, a set of priorities, or any kind of commit-

[1] *Le Pètrole et le Gaz Arabes*, 1 March 1971, pp. 31–5.
[2] Lutfi, *OPEC Oil*, p. 31.

ment to agree on certain subjects by certain dates. It, as well as other resolutions, does have value as a political exhortation. In particular, it exhorts individual member countries to participate in the owner-ship and management of their major oil ventures; to raise posted or tax-reference prices and link their levels to prices of goods imported; and to adopt a 'renegotiation clause' whereby no operator should have 'the right to obtain excessively high net earnings after taxes' and to limit the time periods of fiscal stability. The resolution also urges member countries to settle disputes in national courts (not by international arbitration), and to require accelerated relinquishment schedules and governmental participation in the choice of acreage to be relinquished.

Public and official circles have debated governmental participation in the major oil producing ventures that have vast reserves and low production costs. Certain host countries' policy-makers (primarily Saudi Arabia and Kuwait) have expressed interest in working towards joint-venture alliances between national state companies and international private companies at the production and down-stream levels. Such alliances, their supporters feel, are more conducive to price stability in the markets and tend to promote producer–consumer interdependence to the mutual advantage of the two parties.[1]

Economics aside, the question of participation between national and expatriate companies in one form or another currently has psychological and sociological appeal in certain host countries. It offers an alternative to the ultranationalistic call for outright nationalization, and recognizes that joint enterprises offer a measure of stability in operator-government contractual relations, and is an essential basis for the investment of private foreign capital and know-how. Other host countries (for example, Algeria, Iraq, Iran, Libya) are politically allergic to the presence of powerful expatriate economic interests; these countries would sacrifice a measure of economic gain for the sake of fuller control of their economies.

Some international oil companies are beginning to accept com-petition from, or participation with, agencies of host governments as a fact of life in years to come. M. M. Brisco, the president of the

[1] See, for example, the Saudi Minister of Petroleum and Mineral Resources, Ahmad Zaki Yamani in *MEES Supplement*, 7 June 1968, p. 9; also his talk and discussion on 'Participation versus Nationalization: A Better Means to Survive', reproduced in *Continuity and Change in the World Oil Industry*, pp. 211–33, and Muhammad Joukhdar, Deputy-Governor of the state-owned Saudi oil company Petromin and a former OPEC Secretary-General in: *MEES*, 26 February 1971, p. 10.

world's largest oil company, Jersey, informed the company's shareholders at the 1971 annual meeting: 'In the future, we will see more of the government oil company, sometimes as a competitor and sometimes as a partner . . . we recognize this development as an element of changing times. We have learned to live with such government policies and such government entities.'[1]

Since OPEC's establishment, several achievements have been obtained by member countries individually or collectively in both financial and non-financial matters. Royalty expensing, elimination of tax allowances, and increases in posted or tax-reference prices and in tax rates represent substantial gains in an industry faced with potentially large surplus productive capacity. It is unlikely that some of these gains could have been realized had member countries not co-ordinated their policies and actions within OPEC. Larger government takes have dampened price competition to the extent that they have set rising floors for realized prices on oil exports.

OPEC can also take credit for providing member countries and their national companies with a forum for the exchange of information and experience, with the prospect of possible co-ordination of certain policies in the international market. OPEC's Xth Conference in 1965 had recommended regular meetings for representatives of national companies belonging to it. With utmost concern for the adverse impact of intense competition in the international market on crude oil prices and income tax revenues of member governments, the Secretary-General of OPEC, addressing the first meeting of national companies in Caracas in October 1966, appealed to them as follows:

> It would be cause for the utmost concern and anxiety for all of us if therefore uncontrolled and unplanned entry of our national oil companies into the international market were to aggravate what already is a serious and deplorable situation for us. Your part of this game is to be on our side, the OPEC side. . . .[2]

The possibility of joint international marketing by the national companies has been suggested. But obstacles in the way of that ambitious aim and differences among national companies and their parent nations have yet to be overcome. National companies have differences in their legal constitution and their organizational structure, in the nature and scope of their domestic and foreign activities, and in their financial capacities and their policies (specifi-

[1] *The Wall Street Journal*, 13 May 1971, p. 28.
[2] *OPEC Record*, January 1967.

cally with regard to joint ventures). In addition, they are dissimilar in their commitments to their governments and to national or extranational organizations, whether or not these are commercial in nature.

The Secretariat has also attempted to induce member governments to seek terms and adopt policies and practices *vis-à-vis* concessionary companies in line with the best economic terms prevailing in various member countries. One study commissioned by OPEC analysed on a comparative basis members' posted prices, royalties, taxes, transit and port dues, guarantees and timing of payments, and other economic benefits offered to host countries.[1] The best terms were to be used as guidelines by host governments in their negotiations with concessionaires. Information, studies, and advice, though not of direct immediate financial benefit, have produced far-reaching economic benefits, essentially in the form of improved fiscal terms claimed, and eventually obtained, from oil operators.

The contribution of OPEC to its member countries, especially those with limited oil experience, is notable in the field of analysing conditions in the international petroleum industry, offering advice, and training nationals in the technical and economic aspects of the industry. The OPEC Secretariat has performed a useful function in acting as a clearing house and in filling gaps of information on oil markets. Detailed, accurate, and increasingly comprehensive information, now supplied on a continuous basis, assists top government officials of OPEC governments in formulating appropriate policies and regulations, whether to do with the oil sector or with other related sectors of the economy.

Host countries were and still are generally dissatisfied with the unwillingness of their concessionaires to supply them with certain data on technical and economic matters, particularly prices realized on oil exports. International companies classify such information as trade secrets; after all, national companies of host countries are their active competitors.

In a highly concentrated industry, price and other trade information may have economic value, and would consequently be concealed from competitors, actual and potential, if the firm is to maximize its profits. By comparison, in a perfectly competitive model, knowledge is shared among all parties concerned.[2] As the

[1] Prepared by the author and entitled *Economic Benefits to Host Governments From Major Oil Concessions in the Middle East*, 1965, 58 pp. – not published.
[2] See R. N. Farmer, 'Firm Secrets and their Protection', *Industrial Security*, Washington, D.C., January 1965, pp. 2–9.

structure of the international oil industry becomes less concentrated, and as OPEC countries gain experience through their own national companies or through the help of expatriate and international agencies, more information becomes available.[1] The determined researcher can now dig out some of the required information from trade journals and government publications of oil importing countries and of parent countries of major companies.

It is to the credit of OPEC that it has concerned itself with serious matters, and has not succumbed to the temptation to adopt inflammatory labels – such as 'imperialist companies' – occasionally indulged in by other organizations of developing countries and some individual governments.

OPEC has established itself in the public opinion of several member countries as a positive asset, and political leaders, parliamentarians, and government officials keep the organization in mind when framing their policies and actions. Influential sections of the press and government officials in some OPEC countries, particularly Venezuela and Indonesia, have occasionally questioned the benefits of their membership in OPEC; they have had to face unchecked competition from Middle East oil, and Venezuela's efforts to establish production programming have proved so far fruitless. Nevertheless, these two countries have benefited from tax increases won by Middle Eastern or North African countries. Consequently, they are not willing to leave the organization since it meets their minimum requirements. In the absence of OPEC, all members would be worse off.

It is the author's view that OPEC has contributed, albeit to a limited extent, toward the development of solidarity and a sense of community. Prior to the organization's establishment, oil exporting countries, including those of the Middle East, generally worked in ignorance of each others' oil conditions and problems; suspicion and antagonisms predominated, leading occasionally to conflicts. To say that OPEC's creation has done away with conflicts or their causes is unrealistic; nevertheless, these conflicts have been moderated. Permanent lines of multilateral communication have been established through OPEC and related agencies. Moreover, the fact that ministerial level meetings have been held twice a year, and sometimes more, for over ten years, have led interested OPEC political leaders to become aware of what lies within the scope of common action and the opportune moments for action; it may have convinced them that

[1] See O. C. Herfindahl, *Natural Resource Information for Economic Development*, Resources for the Future, Inc. (Baltimore: The Johns Hopkins Press, 1969).

203

non-oil matters should not be allowed to wreck common oil interests. Conventional diplomatic methods would have led to serious delays in convening meetings and to the loss of a sense of continuity and regularity in relations, and there would have been no Secretariat entrusted with the function of the efficient spreading of information and the co-ordination of policies.

Finally, OPEC's patterns of government–company relations have been emulated by non-OPEC oil exporting countries, such as Abu Dhabi, and Nigeria (which joined OPEC later), Muscat and Oman, Dubai, Brunei, as well as by other developing countries which are exploring for oil. OPEC has also established for the first time in the history of international economic relations the principle of protecting the terms of trade of primary exporting developing countries.

The impact of OPEC has not been limited to countries exporting oil. OPEC has offered other developing countries, particularly the major copper exporting countries (Chile, Peru, Zaire and Zambia), a design of co-operation to improve on. For example, these countries' Inter-Governmental Council of Copper Exporting Countries (CIPEC) has a Conference and a Governing Board with broadly similar functions. However, CIPEC's Executive Director has, as compared with OPEC's Secretary-General, a much longer period of service; it extends for at least four years, once an initial two-year period has elapsed. This beneficial feature of CIPEC statutes enables the Executive Director to plan and implement his administrative programme.

CIPEC's Executive Director need not be (and, in fact, is not in 1971) a national of any member country. He is selected solely on the basis of competence to supervise and represent CIPEC's Information Bureau, and to act as Secretary of the Conference, the Governing Board, and the Executive Committee of the Information Bureau – with the right to speak but not to vote. Moreover, the Governing Board empowers the Executive Director to appoint the technical and administrative staff on a permanent basis over and above those whose appointment must be seconded by member governments. Neither the Executive Director nor any member of the staff may have any financial interest in copper or any other metal industry. No such provision is made in OPEC's statutes for its Secretary-General and its staff.[1]

[1] In March and September 1969, the author held discussions in Paris with CIPEC's Executive Director, Sacha Gueronick, and his staff to learn about the activities of that organization. He also visited in August 1969 officials in Lima, Peru and Santiago de Chile for a study of their copper and other mineral industries.

By comparison with OPEC, strictly Arab attempts at collective co-operation in the oil industry, such as OAPEC, have proved so far of little consequence. On the other hand, a non-Arab scheme for economic co-operation in the Middle East has proved more effective. The Regional Co-operation for Development (RCD), providing multipurpose co-operative effort, groups since July 1964 Iran and two neighbouring non-oil exporting countries, Turkey and Pakistan.[1] All three countries are non-Arab, but are culturally bound through the common heritage of Islam (to which about 90 per cent of their citizens belong), political affinity, and alliance in CENTO. The crucial factor behind RCD's creation and development is the cultural and political affinity of the three constituent nations and, in particular, that of their leaders and their ruling elites. At an RCD meeting in Islamabad in February 1966, this affinity was clearly recognized and extolled by the ex-President of Pakistan who signed the original agreement in 1964. He said:

> RCD is very close to my heart and I take a keen and personal interest in it. I see in it, as I am sure you will do, a most valuable practical basis for fostering close economic and cultural co-operation for the benefit of the people of this region. I see in it also the first step towards establishing close unison amongst the three kindred nations which share a rich and common spiritual, cultural and historical heritage. This bond which binds us is a close affinity among our peoples that transcends governments and political institutions. The benefits of RCD cannot be measured in material terms alone. As a concept the philosophy behind RCD is of a much higher and superior order.[2]

Over its seven years of existence, the RCD community has established some 22 joint industrial projects for various commodities, including machine tools, electrical and agricultural equipment, chemicals, processed jute, sugar, and banknote papers. The establishment of these industries has been governed by conditions in each country and by market prospects at the regional level, coupled with the

[1] See Nurul Islam, 'Regional Co-operation for Development: Pakistan, Iran and Turkey', *Journal of Common Market Studies*, Vol. V, No. 3, pp. 283–301; L. E. Jamal, 'Achievements of R.C.D.' in *Pakistan in the Development Decade, Problems and Performance*, ed. A. M. Ghouse, The Economic Development Seminars, Lahore, 1968, pp. 81–5; M. Rahman and S. M. Rahman, *Economic Development of Pakistan*, Pakistan Book Corporation, Dacca, 1968, pp. 384–8; 'RCD Forges Ahead' in *Morning News*, Karachi, 21 July 1970, p. 8; and *Economic Survey of Asia and the Far East, 1969*, Part One, pp. 158–62.

[2] Quoted by Jamal, *op. cit.*, p. 85.

concern for more or less even distribution of projects among the three countries. To provide an acceptable basis for co-operation, joint-equity participation has been combined with market sharing in each project. Projects which affect only two countries can still be carried out on a bilateral basis within the framework of RCD.

Several other projects are under study or have been approved for implementation, including the construction of an oil refinery in Izmir, Turkey, and laying of a 2,000-kilometre oil pipeline from Ahwaz in Iran to the port of Iskandarun in Turkey. Iran and Pakistan are also studying the joint exploration and production of oil in the Mekran area, and of oil marketing in border areas. For RCD, co-operation in the petroleum field is a major objective. All joint projects are open to the private sector, and are guaranteed outlets in member countries. RCD has also attempted to foster the expansion of trade and the development of joint services in the fields of insurance, banking, air and sea transport, communication, tourism, and technical co-operation.

The performance of RCD is considered disappointing by some observers. One journal charges that the amount of intraregional trade in 1969 – about 1·5 per cent (four-fifths of which is petroleum) of the combined over-all trade – was still 'miserably low'. It attributes this 'disheartening' result to the 'grievous' lack of necessary infrastructure, and the absence of a common market and of a payment union.[1] One student of the subject complains that 'in the field of much-publicized joint-purpose enterprises, an overemphasis on planning, without a respectable record of simultaneous implementation, has led to a *credibility gap*'.[2]

The author feels, however, that the achievements of RCD are, as compared with OAPEC and other Arab economic schemes of regional co-operation, still positive. One would infer from RCD countries' profiles that they are therefore relatively more congruous than those of OAPEC. They have at least the minimum of political and cultural harmony economic integration needs as a prerequisite for take-off and sustained growth; without this harmony, success cannot be achieved, no matter how attractive the economic benefits to be reaped. Other factors which have contributed to the relative success of RCD are the geographical contiguity of the three countries, their

[1] *Pakistan Economist*, 'RCD Trade Performance', Vol. 9, No. 3, Karachi, March 1970, p. 33; also *ibid.*, 12 December 1970, pp. 13–14.
[2] Pervez Tahir, 'Regional Co-operation for Development among Turkey, Iran and Pakistan', *Economic Journal*, Lahore–Pakistan, January 1970, No. 1, Vol. III, p. 99, his *italics*.

comparable levels of development, and the harmonization through the RCD Regional Planning Council of regional projects and national projects within the national development plans.[1]

B. *The Opportunities*

What is the outlook for co-operation among oil exporting countries?

The survival of OPEC does not seem to be in doubt, but its functions may change somewhat. There are several possible alternatives.

First, certain policy makers of oil exporting countries have expressed a wish to see OPEC evolve into an international commodity agreement. A commodity agreement is similar to OPEC, in so far as both are governmental arrangements which reject the openly competitive market mechanism in international trade. Among the basic features for a successful commodity agreement, however, is the participation (formal or informal) of major consuming countries.[2] It was mentioned earlier in the text (pp. 54–8) that industrial countries do not find it generally in their interest to join oil exporting countries in the regulation of prices and output, and accordingly it is unlikely that OPEC will evolve into a commodity agreement.

Industrial countries' support to certain other raw material (non-oil) exporting countries is motivated, in part, by their desire to stabilize the earnings of the poor developing countries exporting these raw materials. Oil exporting countries have been considered since the 1950s to belong to the 'richer' developing countries.

Another difference between OPEC and international commodity agreements pertains to demand–supply conditions.[3] In most commodity agreements, price stabilization is in principle instituted to remedy seasonal or cyclical fluctuations in prices of agricultural and other primary products. No such fluctuations exist in the case of oil prices. Disequilibria have been mostly fundamental in nature, and have resulted – and are likely to continue to result – from trends or shifts in conditions of demand or supply. Historical evidence shows that schemes for the control or correction of such fundamental disequilibria in the oil industry (for example, prorationing in Texas) have not been temporary or oriented towards facilitating adjustments and the most efficient allocation of world resources.

[1] See *Economic Survey of Asia and the Far East, 1969*, pp. 158–62.

[2] See, for example, van Meerhaeghe, *op. cit.*, pp. 218–23.

[3] The author prepared in 1969 a report to OPEC on intergovernmental and intra-industry schemes of co-operation or control in selected mineral exporting industries: bauxite–alluminium, copper, iron ore, and tin. See published excerpt in *MEES*, 24 July 1970.

Moreover, the market structure of operators in the OPEC area is different from that of operators in an international commodity agreement such as the International Tin Agreement. In the case of the tin industry, producers are usually only sellers of a raw material or a semiprocessed commodity. In the case of the oil industry, major international companies explore for, produce, export, transport, process, and manufacture crude oil, distribute and sell petroleum and petrochemical products – mostly within their vertically integrate systems.

Adelman argues that, prior to the establishment of OPEC, there was already some kind of informal world commodity agreement in crude oil, established by oil companies, and condoned by public authorities in consuming countries. He said:

> During most of the 1950s, in effect if not in form or intent, we had a world commodity agreement in crude oil, sponsored by nobody in particular but maintained by the co-operation of the governments in the consuming countries and the international oil companies; the governments each restrained competition at home, the companies did practically nothing, but all refrained from doing what might have brought the agreement to an end.[1]

However, in the 1940s and early 1950s the British government (through the British Navy) and the U.S. government (through the Marshall aid programme to Western Europe) as big buyers exercised effective downward pressures on crude oil prices in the Arabian–Persian Gulf by bargaining successfully for lower prices with the oil supplying companies.[2]

Second, in the absence of a commodity agreement, could OPEC become an effective international cartel of oil exporting countries? Could it also differentiate prices to maximize collective benefits, as has been the practice with some companies?[3] The answer would be

[1] 'The World Oil Outlook', *op. cit.*, p. 86.

[2] See U.S. Federal Trade Commission. *The International Petroleum Cartel* (Washington, 1952), pp. 355–70; UN Economic Commission for Europe, *The Price of Oil in Western Europe* (Geneva, March 1955); and Helmut J. Frank, *Crude Oil Prices in the Middle East, A Study in Oligopolistic Price Behaviour* (New York: Praeger, 1966), pp. 19–60.

[3] Lebanon is one example of a relatively small market whose oil refining and distribution has been hitherto dominated by the majors that supply the country with crude oil at or close to posted prices, while large West European countries have long been billed at about 20 per cent discounts off posted prices. Moreover, the Lebanese government has had to offer refineries a guaranteed non-taxable rate of return of 7½ per cent on gross assets (inclusive of depreciation) which comes close to 14 per cent of net assets (after depreciation). In Western Europe,

positive if OPEC could be turned into a supranational authority endowed with the relevant cartel instruments, such as knowledge of elasticities of demand for petroleum products in various markets, effective control over production and investments in member countries; the power to elaborate specifications and rules, and to set export quotas; and authority to enforce a system of sanctions and rewards. Member countries, however, are unlikely to endow OPEC with such instruments, given their multiple politico-economic differences.

Although prospects for an OPEC price differentiating cartel are not bright, the Secretariat is already looking forward to a time of uniform pricing, when it can neutralize or at least dampen the incentive for price competition among member countries. Production programming is one means; another is an over-all system of posted or tax-reference prices for all countries concerned with a view to eliminating intercountry competition and making international companies with widespread oil interests in the OPEC area indifferent as to sources of supply. The principle of tax parity came up in occasional statements by the OPEC Secretariat[1] and was enunciated in December 1968 by Resolution XVII which 'recommends that Member Countries should seek to ensure that the posted or tax-reference prices of their petroleum exports are consistent with each other, subject to differences in gravity, quality and geographic location'. The 1971 government take settlements between oil companies and the oil exporting countries of the Arabian–Persian Gulf and Libya have aimed at such price consistency, but some member countries question whether this has been effectively achieved.

If OPEC aims at making buyers indifferent as to source of purchase, the levies should be universal and graduated in order to neutralize the cost, location, and quality differentials of the large variety of crudes available in OPEC countries, while maintaining a uniform standard of fair return among oil ventures.[2] The success of such a system is in serious doubt, not only on the grounds of acceptability to all parties concerned but also on the grounds of workability. One difficulty is that variations in quality of crudes, in freight, and in production costs among different areas change continuously over time.

several refining affiliates of major companies have, by comparison, shown losses over a number of years. (The author has been intermittently a consultant to the Government of Lebanon in oil affairs. Lebanon's refinery agreements were in 1971 under renegotiation. See also 'Refining Issues in Lebanon,' *PPS*, February 1971, pp. 55–7; and Penrose, *op. cit.*, pp. 232–4.)

[1] See, for example, OPEC, *Taxation Economics in Crude Production*, March 1965.

[2] J. L. Hartshorn, 'OPEC and Newcomer Governments,' *op. cit.*, pp. 27–37.

Moreover, a certain crude may, at a certain period of time, have different values for different markets, depending on refinery yields and the pattern of product requirements in each. These values could change in the course of time as a result of changes in technological conditions of refining and in market requirements.

Pushed to its logical – and utopian – conclusion, price uniformity should ultimately lead to comparable economic attractiveness of oil rights in all OPEC countries. This uniformity would cover the legal mode of developing oil resources, the role of national interests in oil operations, over-all fiscal obligations, and administrative and conservation matters.[1]

Third, failing to become a producers' cartel, could OPEC establish a sales-purchase alliance between its national companies and the majors, roughly similar to the little-noticed 'Gentlemen's Agreement' in the aluminium industry?[2] In 1957, the major aluminium companies outside the United States agreed to form a consortium in order to absorb aluminium exports of Soviet bloc countries, namely the U.S.S.R., Czechoslovakia, Poland, East Germany, and Hungary.[3] Industry sources admit that if East European suppliers had been left on their own to enter Western markets, they would incur substantial selling expenses; also, world aluminium prices would have been lower than they have actually been.

The agreement involves a dual quota system, one for distribution of exports among Soviet bloc countries, and another for distribution among major companies and major markets outside the bloc.[4] The distribution of export quotas is a lesser problem among Soviet bloc countries than among OPEC countries, because the U.S.S.R. is able to exercise effective pressure or suasion on its partners.

There is also the question of distributing Soviet bloc exports among the major companies. The total quantity of aluminium involved (about 100,000 tons per annum) has been and is likely to remain a relatively small proportion of world aluminium trade (less than 5

[1] See F. R. Parra, 'OPEC: Present and Future Role', in *Continuity and Change in the World Oil Industry*, pp. 135–47.

[2] See International Bank for Reconstruction and Development, *Past and Prospective Trends in the World Aluminium Industry* (Washington, 31 May 1968), Appendix A. The author is grateful for the comments of John Wall, chief economist, British Aluminium Co. Ltd.

[3] Bulgaria does not produce primary aluminium, while Rumania reportedly resisted participation in the agreement. *Metal Bulletin*, London, 14 February 1969, p. 19. Nevertheless, Rumania sells its aluminium to the same group of Western companies.

[4] For example, the quota of Soviet metal to Japan for 1968 was estimated at about 13,000 tons: *Metal Bulletin*, 30 January 1968, p. 20.

per cent). In contrast, the volume of oil expected to be exported by OPEC's national companies in the 1970s and thereafter amounts to several million tons per annum.

The aluminium industry is, moreover, relatively highly concentrated and vertically integrated with extensive multinational facilities; consequently, the major aluminium companies have not found it difficult to arrange for quota distribution among themselves, as well as among various markets, thanks to their world-wide networks of producing and marketing affiliates or associates. Each major company's percentage share in Soviet bloc sales is commensurate with its share of sales in world markets.

The quota system has not, however, precluded attempts to crack the Gentlemen's Agreement, and independent metal dealers have sought to buy Russian metal outside its framework.[1] Nevertheless, one of the merits of the agreement is flexibility; it provides for meetings at least once a year to renegotiate total quantities of aluminium exports from the Soviet bloc, and to distribute quotas of Soviet metal among international companies. Prices are agreed upon from time to time in the light of changing market conditions. Moreover, the agreement is apparently run on a commercial, non-political basis to the extent that quantities and prices are usually set in response to market forces. A commercial firm, Brandeis, Goldschmidt and Co. Ltd (a member of the London Stock Exchange), acts as a collective agent for the group of Soviet companies.

Fourth, sales arrangements among fewer countries are more promising than OPEC-wide gentlemen's co-operation, which was considered by the national companies late in the 1960s. Arrangements among fewer countries need not carry with them restrictions of production in individual countries, but are likely to cover, for example, logistic dealings involving swaps to save in freights and tariffs, combined sales for blended crudes to meet special market requirements, joint use or ownership of certain producing plants or transport media for economies of scale, or joint negotiation on certain sizable long-term contracts for more effective bargaining.

OPEC countries interested in promoting co-operation among their national companies, or even regional sub-OPEC groupings (such as that of OAPEC), should consider examples of export consortia. One interesting example of such co-operation is Malmexport, which involves exporters in the minerals field. This company, established in 1957, is a joint sales company entrusted with the selling of iron ore on behalf of three different enterprises: the Swedish state-owned

[1] *Metal Bulletin*, 30 January 1968, p. 20; *ibid.*, 14 February 1969, p. 19.

Luossavaara-Kirunovaara-Aktiebolag (LKAB), the Swedish privately-owned Grangesberg, and the Liberian company LAMCO–Joint-Venture. The ownership of Venture is shared 75 per cent by LAMCO and 25 per cent by Bethlehem Steel Corporation. LAMCO itself is 50 per cent owned by the Liberian government, and 50 per cent by a mixed group, largely Swedish (74·8 per cent), led by Grangesberg.

Malmexport functions as a negotiator and a drafter of sales contracts, an adviser and informer on current and future developments of market situations, and an executor and a handler of documents and activities relating to sales, inventories, shipping programmes, control of quality and weight, and supervision of contracts. The sales company also provides continuous liaison between parent companies and buyers with respect to such matters as claims and arbitration.

As early as 1918, U.S. legislation permitted export associations. The Export Trade Act of 10 April 1918 (also known as the Webb–Pomerene Act) allows U.S. producers to form export trade associations with a view to raising the export potential of the United States, so long as the association is not used to restrain U.S. exports or interfere with competition in the U.S. domestic market. The Webb–Pomerene Act permits membership in an export association of a majority of the firms in an industry, assignment of stocks in that association in accordance with members' production, and use of the association as the exclusive foreign outlet of members. The act permits the association to refuse to handle the products of U.S. competitors, to determine the price and quantities of exports applying to its members, to fix resale prices applying to an association's foreign distributors, and to require distributors to carry only the members' products.[1]

The Act supports export associations even if they have adverse effects on the foreign commerce of U.S. non-member countries and on domestic competition. According to an officially 'most authoritative' judicial interpretation:

> Now it may very well be that every successful export company does inevitably affect adversely the foreign commerce of those not in the joint enterprise and does bring the members of the enterprise so closely together as to affect adversely the members' competition in domestic commerce. Thus, every export company may be a restraint. But if there are only these inevitable con-

[1] *International Aspects of Antitrust, 1967*, Hearings before the Subcommittee on Antitrust and Monopoly of the Committee on the Judiciary, U.S. Senate, 90th Congress, 1st Session, persuant to S. Res. 26 'Review of the Webb-Pomerene Act of 1918' Washington, D.C., June 1967, p. 298.

sequences an export association is not an unlawful restraint. The Webb–Pomerene Act is an expression of Congressional will that such a restraint shall be permitted. And the Courts are required to give as ungrudging support to the policy of the Webb–Pomerene as to the policy of the Sherman Act. Statutory eclecticism is not a proper judicial function.[1]

Another example of an export arrangement is the Indo-Ceylon Tea Consortium (ICTC), still at the planning stage. Unlike U.S. export associations and Malmexport which are controlled by business interests in one country, ICTC will be controlled by all business interests in the two exporting countries. The objectives of the proposed consortium are to increase exports' proceeds and to ensure a fair return to tea growers in India and Ceylon. To do so, it will engage in joint marketing, establish blending and packaging units overseas, and carry out market surveys and product development. One UN source considers this agreement a model to be emulated in the case of other countries with primary commodities for export.[2] It is too early to predict how well ICTC will work.

The advantages of co-operation among producers of the same commodity for export are economies of scale, sharing in overhead costs and technical know-how, and improved bargaining position *vis-à-vis* buyers. The limitations to such co-operation at a regional or international level arise from rivalry in the sale of identical or substitute products, the absence of a climate of confidence, and differences among national companies.

Fifth, some observers have called for pricing crude oil in open exchanges, such as the London Metal Exchange (LME). Exchanges exist for several primary commodities, notably agricultural products and metals. Businesses dealings in these products are numerous and vertically non-integrated. Most of the international trade in crude oil is, by comparison, conducted by a relatively small number of international firms, moving oil mostly in integrated channels or on long-term contract. Should non-integrated 'independent' operators and newcomer oil companies (including national companies) increase in number and importance, open trading of crude oil could conceivably take place. This change could, however, lead to the destabilization of crude oil prices. Spot quotations of marginal quantities will readily reflect speculative or distress sales in the exchange – as is the case with commodities traded on the LME; and

[1] *Ibid.* pp. 298–9.
[2] *Economic Survey of Asia and the Far East, 1969*, Part One, pp. 163–4.

these sales need not be representative of the bulk of crude oil transactions bypassing that market.

The end result of such open market trading could well prove detrimental to OPEC countries under conditions of a buyers' market, to the extent that it highlights existent price weaknesses; the opposite would be the case in a sellers' market. These reflections suggest that a formal exchange for crude oil could have a significant impact on setting posted or tax-reference prices of host governments, as well as on realized prices of sales by-passing the exchange. It is a moot question whether the economic, strategic, and political significance of oil would make such a formal exchange seem appropriate to the interested governments and companies.

C. *Expected Structural Changes*

Looking into the future beyond the 1970s, one does not see much prospect for further tightening of market control. On the contrary, the international oil oligopoly is likely to weaken further, and the vertical 'dis-integration' movement of the international oil industry will accelerate. National oil companies of exporting countries will get possession of vast crude oil reserves at expiration or renewal dates of major concessions (in 1979 and 1983 in Iran and Venezuela, for example). This development may be intensified if affiliates of expatriate companies are partially or totally nationalized, as has been the policy in some oil exporting countries – notably Algeria.

The Shah of Iran, in particular, would like to see the end of the concession system in his country by 1979.[1] The National Iranian Oil Company (NIOC), he has announced, would then produce oil and sell it at export terminals to foreign companies. This outlook is shared by other OPEC leaders. Another parallel structural change is under way, namely the establishment and growth of national oil companies in consumer countries, both the developed and the developing. These countries are likely to give larger protected shares of their domestic refining and distribution to their national companies.[2]

In the absence of direct oil producing rights, international companies will turn into buyers from national agencies of crude oil (or products) on a contract basis, probably long-term in order to plan their future requirements with a reasonable degree of certainty. Such

---

[1] *The Wall Street Journal*, 26 January 1971, p. 23.

[2] In Japan 30 per cent of oil sales by 1985, see *The Petroleum Industry in Japan, 1969*, p. 6.

purchase arrangements could offer international companies certain advantages, including full managerial freedom in deciding the size and direction of their oil trade; the prospect of being able to play off one host government against another to induce them to cut down their export or tax-reference prices; and lower prices to be derived from forming an oligopsonistic group to counter collectively OPEC countries.

However, one should not overlook factors which will work to prevent oil companies from voluntarily walking away from their concessions and becoming buyers of oil. Among these factors are fiscal advantages to certain companies (the depletion allowance for U.S. companies) to own oil-producing properties; the need for greater flexibility and better assurance of supplies than that offered by purchase contracts; and economies of vertical integration. Indeed, as long as these companies are deriving net incremental benefits from the ownership and operation of their concessions, they are likely to stick to their oil-producing rights.

The decline in the concentration and in the vertical-integration features of the international oil industry would maintain – in the presence of vast low cost reserves – the possibility of price weaknesses in the crude and products markets, thus threatening the unit financial receipts derived by certain host countries. This market situation will remain and probably worsen as a larger number of oil suppliers – their low cost of production permitting – press for market outlets, and as non-oil fuels (nuclear energy, in particular) develop competitiveness.

One can even surmise that some governments of oil exporting countries with large oil reserves are probably tempted or even willing to give their national oil companies tax allowances or rebates on exports in the hope of larger export volumes. Such tax concessions could have serious repercussions on market price levels if they occurred to any significant extent. This would mean that national companies would have larger margins available and could use these to increase their sales volume by price cutting. As a result, the tax concession afforded by a host government to its national company would be passed totally or partially on to the customer in the form of a lower market price.

The private international oil companies, by comparison, have tax-paid costs as a floor, no matter how highly competitive markets turn out to be, until they can wrest from host governments tax allowances similar to those available to national companies. It can also be argued that diversified international companies are not

215

equally pressed, compared with national companies, to dispose of their oil from each of their world-wide oil properties. National companies have no alternative crude oil sources except those in their home country; consequently, they have less flexibility in manipulating production rates for various crudes. They are likely to remain keen rivals among themselves, as well as with international companies. Moreover, they are probably less mindful than international companies of world-wide repercussions of their price reduction policies; as newcomers, they have no international crude oil supplies and long-established sales commitments which they might prejudice.

The future points also to a trend of diversification of international oil companies' activities. An increasing number operating in the OPEC countries and elsewhere are becoming natural resource companies, rather than companies concerned only with oil, petrochemicals, or other energy sources. Such diversification in the minerals field and allied activities arises from company concern for making fuller use of technology, skills, experience, geological surveys and transport facilities available in the petroleum industry operations; for broadening investment opportunities in fields where return on capital is more attractive than in oil. Indeed, companies desire to reduce their vulnerability which arises from geologic risk involved in finding commercial quantities of oil in a restricted geographical area of operation; economic risk arising from the eventual substitution of oil, at least partially; and political risks.

Among oil companies going into minerals other than oil are Gulf Oil Corporation with its 100 per cent subsidiary, Gulf Mineral Resources Co.; Shell which has taken over Billiton, a leading ore mining and metallurgy concern; Cities Services with copper and zinc interests; Union Oil Co. and Continental Oil Co., each with copper interests; Standard Oil Co. (Indiana) with iron ore interests; Occidental, Superior Oil Co., and Phillips Petroleum Co., each with interests in several minerals – to mention a few.[1]

With these expected structural developments in the world oil industry, what then is to become of OPEC? Will it become a quasi-cartel; a bargaining agent for its members asking for better terms from international oil companies; a trade association propagating information; a political pressure group lobbying with governments of oil importing countries for reductions in trade and fiscal barriers, and for better terms of trade; or a staff-agency acting as a clearing house

[1] See *Petroleum Outlook*, December 1968; The *Financial Times*, London, 15 February 1971; *PPS*, January 1971, p. 10 and 33, and Royal Dutch *Annual Report 1970*, p. 2.

for information and ideas, conducting research, and offering advice to member countries?

Much of the evidence in this study suggests that the OPEC organization has assumed, at various points of time, one or more of the foregoing roles. More often than not, however, it has acted as an effective international advisory organization for the co-ordination of member countries' policies and actions, and it is likely to maintain this as a dominant role. Factors that have limited and will continue to limit the prospects of greater power for OPEC are fear of internal defection or non-compliance by members, threat of outside competition, technological–economic displacement by other sources of energy, and fear of active opposition by major oil importing countries.[1] The organization's weaknesses are, however, primarily attributable to the fact that it is composed of national governments with disparate economic and political interests, each jealously guarding its sovereign prerogatives.

The threat of a collapse in petroleum prices and in host countries' oil income, or of a deterioration in their terms of trade – which is likely to prevail for several years to come – is one of the best reasons for oil exporting countries to stick with an organization like OPEC. Indeed, OPEC seems to have had a remarkable effect in forestalling such a collapse, and, since 1970, in reversing the trend of price decline. If OPEC can continue to be effective to this degree, and if member countries do not have inflated ideas of what OPEC is able to do, it will remain a useful organization.

While OPEC countries have achieved a significant measure of policy co-ordination concerning fiscal measures on oil exports made by expatriate concessionaires, this has not yet led to any substantive co-operation in, or integration of, policies and activities in other fields. By comparison, OAPEC, which represents a 'spill-over' from OPEC, has been set up for the purpose of regional co-operation in the oil sector to begin with, as part of a longer term goal of regional unity among its members. OAPEC has still to translate hopes into actions. As one student of integration pertinently pointed out:

> A region does not hang together if its constituent countries or states cohere simply in regard to copper or wheat or coal [or oil, one may add]. They must cohere in many respects – in many transactions and commodities, in the flow of labour, management,

[1] See also Z. Mikdashi, 'A Future Vision of the Oil Industry, and the Oil Policy of Petroleum Exporting Countries', Supplement to *Energy in Japan* No. 11, Tokyo, October 1970, p. 4.

217

and capital, in economic structure, in education, in culture, in science, in politics, in intermarriage and migration, and in still other ways. The more varied and numerous the transactions that hold a region together are, the more solid the region is likely to be.[1]

Closer co-operation among developing countries, among OPEC and OAPEC countries in particular, has been impeded by countless individual considerations. Nevertheless, national divergencies and hesitations among these countries could well give way to a growing solidarity. This can highlight and crystallize common interests, promote an awareness of common threats to members' prosperity, and a perception of benefits from collective action. As events of 1970–71 have very well shown, such solidarity can pay handsomely.

[1] Deutsch, *Nationalism and its Alternatives*, p. 102.

Appendix 1

BIOGRAPHICAL NOTES ON OPEC'S SECRETARIES-GENERAL*

1. *Fuad Rouhani*
(Iran)

Staff member of Anglo-Iranian Oil Co., prior to 1951;
Chief Legal Adviser, National Iranian Oil Co. (NIOC), 1951–54;
Director of NIOC, 1954;
Managing Director and Deputy Chairman of NIOC, 1956;
Secretary General and Chairman of the Board of Governors of OPEC, 1961–64;
Professor of Iranian Studies at Columbia University, 1964–65;
Secretary-General of the organization of Regional Co-operation for Development (RCD), 1966;
Consultant to the UN Energy Section, 1970.

2. *Abdul Rahman Bazzaz*
(Iraq)

Graduated from Baghdad Law College, 1935, and from London University (LLB), 1939;
Assistant Professor at Baghdad Law College, 1940;
Court judge, Baghdad, 1945–55;
Dean of Law College, Baghdad, 1955;
Judge in Supreme Court, Baghdad, 1959;
Director of Arab League Institute for Higher Studies, Cairo, 1962;
Ambassador to U.A.R. in February 1963, and to Britain late in 1963;
Secretary-General of OPEC, January 1964-April 1965;
Deputy Prime Minister, Minister of Foreign Affairs, Acting Minister of Oil, and Prime Minister of Iraq, 1965–67;
Jailed in Baghdad by British in 1941–44, by Nuri al-Sa'id's regime in

* See also Table 4.1.

1956, by Qasem's regime in 1961, by al-Bakr's regime since 1969; Author of several books on Arab nationalism.

3. *Ashraf Lutfi*
(Kuwait)

Originally Palestinian, naturalized Kuwaiti;
Entered into service of Kuwait Government Secretariat, 1948;
Reached later the post of Under-Secretary in that department;
Took part in oil negotiations and policy matters;
Member of the Board of Directors of the Kuwait National Petroleum Co., 1960–8;
Secretary-General of OPEC, May 1965–December 1966;
Wrote two books *Arab Oil: a Plan for the Future* in 1960, and *OPEC Oil* in 1968.

4. *Mohammad Joukdhar*
(Saudi Arabia)

Graduated from University of California in Los Angeles B.A. (Economics), 1956;
Received M.A. from the University of Southern California, 1958;
Economic adviser to the Saudi Government Directorate of Petroleum and Mineral Affairs, 1958;
Spent one year with the Venezuelan Ministry of Mines and Hydrocarbons, 1960;
Nominated as Saudi Government representative on the Board of Directors of the Arabian Oil Company;
Director-General of the Saudi Ministry of Petroleum and Mineral Resources, 1963;
Secretary-General of OPEC, 1967;
Deputy-Governor of Petromin since 1971.

5. *Francisco Parra*
(Venezuela)

Graduated from the University of Geneva with a degree in political Science;
Economic analyst with Crèole Petroleum Corporation, Venezuela, 1951–60;
Petroleum economist with the consulting firm of Arthur D. Little, Inc., 1960–62;

Joined OPEC as Economic Adviser to Secretary-General, Chief of Economic Department, and as Secretary-General, 1962–68;
Consultant in international petroleum economics since 1969;
Author of several articles and published addresses on oil.

6. *Elrich Sanger*
(Indonesia)

Graduated from the Faculty of Law and Social Science at the University of Indonesia, 1954;
Received a Ph.D. in law from Bonn University, 1959;
Headed the Legal Department of the Bureau of Oil Affairs at the Ministry of Industry, Indonesia, 1959.
Member of the Board for the Distribution of Oil Products, Indonesia, 1960;
Secretary-General of the Indonesian Co-ordinating Commission for National Oil Companies, 1961;
Chief of Staff of the Indonesian national oil company, Permina, 1964;
Under-Secretary of the Indonesian Oil Ministry, 1964–67;
Director of Permina in charge of legal affairs, foreign relations and international marketing, 1967–68;
Secretary-General of OPEC, 1969;
Chief Delegate of Indonesia to OPEC Conferences, 1970–71

7. *Omar al-Badri*
(Libya)

Graduated from Dublin University with a B.A. in economics and political science, 1961;
Worked with an oil company in Libya, and as consulting correspondent for the Economist Intelligence Unit of London, 1962–69;
Secretary-General of OPEC, 1970.

8. *Nadim Pachachi*
(Abu Dhabi)

Ph.D.;
Director of Oil and Mines in the Ministry of Economics, Iraq, 1940–43;
Director–General of the Ministry of Economics, Iraq, 1943–52;
Minister of Economics, of Development, and of Finance in Iraq, intermittently in 1952–58;

Member of the Iraqi Parliament, 1952–58;
Oil Adviser to the Libyan Government, 1960–64;
Oil Adviser to the Kuwait Government, 1966–68;
Oil Adviser to the Ruler of Abu Dhabi, 1966–71;
Chairman of OPEC Board of Governors, 1970;
Secretary-General of OPEC, 1971–72.

Sources: Various publications, primarily *MEES*.

Appendix 2
SELECTED BIBLIOGRAPHY

The author has done extensive research for this work, which comes at the end of some 15 years of close association in one way or another with energy questions. In his capacity as consultant to OPEC on several occasions, over 1964–70, he has been able to know intimately the organization, its staff, and its activities.

As resident adviser in oil affairs to the Government of Kuwait and as Secretary of Kuwait's Oil Policy Planning Committee in 1966–67, he has had access to primary information available to the few highly placed officials. In 1971, he was invited to join a UN 'Panel of Experts' on the petroleum industry, and to serve as a UN consultant in energy matters.

The author has also been involved in research on other minerals since 1968, and has visited a number of leading mineral exporting countries. In addition, he has participated in several congresses, symposia or seminars on extractive industries, or on developing countries generally. These experiences have contributed to broadening and enriching his knowledge of the subject under study.

The analysis depends basically on primary sources, whether these are published or unpublished. Secondary sources have been used in the text when the author could not quote primary sources of a confidential nature available to him. Secondary sources, whenever used, have been checked for the trustworthiness of information they carry.

Primary sources are either official or private. The first category covers reports, proceedings of conferences or negotiations, studies, memoranda, legislation and other works made by, or on behalf of, international organizations or governmental departments and agencies. International sources comprise essentially those of OPEC, the United Nations and its specialized agencies, the Arab League and its seven Petroleum Congresses held between 1959 and 1970. Inter-

223

national treaties, pacts or conventions, mining codes, fiscal and other legislation, as well as most of the company–government agreements (with their amendments) are published in official journals, or separately.

Private sources of a primary nature used in this study cover those of oil companies operating internationally. These documents (published and unpublished) include audited annual reports or other authentic documents submitted to the regulatory authorities in oil exporting or oil importing countries, such as the fiscal authorities. Oil companies, moreover, publish annual and other periodical reports on their financial and operational conditions, as well as occasional statements, papers, pamphlets, studies, manuals, handbooks, and so on. A number of these companies also publish individually or collectively statistical reviews or factual surveys of the world oil industry.

In addition to oil companies, firms which provide services to the oil industry offer valuable information. Among these firms are tanker brokers, banks and other financial institutions, and equipment manufacturers. Trade associations or research institutions constitute another valuable source of reference. Besides information published by the protagonists of the oil industry, a number of authors have come out with valuable source materials.

The author wishes to caution the reader that the subject matter of this study covers a number of complex and controversial issues, and many of the *obiter dicta* or information issued by various interested parties lack objectivity. They often contain partisan views, and sometimes bristle with factual errors; personal views in quotation marks in this study should therefore be used as evidence only of subjective attitudes. For an analytical assessment of sources on the Middle East oil industry, see also the author's 'The Profitability of Middle Eastern Oil Ventures: a Historical Approach', in *Studies in the Economic History of the Middle East from the Rise of Islam to the Present Day*, ed. M. A. Cook, Oxford University Press, pp. 468–84.

In addition to works consulted, the author has interviewed several political leaders, and numerous government and industry officials. These discussions have shed light on events, and on the behaviour and motives of decision makers. To carry out these interviews, the author has made field trips to most major oil exporting countries and to major oil importing countries.

The following bibliography does not purport to be comprehensive or exhaustive. It excludes materials consulted in the fields of history, politics, economic development, international and regional relations, and multi-national business. Its purpose is to present major relevant source materials on the petroleum industry published since OPEC's establishment in 1960. This selected list does not cover all the documents quoted in the text. Moreover, it should be considered as supplemental to the author's bibliography in his earlier book.[1]

A. *Published Official*

1. *European Communities:*
European Economic Community, *L'influence économique du prix de l'énergie*, Brussels, 1966.
Bulletin de la Communauté Européenne du Charbon et de l'Acier, *Nouvelles réflexions sur les perspectives énergétiques à long terme de la Communauté européenne*, Brussels, April 1966.
Communauté Européenne, Service d'information, *L'Europe et l'Energie*, Luxembourg, 1967.
La C.E.C.A. Première Assise d'Une Communauté plus Large et plus Profonde, Luxembourg, June 1967.

2. *OPEC:*
Explanatory Memoranda on OPEC Resolutions IV.32, IV.33, IV.34. June 1962.
Natural Gas in the OPEC Area: paper presented by G. al-Ukaili at ECAFE Symposium in Tehran, September 1962.
Definition of Petroleum Resources: paper presented by Anibal R. Martinez at ECAFE Symposium in Tehran, September 1962.
OPEC and the Oil Industry in the Middle East: based on talk by Francisco Parra at Middle East seminar, Johns Hopkins University, October 1962.
Demand Patterns and Crude Gravities: based on talk by Francisco Parra at oil industry seminar, London School of Economics, January 1963.
Speech Delivered by Fuad Rouhani, Secretary General, at the IInd Consultative Meeting, Geneva, 1 July 1963.
Pricing Problems, Further Considerations: September 1963.
The Price of Crude Oil, a Rational Approach: OPEC paper presented at Fourth Arab Petroleum Congress, Beirut, November 1963.
Radical Changes in the International Oil Industry During the Past Decade: OPEC paper presented at Fourth Arab Petroleum Congress, Beirut, November 1963.

[1] *A Financial Analysis of Middle Eastern Oil Concessions: 1901–1965, op. cit.*, pp. 329–40.

The Oil Industry's Organization in the Middle East and Some of its Fiscal Consequences: based on talk by Francisco Parra at Business Administration Seminar, American University of Beirut, November 1963.

Exporting Countries and International Oil: based on talk by Francisco Parra at Imperial Defence College, London, May 1964.

Elasticity of Demand for Crude Oil: its Implications for Exporting Countries: based on talk by Isam Kabbani at oil industry seminar, London School of Economics, May 1964.

The Development of Petroleum Resources under the Concession System in Non-Industrialized Countries: based on talk by Francisco Parra to Iraqi Engineers Association and Iraqi Economists Society, Baghdad, June 1964.

Background Information: June 1964.

OPEC and the Principle of Negotiation: OPEC paper presented at Fifth Arab Petroleum Congress, Cairo, March 1965.

Taxation Economics in Crude Production: OPEC paper presented at Fifth Arab Petroleum Congress, Cairo, March 1965.

From Concessions to Contracts: OPEC paper presented at Fifth Arab Petroleum Congress, Cairo, March 1965.

Offshore Oil Concession Agreements in OPEC Member Countries: paper presented by E. A. Mabruk at First International Congress on Petroleum and the Sea, Monaco, May 1965.

Note on Resolution IX.61: July 1965.

Cheap Energy, Diversification of Sources and Security of Supply: based on talk by Nameer Jawdat at Loughborough College of Technology, November 1965.

Collective Influence in the Recent Trend Towards the Stabilization of International Crude and Product Prices: OPEC paper presented at Sixth Arab Petroleum Congress, Baghdad, March 1967.

OPEC as an Instrument of Moderation: talk by OPEC Secretary General Muhammad Joukhdar to group of institutional security analysts, New York, April 1967.

OPEC and the Consuming Countries, Vienna, May 1967.

Annual Statistical Bulletin, 1965 to 1970.

OPEC Resolution XVI.90: Its Background and Some Analytical Comments, text of three lectures given by Hasan S. Zakariya at the Petroleum Economics Seminar organized by the Norwegian Petroleum Council held at Ustaoset, Norway, January 1969.

International Oil and the Energy Policies of the Producing and Consuming Countries, A collection of papers presented at OPEC's Seminar held in Vienna in July 1969.

226

Selected Documents of the International Petroleum Industry, 1967, 1968, and 1969.

Contribution of OPEC-Based Crude Oil to the National Incomes of OECD Countries, presented by Farouk al-Husseini, VIIth Arab Petroleum Congress, Kuwait, March 1970.

Progressive Relinquishment Under OPEC Declaratory Statement of Policy of 1968, by Hasan S. Zakariya, VIIth Arab Petroleum Congress, Kuwait, March 1970.

3. *OPEC Countries:*

Algeria's Ministère des Finances et du Plan, *L'Algérie et les Hydrocarbures*, extract from 'l'Annuaire de l'Afrique du Nord, 1965'.

—— *Caractéristiques de la Politique de l'Algérie en Matière d'Hydrocarbures*, 1 June 1967.

Indonesia, Ibnu Sutowo, *The Role of Oil in the National Life*, Hong Boon Printing Company, Djakarta, 1966,

Iran, *Press Conferences of His Imperial Majesty Mohammad Reza Shah Pahlavi of Iran, 1960–1961.*

—— The Shah's speech to the Majlis on 6 October 1967, published in *The Revolution: New Dimensions*, Transorient, London, 1967.

Iraq, 'Compte Rendu on the Negotiations between the Government of Iraq and the Iraq Petroleum Co. Ltd from 2 May 1964 to 3 June 1965', in Arabic in *Dirassat 'Arabiyah*, Beirut, December 1966.

Venezuela, Republic of, *Venezuela and OPEC*, Imprenta Nacional, Caracas, 1961.

Pérez-Alfonzo, Juan Pablo, Memorandum sent to President Marcos Pérez-Jiménex from Washington in 1954, reproduced in his study *Oil, Juice of the Earth*, Caracas, 2 January 1961.

Pérez-Guerrero, Manuel, Minister of Mines and Hydrocarbons, *Oil Problems in Venezuela and the Solution of Same*, speech read over the Venezuelan National Television Network and the Commercial Radio Stations on October 6, 1966 – translated by Traductores Técnicos Asociados in Caracas.

Venezuela CVP, *The National Oil Company and Public Opinion*, Caracas, May 1967.

4. *United Nations, and Specialized Agencies:*

International Monetary Fund-International Bank for Reconstruction and Development, A Joint Staff Study (Part I), *The Problem of Stabilization of Prices of Primary Products* (Washington, 1969).

International Bank for Reconstruction and Development, *Stabilization of Prices of Primary Products* Part II (Washington, 1969).

227

UN General Assembly, Report of the Secretary General, *Sovereignty over Natural Resources*, 14 September 1970.

UN Economic and Social Council, *Natural Resources Development and Policies, Including Environmental Considerations*, New York, 12 January 1971.

5. United States:

National Petroleum Council, *Impact of Oil Exports From the Soviet Bloc*, 2 vols., Washington, 1962; and *Supplement*, 1964.

Moore, J. Cordell, U.S. Department of the Interior, Assistant Secretary, *Observations and Remarks on United States Energy Policy*, presented to OECD's Energy Committee, January 1967.

U.S. Senate, *Governmental Intervention in the Market Mechanism, The Petroleum Industry, Part 1*, Hearings before the Subcommittee on Antitrust and Monopoly of the Committee on the Judiciary, Washington, March–April 1969.

U.S. Cabinet Task Force on Oil Import Control, *The Oil Import Question, A Report on the Relationship of Oil Imports to the National Security*, Washington, February 1970.

U.S. Congress, *Oil Import Controls*, Hearings before the Subcommittee on Mines and Mining of the Committee on Interior and Insular Affairs, House of Representatives, 91st Congress, Washington, D.C., March–April 1970.

—— *Tariff and Trade Proposals*, Hearings before the Committee on Ways and Means, House of Representatives, 91st Congress, Washington, D.C., June 1970, Part 8.

6. Other Consumer Countries:

Government of India, Ministry of Steel, Mines and Fuel, *Report of the Oil Price Inquiry Committee*, July 1961.

Japan, Advisory Committee for Energy, *Report on Energy Policy*, 20 February 1967.

The Japanese National Committee of the World Petroleum Congress, *The Petroleum Industry in Japan, 1969*, Tokyo, October 1969.

U.K. Ministry of Power, *Fuel Policy*, October 1965 and November 1967 in Cmds 2798 and 3438 respectively.

OECD, *Energy Policy, Problems and Objectives*, Paris, July 1966.

B. *Published Private*

Adelman, M. A., 'Oil Prices in the Long Run (1963–75)', *The Journal of Business* of the University of Chicago, April 1964.

—— 'Efficiency of Resource Use in Crude Petroleum', *The Southern Economic Journal*, October 1964.

—— 'The World Oil Outlook', *Natural Resources and International Development*, ed. Marion Clawson, Resources for the Future, Inc., The Johns Hopkins Press (Baltimore, 1964).

—— Speech delivered at the 'Economics of Petroleum Distribution' Conference, The Transportation Center of Northwestern University, 1 April 1965.

—— *Oil Production Costs in Four Areas*, paper delivered at the American Institute of Mining, Metallurgical, and Petroleum Engineers, 28 February–2 March 1966.

—— *The Future of World Oil*, Parts I & II, The Transportation Center of Northwestern University, 27 and 28 March 1966, edited transcript.

Helmut, Frank, *Crude Oil Prices in the Middle East, A Study in Oligopolistic Price Behavior*, Praeger (New York, 1966).

Hirst, David, *Oil and Public Opinion in the Middle East*, London, Faber & Faber, 1966.

Kitzinger, Uwe, 'Regional and Functional Integration', in *The Common Markets*, The Lebanese Association of Political Sciences, IVth International Congress of Political Sciences (Beirut, November–December 1965).

Knapp, Wilfred, *A History of War and Peace, 1939–1965*, Oxford University Press, 1967.

Law, Elston R., Middle East Co-ordinator, Gulf Oil Corporation, *Financing of Integrated International Oil Companies*, Kuwait Institute of Economic and Social Planning in the Middle East, 22 November 1967.

Lovejoy, W. F. and Homan, P. T., *Economic Aspects of Oil Conservation Regulation*, Resources for the Future, Inc. (The Johns Hopkins Press, Baltimore, 1967).

Lutfi, Ashraf T., *OPEC Oil*, Middle East Research and Publishing Centre (Beirut, 1968).

—— *OPEC and its Problems*, Kuwait Institute of Economic and Social Planning in the Middle East, October 1967.

McLean, John G., President and Chief Executive, Continental Oil Company, 'The Importance of the Newcomers in the International Oil Business', paper presented at the American University of Beirut, 8 April 1968, reproduced in *MEES Supplement*, 12 April 1968.

El Mallakh, Ragaei, *Some Dimensions of Middle East Oil: The Producing Countries and the United States*, American-Arab

229

Association for Commerce and Industry, New York, March 1970.

R. F. Mikesell *et al.*, *Foreign Investment in the Petroleum and Mineral Industries*, Case Studies of Investor-Host Country Relations, The Johns Hopkins Press, Baltimore, 1971.

Brouwer, L. E. J., Managing Director of Royal Dutch/Shell, *Some Basic Issues in the Oil Industry's Relations With Governments*, talk given to the Iraqi Engineers' Association in Baghdad on 28 May 1964.

Chandler, Geoffrey, Trade Relations Co-ordinator, Shell International Petroleum Co., 'The Myth of Oil Power – International Groups and National Sovereignty', in *International Affairs*, London, October 1970, Vol. 46, No. 4.

Hartshorn, J. E., *Oil Companies and Governments, an Account of the International Oil Industry in its Political Environment*, Faber & Faber (London, 1967).

—— 'OPEC and Newcomer Governments', in *Continuity and Change in the World Oil Industry*, eds. Mikdashi, Z., Cleland, S. and Seymour, I; Middle East Research and Publishing Centre, Beirut, 1970.

Mikdashi, Zuhayr, *A Financial Analysis of Middle Eastern Oil Concessions: 1901–65* New York, Praeger, 1966.

—— 'Problems of a Common Production Policy among OPEC Member Countries', *Organization of the Petroleum Exporting Countries* (Vienna, July 1969) and *Middle East Economic Papers, 1969*.

—— Cleland S. and Seymour I. eds., *Continuity and Change in the World Oil Industry*, Middle East Research and Publishing Centre, Beirut, June 1970.

—— 'The Profitability of Middle Eastern Oil Ventures: A Historical Approach', in *Studies in the Economic History of the Middle East From the Rise of Islam to the Present Day*, ed. M. A. Cook, Oxford University Press, 1970.

—— 'A Future Vision of the Oil Industry, and the Oil Policy of Petroleum Exporting Countries', Supplement to *Energy in Japan*, No. 11, Tokyo, September 1970.

Penrose, E. T. 'Profit Sharing Between Producing Countries and Oil Companies in the Middle East' *The Economic Journal*, London, June 1959.

—— 'Middle East Oil: The International Distribution of Profits and Income Taxes', *Economica*, London, August 1960.

—— 'Vertical Integration with joint Control of Raw Material Production', *Journal of Development Studies*, April 1965.

—— 'Government Partnership in the Major Concessions of the Middle East: the Nature of the Problem', *MEES Supplement*, 30 August 1968.

—— *The Large International Firm in Developing Countries: The International Petroleum Industry* (London: Allen & Unwin, 1968).

Pérez Alfonzo, Juan Pablo, *El Pentagono Pétrolero*, Ediciones Revista Politica, Caracas 1967.

Schuman, Robert 'Origine, objectif et élaboration de la Communauté du Charbon et de l'Acier' in *Pour l'Europe* (Nagel, Paris, 1963).

Stocking, G. W., *Middle East Oil, A Study in Political and Economic Controversy*, Vanderbilt University Press, Nashville, Tenn.: 1970.

Suzuki, M., *Competition and Monopoly in the World Oil Markets – A Review in the Light of Price Analysis of Imported Crude Oils in Japan*, The Institute of Energy Economics, Supplement to *Energy in Japan No. 4* (Tokyo, February 1968).

Swerling, Boris C., Princeton University Essays in International Finance, *Current Issues in Commodity Policy*, June 1962.

C. Selected Trade Journals and Periodicals

Articles, talks, interviews, reviews, and statistics on the world petroleum industry are published by a large number of journals, petroleum companies, industry groups, and financial institutions (such as Chase Manhattan Bank and First National City Bank – both of New York). The following is a selected list of major specialized oil trade journals and periodicals which contain material of direct relevance to the subject matter of this study.

Arab Oil Review, Tripoli–Libya.
Bulletin de l'Industrie Pétrolière, Paris.
Energy in Japan, Tokyo.
Iran Oil Journal, Tehran.
Middle East Economic Survey, Beirut.
Naft El Arab, previously *Arab Oil & Gas Journal*, Beirut.
Oil and Gas Journal, Tulsa, Oklahoma.
OPEC, *Annual Review and Record*;
—— *Annual Statistical Bulletin*; and
—— *OPEC Bulletin*, Vienna.
Le Pétrole et le Gaz Arabes, Beirut.
Petroleum and Economic Digest, Dublin.
Petroleum Intelligence Weekly, New York.
Petroleum Press Service, London.
Platt's Oilgram, New York.

D. *Unpublished*

Adelman, M. A., *Eastern Hemisphere Oil Profits – The Next Five Years*, Annual Convention – The Financial Analysts Federation, 24 May 1966, New York.

—— *Oil Demand, Supply, Cost and Prices in the World Market*, paper submitted to the U.N. *ad hoc* Panel of Experts on Projections of Demand and Supply of Crude Petroleum and Products, 2 March 1971, New York.

Bharier, Julian, *Capital Formation in Iran, 1900–1965*, Ph.D. thesis, University of London, June 1969.

Burnett, Carl, Mobil Oil, *Significance of New Trends in Crude Oil Pricing*, 1 March 1971 – paper submitted to the UN Panel of Experts on Projections of Demand and Supply of Crude Petroleum and Products, New York, 9–18 March 1971.

Institut Français du Pétrole, Division des Applications Industrielles, *Relative Values of Crude Oils*, Study prepared for the Organization of the Petroleum Exporting Countries, April 1966.
> (1) 'Executive Summary'
> (2) Vol. 1: 'Market Survey – Basis of the Study'
> (3) Vol. 2: 'Technical and Economic Calculations, Western Europe 1965'
> (4) Vol. 3: 'Technical and Economic Calculations, Western Europe 1970'.

Itayim, Fuad, W., 'Middle East Conflict and the Continuity of Oil Supplies', address delivered on 7 May 1970 at Harvard University Center for Middle Eastern Studies.

Leeman, Wayne, *The Future Structure of the Market for Middle East Oil*, paper presented at the Princeton University Conference on 'Arab Development in the Emerging International Economy'; and *Comments* by H. W. Page, Vice President and Director, Standard Oil Co. (N.J.), 26 April 1963.

Little, Arthur D., Inc. *Economic Aspects of the International Petroleum Industry – Summary and Conclusions*, Cambridge, Massachusetts, 15 December 1961. (Report to OPEC.)

—— *Economic Aspects of the International Petroleum Industry*, Report to the Organization of the Petroleum Exporting Countries, and *Appendices A, B, C, D*. Cambridge, Massachusetts, 15 January 1962.

—— *Aspects of Government Revenue from Petroleum Industry Operations*, Memorandum Report to OPEC, Cambridge, Mass., 1 June 1962.

Mikdashi, Zuhayr, *Economic Benefits to Host Governments From Major Oil Concessions in the Middle East*, December 1964 – prepared for OPEC, 60 pp.

—— *A Comparative Analysis of Selected Mineral Exporting Industries*, December 1969 – prepared for OPEC, 182 pp.

OPEC, *OPEC: An Example of Sub-Regional Co-operation and Trade Expansion*, a paper prepared by OPEC Economics Department for the benefit of the UNCTAD International Group on Trade Expansion, Economic Co-operation and Regional Integration among Developing Countries, Vienna, July 1970.

—— *Economic Desirability and Feasibility of Participation Upstream and Downstream*, Vienna, May 1970.

Page, Howard, then Vice President and Director of Standard Oil Company (New Jersey), *Address* at the Staff Information Meeting, 17 October 1962.

Shell International Petroleum Co. Ltd, *The Role of Government in Economic Affairs*, 6 December 1960.

—— *International and Multinational Nature of the Oil Industry*, October 1961.

—— *International Oil Prices*, October 1961; *ibid.*, June 1968.

—— *Current International Oil Pricing Problems*, 29 August 1963.

—— *Some Current Issues Facing the Oil Industry*, September 1963.

—— *The Economic Impact of Oil Operations in Producing Countries*, February 1969.

Standard Oil Co. of New Jersey, *Middle East Oil Revenues in Relation to the Price of Imported Goods*, 16 September 1964.

U.S.S.R. Delegation, *Oil Production Industry of the U.S.S.R. and Co-operation with the Arab Countries in Developing Their National Oil Industry*, Report to the VIIth Arab Petroleum Congress, Kuwait, March 1970.

White, J. R., Director and Senior Vice President, Standard Oil Company (New Jersey), *Remarks* presented at the Sixth Annual Student Conference on Foreign Affairs, United States Naval Academy, Annapolis, Maryland, 22 April 1966.

INDEX

Abu Dhabi, 21, 80, 82, 151, 153, 155; income from oil, 131, 183; and OAPEC, 104, 105; and OPEC membership, 18, 97, 128, 130, 204
Abu Musa, 81
Adelman, M. A., 17*n*, 37*n*, 112–13*n*, 118–19, 135, 208
al-Atiqi, Abdel-Rahman, 83
Alexandria Protocol (1944), 27
Alfonzo, Pérez, 31, 32, 33, 57, 93, 96
Algeria, 27, 83, 89, 104; and income from oil, 162–3, 173, 183; and OAPEC, 86–8, 90–1, 94; and OPEC membership, 18, 97, 155–6; nationalization, 200, 214
aluminium industry: Gentlemen's Agreement, 210–11
Amerada, 148, 153
Amouzegar, Jamshid, 83
Anglo-Iranian Oil Co., 23–4; *see also* BP
antitrust legislation, 36–7, 152
Arab League (1945), 27–9, 31, 77, 88, 91, 104; objectives, 27–9, and oil schemes, 27–9, 93–4; and OAPEC, 104–7; Summit Conference, 86–8
Arab Oil Congress, 29, 31; Arab Petroleum Congress: Second, 124; Fifth, 78, 198
Arab unity, 90–4
Aramco, 25–6, 80
arbitration, 43–4
Argentina, 93
ARPEL, 93–4
Australia, 122, 140

Bahrain, 81, 104, 105
balance of payments, 50, 55–6, 151, 157, 178, 197
bargaining strength, 44, 111–14, 137, 191–3, 213; Libyan, 146–9
Bellmon, H., 152
Bolivia, 93
Boulding, K. E., 159
Boumedienne, President, 162–3
BP, 29–30, 36, 50, 55–6, 61, 153
Brazil, 93
Brunei, 140, 204
Buraimi oasis, 82

Caltex, 148
cartels, 78, 96–7, 208–9; *see also* OPEC
CENTO, 45, 81–2, 205
CFP, 35, 36, 140, 153
CIPEC, 18, 160, 204
Cold War, 45
Colombia, 93
competition, 123, 127–8, 150, 202–3, 209; and free enterprise, 125; model of, 159, 202; between oil companies, 36–7, 39, 41–2, 45
concession system, 47, 53, 122–3, 130, 161–2; financial terms, 23–6, 145; and governmental participation, 199–203, 214–15; in Middle East, 42–5
Conference of Arab Ministers (1967), 84, 86, 107
Conference, OPEC, 51, 62, 68, 133, 142, 209; IV, 162; IX, 112; X, 201; XI, 114; XII, 130; XV, 144; XVIII, 58; XX, 162; XXI, 151, 174;

234

Conference, OPEC (*cont.*)
XXII, 155; function, 96–103; mandatory resolution (1971), 155–6
consumer surplus, 173
Continental, 148, 153, 216
co-operation: and collective policies, 62–8, 69, 83, 113; and countries' compatibility, 70, 72, 76–7; critical factors and variables, 70; for defence, 27–8; among oil companies, 36–9, 76–7, 88–9, 122, 151–6; among oil exporting countries, 22–6, 69–94, 160, 201–18; *see also* OAPEC and OPEC; among oil importing countries, 56–7, 76–7, 122
crude oil, 123, 208, 209–10; price of, 116, 179; and price of petroleum products, 116, 151; from various sources, 141–2, 147

Delphi Technique, 74–6
Deminex, 55
developing countries, 44, 80, 108–10; dependency on oil for income, 44, 157, 172–3, 191–5; and price of imports, 172–6; and price of oil, 52–3, 59, 174; and trade, 160–5, 178–84, 207
diversification, 50, 122, 216; of economic resources, 113, 194; geographic, 38
Drake, E., 61
Dubai, 104, 105, 204

Economic Commission (OPEC), 72, 74, 112, 128–30
economic integration, 69, 70–1, 90–1, 92–4; by agriculture, 94; and political union, 71, 92; sector-by-sector approach, 92–4
ECSC: and OAPEC, 107–9; and OPEC, 95–6
Ecuador, 93
EEC, 56–7, 58, 71, 95, 106, 165; and OAPEC, 107–9
Egypt *see* U.A.R.
elasticity: cross-elasticity, 119; income, 119–21; price, 41, 47, 116–19
energy, 51, 119, 148, 191; alternative sources of, 55, 122, 172–3, 194,

215–16; comparative costs of, 119, 127, 146, 162
ENI, 55, 58, 79*n*
Epley, M. J., 60
ERAP, 55, 58
Euratom, 107
expert opinion, 74–6; agreement of, 74–5
export consortia: Indo-Ceylon, 213; Malmexport, 211–12; OAPEC, 211; in U.S., 212–13

Faisal, King, 91
First National City Bank of New York, 138–42
Fisher ideal index, 186
foreign exchange, 55, 131, 159, 183, 190
France, 55, 119, 152

Gadhafi, President, 89*n*, 91, 146
Gaulle, General de, 108*n*, 152
government revenue, 130–1, 183–90; decline in, 193, 215; from oil, 21–3, 50–1, 137–57, 171–2, 180, 191, 196–204; *see also* income tax and royalties
gross national product, 50, 194, 197
Gulf, 35–6, 153, 216; and Kuwait oil, 26, 168–71, 179

Haas, E. B., 70–1
Haider, M. H., 59, 60
Hammadi, Sa'doun, 83
Hispanoil, 55, 153
Holland *see* Netherlands
Hoveyda, Amir Abbas, 130, 151
Hussein, King, 85, 91

Ikard, F. N., 126
imports: to oil producing countries, 52–3, 55, 157–95
income tax, 48, 78–80, 113, 142–56, 171, 184–5; system operating in Middle East, 23–5, 40, 44
independent oil companies, 42, 46–50, 58, 112, 140; in Libya, 79, 147–8
India, 52, 213; Indo-Ceylon Tea Consortium, 213

Indonesia, 43, 129, 153, 173, 203; and OPEC membership, 20, 97, 105, 128; population, 130-1
industrialization, 50, 58, 88
inflation, 172, 175, 198
INOC, 87, 88, 90
integration: analysis of concept, 109-10; economic, 69; political, 70; sectoral, 91-4
international oil companies, 53-4, 79, 90, 122-3, 214-15; bargaining position of, 111-14, 137, 215; concentrated structure of, 36-40; influence of national interests on, 58-62, 151-6, 167, 181-2; interlocking directorates, 37; international production programming, 111-27; joint ventures, 36, 37-8, 62-8; and posted prices, 42, 168-71, 174; relations with host countries, 36-7, 137-56, 180, 183, 200-3; share of market, 36, 49-50
International Tin Agreement, 57, 127, 208
Iran, 53, 80, 85, 165; and CENTO, 81; income from oil, 23, 141, 150-5, 173, 183, 190; nationalization of oil companies, 23-4, 44, 168, 194, 200; and OPEC membership, 20, 31, 33, 105, 128, 130-3; politics of, 32, 81-2, 104, 129; profile of, 72-3; and RCD, 82, 205-6
Iran Consortium, 53, 131, 150
Iraq, 32, 81, 153, 155, 173; and Arab League, 27, 86, 91; income from oil, 24-5, 78, 141, 149, 173, 183, 190; and OAPEC, 88, 90, 94, 104; and OPEC membership, 18, 33, 82, 130; revolutionary regime in, 83, 89, 200
Iraq Petroleum Co. Ltd, 25n, 33, 149
Israel, 28, 81, 82, 84-5

Japan, 21, 80, 118, 119, 152, 193
Jersey, 35-6, 50, 79, 117-18, 201; imports price index, 167-8, 172; and posted prices, 145, 153; and U.S. interests, 58-61
Johnson, President, 85
Joint Defence and Economic Co-operation Treaty (1950), 27-8

Jordan, 84, 87, 91; Trans-Jordan, 27
judicial control, 43-4; OAPEC court, 106; OPEC High Court, 106

Kassem, General, 32, 33, 78, 82
Kindleberger, C. P., 164, 178
Korean War, 167-8
Kosygin, A., 85
Kuwait, 21, 56, 82, 200; and Arab League, 27, 86-7, 91; and Gulf Oil Corporation, 26, 168-71, 179; income from oil, 129-31, 141, 151-5, 179, 183, 190; and OAPEC, 83, 103, 105, 106; and OPEC membership, 18, 33, 45, 130; profile of, 72-3

Laspeyres index, 186
Lebanon, 27, 208-9n
Libya, 27, 131, 175, 199-200, 209; and Arab League, 86-7; income from oil, 131, 183, 190; and OAPEC, 83, 89-91, 94; and OPEC membership, 18, 97, 103, 130; and OPEC settlement (1964), 78-80; and posted price revision (1970), 146-50, 154-6
Linoco, 90
London Metal Exchange, 213-14
Lutfi, Ashraf, 48-9, 52, 100-1, 102, 199

Maghrabi, Mahmoud, 146
Malmexport, 211-13
Marathon, 148, 153
market prices, 40-2, 45-9, 52, 145-6, 168; deterioration in, 45-7, 162, 215, 217
matrix model, 62-8
Mayobre, J. A., 57
Mediterranean terminals, 147-8, 149
Mexico, 93
Middle East War (June 1967), 82, 84-5, 108, 128, 194; oil embargoes, 84-6, 86-7, 128
Mobil, 35-6, 123, 153
Monnet, J., 95
Morocco, 27
Muscat and Oman, 20, 104, 140, 151, 204
Myint, H., 182
Mydral, G., 160-1

Nasser, President, 85; Nasserite tradition, 91
national oil companies, 88–9, 93, 114, 201–2, 211–16; effect on oil price, 42, 46–9; national and expatriate company co-operation, 50, 103, 200–1
nationalization of oil industry, 200; Algeria, 214; Iran, 23–4, 44, 168, 194
Netherlands, The, 52, 55, 140
neutralism, 82
Newton, W. L., 179
Nigeria, 20, 140, 151, 153, 173, 204
NIOC, 48, 214
Nixon, President, 152
North Sea, 122, 140
North Slope, 122
Nurkse, R., 193
Nye, J. S., 109–10

OAPEC, 29, 217–18; analysis of structure, 103–10; conservative basis, 83, 87, 89–91, 105; establishment and aims, 29, 69, 82–90, 93–4, 103–4; and ECSC and EEC, 107–9; membership requirements, 87–8, 90, 91, 104; and OPEC, 83, 105–6, 197, 205–6
Occidental, 147–8, 149, 150, 153, 216
OECD, 47, 56
Oil Consultation Commission, 31–2
oil exporting countries, 39, 87–8, 127; bargaining position, 111, 113–14, 122, 137–56, 191–3, 201; fiscal system, 140; and international trade, 157–95; objectives, 54–5, 131–3, 178; profile, 69, 76–7; see also OPEC
oil importing countries, 83, 111, 151–3, 161, 172; co-operation with producers, 57, 58; and independent oil companies, 46–7; interests of, 54–62; without international oil companies, 167; and non-Arab oil, 85–6; profile, 76–7
oil industry: importance to national income, 157; international basis, 35, 38, 39, 52–3; joint projects, 92
oil resources, 20, 38, 86–7, 93, 127–34; conservation of, 146–7; decline in, 193; development of, 42–3; and economic benefits, 88, 128

oil rights, 42–3, 45, 79
oligopoly, 35–9, 111, 150; bilateral, 39–40, 137, 159; undermining of, 45–50, 214
Onitri, H. M. A., 182, 183
OPEC: achievements, 18, 196–207; analysis of structure, 96–103, 107–10; bargaining and government revenues, 137–56, 196–204; as cartel, 18, 54, 57, 62, 96–7, 124, 208–10, 216; compromises in, 51–2, 83, 101–3, 144, 198; conferences, 80, 82–3, 96–103; co-operation in, 18, 45, 50–3, 69–70, 78–83; differences in, 50–1, 78–83, 102–3, 115, 127–33; establishment of, 22–4, 44–5; and external constraints, 62–8; joint production programming, 111–34; membership, 18, 97; objectives, 17, 35, 50–3, 96–7, 111; possible alternative functions, 207–18; Secretariat, 96–107, 111, 130, 165–6, 204; Secretary-General, 98–101; shortcomings of, 102, 199; solidarity in, 34, 78–83, 105, 127, 197

Paasche index, 186
Pachachi, Nadim, 25n, 53, 100
Pahlavi, Shah Mohammed Riza, 33, 44–5, 52, 83
Pakistan, 81, 82, 205–6
Palestine/Palestinians, 82, 87, 104; war (1948), 27, 194
Parra, Francisco, 52, 53, 101
Penrose, Edith, 49
Petroleum Information Foundation, 171–2
political risks, 70
population, 129, 194
poverty, 160–4, see also developing countries
Prebisch, R., 160–1, 182
price of oil: competition between companies, 32–3, 36–7, 43–9, 112–14, 127–8, 168–71; discounts off, 25–6, 40–1, 47–8, 79, 141–5, 198; elasticity, 41, 47, 116–19; posted prices, 25n, 40–8, 78–80, 143–56, 167–71, 209 (reduction of), 29–33, 40–1, 44, 208; realized prices, 80, 167, 171, 179 (erosion of), 46–8,

237

price of oil (*cont.*)
112–13, 133, 137–8; stabilization, 32, 50–1, 96–7, 112–14, 134–5, 207; transfer, 48, 141, 183
production of oil, 20, 36, 38, 43; cost of, 133, 138; programme (OPEC), 72–5, 96–7, 103, 111–36, 209
profile model, 69, 72–7
profits: by oil companies, 37–42, 46–9, 60, 130, 137–56, 182, 202; profit-sharing system, 23, 40
prorationing *see* production programme

Qatar, 21, 80, 115, 153, 155; income from oil, 131, 141, 183, 190; and OAPEC 104, 105; and OPEC membership, 18, 97, 130
quota system *see* production programme

Ramazani, R. K., 82
Rambin, J. H., 59–60
Rathbone, M. J., 59
RCD, 82, 197, 205–7
restrictive practices, 122
revolutionary regimes, 33, 83, 87–91, 200
risk spreading, 38
Rouhani, Fuad, 53, 100, 101, 161
royalties, 23, 113, 123, 151, 201; royalty expensing, 78–9, 142–5, 151, 201

Sa'dawi, Suhail, 104n, 106
Sarkis, N., 198–9
Saudi Arabia, 24–5, 56, 82, 115, 133, 200; and Arab League, 27, 86–7, 91; and government revenue, 24–5, 80, 141, 151–3, 190; and oil embargoes, 84–5, 155; and OAPEC, 83, 103–5; and OPEC membership, 18, 33, 45, 130; terms of trade, 173, 174, 183
Schmitter, Philippe C., 70–1
Schuman, R., 95
selling expense allowance, 25, 145
Shah of Iran, 81, 83, 133, 150, 214; quoted, 44–5, 52–3, 130–1, 153, 175
Shell, 35–6, 49–50, 70, 168, 193, 216; and OPEC policies, 124–5, 153, 165

Singer, H. W., 181
Socal, 35, 148, 153
socio-economic development, 44, 149, 157, 180–2; in OPEC countries, 128–31, 152–3, 173
Sonatrach, 88
sovereignty, 43–4, 92, 137
Soviet Union, 82, 89, 150, 210; as oil exporter, 20, 46, 97, 124
Suez Canal, 32; closure, 145, 147, 156; war, 194
Sudan, 27, 91
sulphur content, 138, 148, 149
Syria, 27, 84, 88–9, 91, 147

tanker freight, 148–9
Tapline, 147–8
Tariki, A., 23n, 25–6, 31, 32, 33, 198–9
technological development, 193–4
Tehran Agreement (1971), 156, 198–9
terms of trade, 157–95; defined, 157–60, 176–82; measures of, 165–76, 183–91; and OPEC solidarity, 217; worsening of, 159–66
Texaco, 35, 59–60, 125, 148, 153
trade creation, 94
trade restrictions: against OPEC area oil, 50–1; *see also* United States (import restrictions)
Tumbs, 81
Tunisia, 27
Turkey, 81, 82, 205–6

U.A.R. (Egypt) 20, 27, 31–2, 84, 87–91, 97
United Kingdom, 55–6, 84–5, 117–18, 150, 208; and CENTO, 45, 81
United Nations, 21, 74n, 163, 182; Conference on Trade and Development, 160–1; export index of manufactured goods, 165–8; import price index, 184, 186
United States, 36, 49, 55, 117–18, 128, 150–3; and capitalism, 58–9; and CENTO 81–2; commodity policy, 164, 208; dollar devaluation, 176; export associations, 212–13; import restrictions, 46, 51, 86, 125–6, 136; and Middle East War, 84–6; oil companies, 23, 35–6, 45, 153; oil and national security, 59, 125–6; oil

United States (*cont.*)
production, 21, 30–1; production programme, 134–6
Uruguay, 52, 93

Valery, M., 134
Venezuela, 56–7, 112, 140, 155, 173, 183; and cost of Middle East Oil, 32, 128, 133, 141; income from oil, 23, 29–33, 80, 151–3, 190, 191; national oil company, 93; oil sales, 46, 85, 93; and OPEC membership, 20, 31, 33, 45, 105, 130, 203
vertical integration, 35, 41–2, 46, 215; profits under, 141–2; undermining of, 45–50, 103
Vienna: OPEC headquarters, 52, 98

West Germany, 84, 153, 176

Yamani, Ahmad Zaki, 57, 83, 104–7
Yemen, 27, 91

For Product Safety Concerns and Information please contact our EU
representative GPSR@taylorandfrancis.com
Taylor & Francis Verlag GmbH, Kaufingerstraße 24, 80331 München, Germany

www.ingramcontent.com/pod-product-compliance
Ingram Content Group UK Ltd.
Pitfield, Milton Keynes, MK11 3LW, UK
UKHW020930280425
457818UK00025B/138